*The Programmer's Brain*

## Get the eBook FREE!

(PDF, ePub, Kindle, and liveBook all included)

We believe that once you buy a book from us, you should be able to read it in any format we have available. To get electronic versions of this book at no additional cost to you, purchase and then register this book at the Manning website.

Go to https://www.manning.com/freebook and follow the instructions to complete your pBook registration.

## That's it!
## Thanks from Manning!

# The Programmer's Brain

WHAT EVERY PROGRAMMER NEEDS TO KNOW ABOUT COGNITION

FELIENNE HERMANS
FOREWORD BY JON SKEET

MANNING
SHELTER ISLAND

For online information and ordering of this and other Manning books, please visit
www.manning.com. The publisher offers discounts on this book when ordered in quantity.
For more information, please contact

    Special Sales Department
    Manning Publications Co.
    20 Baldwin Road
    PO Box 761
    Shelter Island, NY 11964
    Email: orders@manning.com

Manning Publications Co.
20 Baldwin Road
PO Box 761
Shelter Island, NY 11964

| | |
|---|---|
| Development editor: | Tricia Louvar |
| Technical development editor: | Jerry Kuch |
| Review editor: | Mihaela Batinić |
| Production editor: | Keri Hales |
| Copy editor: | Michele Mitchell |
| Proofreader: | Melody Dolab |
| Technical proofreader: | Sébastien Portebois |
| Typesetter: | Gordan Salinovic |
| Cover designer: | Marija Tudor |

ISBN 9781617298677

Printed in the United States of America

# brief contents

PART 1   ON READING CODE BETTER...................................................1

     1 ■ Decoding your confusion while coding   3

     2 ■ Speed reading for code   13

     3 ■ How to learn programming syntax quickly   33

     4 ■ How to read complex code   46

PART 2   ON THINKING ABOUT CODE...............................................65

     5 ■ Reaching a deeper understanding of code   67

     6 ■ Getting better at solving programming problems   91

     7 ■ Misconceptions: Bugs in thinking   110

PART 3   ON WRITING BETTER CODE............................................125

     8 ■ How to get better at naming things   127

     9 ■ Avoiding bad code and cognitive load: Two
        frameworks   147

   10 ■ Getting better at solving complex problems   160

Part 4  On collaborating on code ....................................... 177

11  ■  The act of writing code   179

12  ■  Designing and improving larger systems   191

13  ■  How to onboard new developers   205

# contents

*foreword    xiii*
*preface    xv*
*acknowledgments    xvii*
*about this book    xix*
*about the author    xxii*
*about the cover illustration    xxiii*

PART 1 ON READING CODE BETTER ....................................1

**1**  *Decoding your confusion while coding*    **3**

1.1  Different kinds of confusion in code    4
   *Confusion type 1: Lack of knowledge    5 ▪ Confusion type 2: Lack of information    5 ▪ Confusion type 3: Lack of processing power    6*

1.2  Different cognitive processes that affect coding    6
   *LTM and programming    7 ▪ STM and programming    7*
   *Working memory and programming    8*

1.3  Cognitive processes in collaboration    9
   *A brief dissection of how the cognitive processes interacted    9*
   *Cognitive processes regarding programming tasks    10*

## 2   Speed reading for code   13

**2.1**   Quickly reading code   14

*What just happened in your brain?   15 ▪ Reexamine your
reproduction   16 ▪ Reexamining your second attempt at
reproducing code   17 ▪ Why is reading unfamiliar code hard?   18*

**2.2**   Overcoming size limits in your memory   18

*The power of chunking   19 ▪ Expert programmers can remember
code better than beginners   22*

**2.3**   You see more code than you can read   23

*Iconic memory   23 ▪ It's not what you remember; it's the way you
remember it   25 ▪ Practice chunking   30*

## 3   How to learn programming syntax quickly   33

**3.1**   Tips for remembering syntax   34

*Disruptions play havoc with your workflow   34*

**3.2**   How to learn syntax quickly with flashcards   35

*When to use the flashcards   36 ▪ Expanding the set of
flashcards   36 ▪ Thinning the set of flashcards   36*

**3.3**   How to not forget things   37

*Why do we forget memories?   38 ▪ Spaced repetition   39*

**3.4**   How to remember syntax longer   40

*Two forms of remembering information   40 ▪ Just seeing
information is not enough   41 ▪ Remembering information
strengthens memories   42 ▪ Strengthen memories by actively
thinking   42*

## 4   How to read complex code   46

**4.1**   Why it's hard to understand complex code   47

*What's the difference between working memory and STM?   48
Types of cognitive load as they relate to programming   49*

**4.2**   Techniques to reduce cognitive load   51

*Refactoring   51 ▪ Replacing unfamiliar language constructs   52
Code synonyms are great additions to a flashcard deck   55*

**4.3**   Memory aids to use when your working memory is
overloaded   56

*Creating a dependency graph   56 ▪ Using a state table   59
Combining dependency graphs and state tables   61*

PART 2   ON THINKING ABOUT CODE ........................................65

**5** *Reaching a deeper understanding of code   67*

    5.1   Roles of variables framework   68
          *Different variables do different things   68* ▪ *Eleven roles to cover almost all variables   69*

    5.2   Roles and paradigms   71
          *Benefits of roles   72* ▪ *Hungarian notation   73*

    5.3   Gaining a deeper knowledge of programs   75
          *Text knowledge vs. plan knowledge   75* ▪ *Different stages of program understanding   76*

    5.4   Reading text is similar to reading code   79
          *What happens in the brain when we read code?   79* ▪ *If you can learn French, you can learn Python   81*

    5.5   Text comprehension strategies applied to code   84
          *Activating prior knowledge   84* ▪ *Monitoring   85* ▪ *Determining the importance of different lines of code   86* ▪ *Inferring the meaning of variable names   87* ▪ *Visualizing   88* ▪ *Questioning   89* Summarizing code   90*

**6** *Getting better at solving programming problems   91*

    6.1   Using models to think about code   92
          *The benefits of using models   92*

    6.2   Mental models   94
          *Examining mental models in detail   96* ▪ *Learning new mental models   97* ▪ *How to use mental models efficiently when thinking about code   97*

    6.3   Notional machines   102
          *What is a notional machine?   103* ▪ *Examples of notional machines   103* ▪ *Different levels of notional machines   105*

    6.4   Notional machines and language   106
          *Expanding sets of notional machines   106* ▪ *Different notional machines can create conflicting mental models   107*

    6.5   Notional machines and schemata   108
          *Why schemata matters   108* ▪ *Are notional machines semantics?   109*

**7** *Misconceptions: Bugs in thinking* **110**

 7.1  Why learning a second programming language is easier than learning the first one  *111*

 *How to increase the chances of benefiting from existing programming knowledge  113  ▪  Different forms of transfer  114  ▪  Already knowing something: Curse or blessing?  115  ▪  The difficulties of transfer  116*

 7.2  Misconceptions: Bugs in thinking  *117*

 *Debugging misconceptions with conceptual change  118 Suppressing misconceptions  119  ▪  Misconceptions about programming languages  120  ▪  Preventing misconceptions while learning a new programming language  122  ▪  Diagnosing misconceptions in a new codebase  122*

**PART 3  ON WRITING BETTER CODE** .......................................**125**

**8** *How to get better at naming things* **127**

 8.1  Why naming matters  *128*

 *Why naming matters  129  ▪  Different perspectives on naming  129  ▪  Initial naming practices have a lasting impact  131*

 8.2  Cognitive aspects of naming  *133*

 *Formatting names supports your STM  133  ▪  Clear names help your LTM  134  ▪  Variable names can contain different types of information to help you understand them  135  ▪  When to evaluate the quality of names  136*

 8.3  What types of names are easier to understand?  *137*

 *To abbreviate or not to abbreviate?  137  ▪  Snake case or camel case?  140*

 8.4  The influence of names on bugs  *141*

 *Code with bad names has more bugs  141*

 8.5  How to choose better names  *142*

 *Name molds  142  ▪  Feitelson's three-step model for better variable names  145*

**9** *Avoiding bad code and cognitive load: Two frameworks* **147**

 9.1  Why code with code smells creates a lot of cognitive load  *148*

 *A brief intro to code smells  148  ▪  How code smells harm cognition  151*

9.2 The influence of bad names on cognitive load 153

*Linguistic antipatterns 154 ▪ Measuring cognitive load 155
Linguistic antipatterns and cognitive load 158 ▪ Why linguistic
antipatterns cause confusion 159*

10 **Getting better at solving complex problems 160**

10.1 What is problem solving? 161

*Elements of problem solving 161 ▪ State space 161*

10.2 What is the role of the LTM when you solve programming
problems? 162

*Is problem solving a cognitive process on its own? 162 ▪ How to
teach your LTM to solve problems 164 ▪ Two types of memories
that play a role in problem solving 164*

10.3 Automatization: Creating implicit memories 167

*Implicit memories over time 168 ▪ Why automatization will make
you program quicker 170 ▪ Improving implicit memories 171*

10.4 Learning from code and its explanation 172

*A new type of cognitive load: Germane load 173 ▪ Using worked
examples in your working life 175*

PART 4 ON COLLABORATING ON CODE ..............................177

11 **The act of writing code 179**

11.1 Different activities while programming 180

*Searching 180 ▪ Comprehension 181 ▪ Transcription 181
Incrementation 181 ▪ Exploration 182 ▪ What about
debugging? 182*

11.2 Programmer interrupted 183

*Programming tasks require a warm-up 183 ▪ What happens after an
interruption? 184 ▪ How to better prepare for interruptions 185
When to interrupt a programmer 187 ▪ Some thoughts on
multitasking 189*

12 **Designing and improving larger systems 191**

12.1 Examining the properties of codebases 192

*Cognitive dimensions 192 ▪ Using CDCB to improve your
codebase 200 ▪ Design maneuvers and their trade-offs 201*

12.2 Dimensions and activities 202

*Impact of dimensions on different activities 202 ▪ Optimizing your
codebase for expected activities 204*

## 13 *How to onboard new developers* 205

13.1 Issues in the onboarding process 206

13.2 Differences between experts and novices 207

*Beginners' behavior in more depth 207 ▪ Difference between seeing concepts concretely and abstractly 211*

13.3 Activities for a better onboarding process 213

*Limit tasks to one programming activity 213 ▪ Support the memory of the onboardee 214 ▪ Read code together 216*

13.4 Some words to close this book 221

*epilogue 221*

*index 223*

# *foreword*

I've spent a lot of my life thinking about programming, and if you're reading this book you probably have too. I haven't spent nearly as much time thinking about thinking, though. The concept of our thought processes and how we interact with code as humans has been important to me, but there has been no scientific study behind it. Let me give you three examples.

I'm the main contributor to a .NET project called Noda Time, providing an alternative set of date and time types to the ones built into .NET. It's been a great environment for me to put time into API design, particularly with respect to naming. Having seen the problems caused by names that make it sound like they change an existing value, but actually return a new value, I've tried to use names that make buggy code sound wrong when you read it. For example, the `LocalDate` type has a `PlusDays` method rather than `AddDays`. I'm hoping that this code looks wrong to most C# developers

```
date.PlusDays(1);
```

whereas this looks more reasonable:

```
tomorrow = today.PlusDays(1);
```

Compare that with the `AddDays` method in the .NET `DateTime` type:

```
date.AddDays(1);
```

That looks like it's just modifying date, and isn't a bug, even though it's just as incorrect as the first example.

The second example is also from Noda Time, but it's not quite as specific. Whereas many libraries try (for good reason) to do all the hard work without developers having to think much, we explicitly want the users of Noda Time to put a lot of thought into their date and time code up front. We try to force users to put thought into what they're really trying to achieve, with no ambiguity—and then we try to make it easy to express that clearly in the code.

Finally, there's the one conceptual example of what values variables hold in Java and C# and what happens when you pass an argument to a method. It feels like I've been trying to counter the notion that objects are passed by reference in Java for most of my life, and when I do the math, that's probably the case. I suspect I've been trying to help other developers fine-tune their mental models for about 25 years now.

It turns out that how programmers think has been important to me for a long time, but with no science behind it, just guesswork and hard-won experience. This book helps to change that, although it isn't quite the start of this process for me.

I first came across Felienne Hermans at the NDC conference in Oslo in 2017 when she gave her presentation "Programming Is Writing Is Programming." My reaction on Twitter says it all: "I need a long time to let it all sink in. But wow. Wow." I've seen Felienne give this presentation (evolving over time, of course) at least three times now and have taken something new out of it each time. Finally there were some cognitive explanations for the things I had been trying to do—and also some surprises that challenged me to tweak my approach.

Alternating reactions of "Ah, that makes sense now!" and "Oh, I hadn't thought of that!" have been the background rhythm when reading this book. Aside from some immediate practical suggestions such as using flashcards, I suspect the impact of the book will be more subtle. Maybe it's a little more deliberation about when to put a blank line in code. Maybe it's a change in the tasks we give to new members of the team, or even just a change in the timing of those tasks. Maybe it's how we explain concepts on Stack Overflow.

Whatever the impact, Felienne has provided a treasure chest of ideas to think about and to process in working memory and move to long-term memory—thinking about thinking is addictive!

—JON SKEET
STAFF DEVELOPER RELATIONS ENGINEER, GOOGLE

# *preface*

When I started to teach children to program about 10 years ago, I quickly realized I didn't have the faintest idea how people use their brains for anything, especially for programming. While I learned a lot about programming in university, no course in my computer science education had prepared me to think about thinking about programming.

If you followed a computer science program like I did, or if you learned programming by yourself, you most likely did not learn about the cognitive functions of the brain. Therefore, you might also not know how to improve your brain to read and write code in a better way. I certainly did not, but while teaching kids to program, I realized I needed a deeper understanding of cognition. I then set out to learn more about how we think and how we learn. This book is the result of the last few years of me reading books, talking to people, and attending talks and conferences about learning and thinking.

Understanding how your brain works is interesting in its own right, of course, but it also matters for programming. Programming is seen as one of the most demanding cognitive activities there is: you are both solving a problem in an abstract way and manipulating a program, which requires a level of attention that does not come naturally to most people. Missed a space? Error. Miscalculated where to start the array indexing? Error. Misunderstood the precise workings of an already existing code? Error.

There are so many ways in which you can shoot yourself in the foot while programming. As you will see in this book, many of the errors you make are rooted in cognitive issues. For example, missing a space might mean you have not mastered the programming language's syntax in enough detail. Miscalculating where to index an array might indicate you have wrong assumptions about the code. Misunderstanding existing code could be caused by a lack of skills in how to read code.

The aim of this book is to first help you understand how your brain processes code. Understanding what your brain does when presented with new information will help you be a better programmer because professional programmers are faced with new information often. Once we know how code affects the brain, we will talk about methods to improve your code processing skills.

# acknowledgments

I fully realize how tremendously lucky I am to be able to complete a book on a topic I love. There are so many things in my life that happened in the exact right way at the exact right moment, without which my life would have been a lot different, and this book certainly would have not been written. Dozens of small and large encounters with amazing people have all contributed to this book and to my career. I want to name a few very important ones.

Marlies Aldewereld first put me on the path of programming and language learning. Marileen Smit taught me enough psychology to write this book. Greg Wilson made the topic of programming education mainstream again. Peter Nabbe and Rob Hoogerwoord set world-class examples of how to be a great teacher. Stefan Hanenberg gave me advice that shaped the trajectory of my research. Katja Mordaunt kickstarted the first ever code reading club. Llewellyn Falco's thinking on koans shaped my thinking on learning extensively. And Rico Huijbers is my beacon in any storm.

In addition to these people, of course, I need to thank the people at Manning—Marjan Bace, Mike Stephens, Tricia Louvar, Bert Bates, Mihaela Batinić, Becky Reinhart, Melissa Ice, Jennifer Houle, Paul Wells, Jerry Kuch, Rachel Head, Sébastien Portebois, Candace Gillhoolley, Chris Kaufmann, Matko Hrvatin, Ivan Martinović, Branko Latincic, and Andrej Hofšuster for taking on this vague book idea and making it into something readable and sensible.

To all the reviewers: Adam Kaczmarek, Adriaan Beiertz, Alex Rios, Ariel Gamiño, Ben McNamara, Bill Mitchell, Billy O'Callaghan, Bruno Sonnino, Charles Lam, Claudia Maderthaner, Clifford Thurber, Daniela Zapata Riesco, Emanuele Origgi, George

Onofrei , George Thomas, Gilberto Taccari, Haim Raman, Jaume Lopez, Joseph Perenia, Kent Spillner, Kimberly Winston-Jackson, Manuel Gonzalez, Marcin Sęk, Mark Harris, Martin Knudsen, Mike Hewitson, Mike Taylor, Orlando Méndez Morales, Pedro Seromenho, Peter Morgan, Samantha Berk, Sebastian Felling, Sébastien Portebois, Simon Tschöke, Stefano Ongarello, Thomas Overby Hansen, Tim van Deurzen, Tuomo Kalliokoski, Unnikrishnan Kumar, Vasile Boris, Viktor Bek, Zachery Beyel, and Zhijun Liu, your suggestions helped make this a better book.

# about this book

*The Programmer's Brain* is a book for programmers of all levels who want to gain a deeper understanding of how their brains work and how they can improve their programming skills and habits. Code examples in various languages will be shown, including JavaScript, Python, and Java, but you do not need deep knowledge of any of the languages as long as you are comfortable reading source code in programming languages you might not have seen before.

To get the most out of reading this book, you should have experience working in a development team or on larger software systems and onboarding people to a team. We will refer to these types of situations often, and you will gain a deeper understanding if you can relate those to your own experiences. In fact, learning increases when you can connect new information to existing knowledge and experiences, which I cover in this book.

While this book presents many topics from cognitive science, it is ultimately a book meant specifically for programmers. We will always contextualize the workings of the brain with results from studies on programming and programming languages specifically.

## How this book is organized: A roadmap

This book consists of 13 chapters divided into 4 parts. The chapters should be read in order because they build on each other. Each chapter offers applications and exercises that will help you process the material and understand it more deeply. In some cases, I will ask you to find a code base to perform the exercises on to make sure the context is best for you.

Your daily practice is also a place where the knowledge should be applied. I imagine you can read this book over a prolonged period and apply the lessons from one chapter to your programming practice before you move on to read more chapters:

- Chapter 1 examines the three cognitive processes that play a role when programming and how each is associated with its own type of confusion.
- Chapter 2 discusses how to quickly read code and get a sense of its workings.
- Chapter 3 teaches you how to learn programming syntax and concepts better and more easily.
- Chapter 4 helps you read complex code.
- Chapter 5 shows techniques that help you reach a deeper understanding of unfamiliar code.
- Chapter 6 covers techniques to get better at solving programming problems.
- Chapter 7 helps you avoid bugs in code and in thinking.
- Chapter 8 discusses how to select clear variable names, especially across a code base.
- Chapter 9 focuses on code smells and the cognitive principles behind them.
- Chapter 10 discusses more advanced techniques to solve complex problems.
- Chapter 11 covers the act of coding and explores the variety of tasks in programming.
- Chapter 12 teaches you ways to improve large code bases.
- Chapter 13 helps you make the onboarding process of new developers less painful.

This book contains many examples of source code both in numbered listings and in line with normal text. In both cases, source code is formatted in a `fixed-width font like this` to separate it from ordinary text. Sometimes code is also **in bold** to highlight code that has changed from previous steps in the chapter, such as when a new feature adds to an existing line of code.

In many cases, the original source code has been reformatted; we've added line breaks and reworked indentation to accommodate the available page space in the book. In rare cases, even this was not enough, and listings include line-continuation markers (➡). Additionally, comments in the source code have often been removed from the listings when the code is described in the text. Code annotations accompany many of the listings, highlighting important concepts.

## liveBook discussion forum

Purchase of *The Programmer's Brain* includes free access to a private web forum run by Manning Publications where you can make comments about the book, ask technical questions, and receive help from the author and from other users. To access the forum, go to https://livebook.manning.com/#!/book/the-programmers-brain/discussion. You can also learn more about Manning's forums and the rules of conduct at https://livebook.manning.com/#!/discussion.

Manning's commitment to our readers is to provide a venue where a meaningful dialogue between individual readers and between readers and the author can take place. It is not a commitment to any specific amount of participation on the part of the author, whose contribution to the forum remains voluntary (and unpaid). We suggest you try asking the author some challenging questions lest their interest stray! The forum and the archives of previous discussions will be accessible from the publisher's website as long as the book is in print.

# *about the author*

**Dr. Felienne Hermans** is an associate professor at Leiden University in the Netherlands where she researches programming education and programming languages. She also is a teacher-educator at the teachers' academy of Vrije Universiteit Amsterdam, specializing in didactics of computer science, and teaches at the Lyceum Kralingen high school in Rotterdam.

Felienne is also the creator of the Hedy programming language for novice programmers and is a host of the Software Engineering Radio podcast, one of the largest podcasts about software on the web.

# *about the cover illustration*

The figure on the cover of *The Programmer's Brain* is captioned "femme Sauvage du Canada," or native woman of Canada. The illustration is taken from a collection of dress costumes from various countries by Jacques Grasset de Saint-Sauveur (1757–1810), titled *Costumes civils actuels de tous les peuples connus,* published in France in 1788. Each illustration is finely drawn and colored by hand. The rich variety of Grasset de Saint-Sauveur's collection reminds us vividly of how culturally apart the world's towns and regions were just 200 years ago. Isolated from each other, people spoke different dialects and languages. In the streets or in the countryside, it was easy to identify where they lived and what their trade or station in life was just by their dress.

The way we dress has changed since then and the diversity by region, so rich at the time, has faded away. It is now hard to tell apart the inhabitants of different continents, let alone different towns, regions, or countries. Perhaps we have traded cultural diversity for a more varied personal life—certainly for a more varied and fast-paced technological life.

At a time when it is hard to tell one computer book from another, Manning celebrates the inventiveness and initiative of the computer business with book covers based on the rich diversity of regional life of two centuries ago, brought back to life by Grasset de Saint-Sauveur's pictures.

# Part 1

## On reading code better

Reading code is a core part of programming, but as a professional developer, you might not know how. Code reading is not taught or practiced often, and getting to know code is confusing and often hard work. The first chapters of this book will help you to understand why code reading is so hard and what you can do to get better at it.

# Decoding your confusion while coding

*1*

**This chapter covers**

- Discriminating the different ways you may be confused while coding
- Comparing three different cognitive processes that play a role when coding
- Understanding how different cognitive processes complement each other

Confusion is part of programming. When you learn a new programming language, concept, or framework, the new ideas might scare you. When reading unfamiliar code or code that you wrote a long time ago, you might not understand what the code does or why it was written the way it was. Whenever you start to work in a new business domain, new terms and jargon can all bump into each other in your brain.

It's not a problem to be confused for a while, of course, but you don't want to be confused for longer than needed. This chapter teaches you to recognize and decode your confusion. Maybe you've never thought about this, but there are different ways to be confused. Not knowing the meaning of a domain concept is a different sort of confusion than trying to read a complicated algorithm step by step.

Different types of confusion relate to different kinds of cognitive processes. Using various code examples, this chapter will detail three different kinds of confusion and explain what happens in your mind.

By the end of this chapter, you will be able to recognize the different ways that code might cause confusion and understand the cognitive process happening in your brain in each case. Once you know about the three different types of confusion, and the three related cognitive processes, later chapters will teach you how to improve these cognitive processes.

## 1.1    *Different kinds of confusion in code*

All unfamiliar code is confusing to a certain extent, but not all code is confusing in the same way. Let's illustrate that with three different code examples. All three examples translate a given number N or n to binary. The first program is written in APL, the second one in Java, and the third one in BASIC.

Give yourself a few minutes to deeply inspect these programs. What type of knowledge do you rely on when reading them? How does that differ for the three programs? You might not have the words at this point to express what happens in your brain when you read these programs, but I would guess it will feel differently for each. At the end of this chapter, you will have the vocabulary to discuss the different cognitive processes that take place when you read code.

The example in listing 1.1 is a program converting the number n into a binary representation in APL. Unless you are a mathematician from the 1960s, you've probably never used APL (a programming language). It was designed specifically for mathematical operations and is hardly in use anywhere today. As you can see, this program is very compact, and not at all self-explanatory for the uninitiated.

---

**Listing 1.1    Binary representation in APL**

```
2 2 2 2 2 T n
```

The second example is a Java program that also converts the number n into a binary representation. In this case, the program uses the Java method toBinaryString() to accomplish the transformation.

---

**Listing 1.2    Binary representation in Java**

```java
public class BinaryCalculator {
    public static void mian(Integer n) {
        System.out.println(Integer.toBinaryString(n));
    }
}
```

The final example is yet another program, this time in BASIC, that converts the number N into a binary representation. This code implements an algorithm involving several steps to transform the number.

```
     Listing 1.3   Binary representation in BASIC
  1   LET N2 =  ABS (INT (N))
  2   LET B$ = ""
  3   FOR N1 = N2 TO 0 STEP 0
  4       LET N2 =  INT (N1 / 2)
  5       LET B$ =  STR$ (N1 - N2 * 2) + B$
  6       LET N1 = N2
  7   NEXT N1
  8   PRINT B$
  9   RETURN
```

### 1.1.1   Confusion type 1: Lack of knowledge

Now let's dive into what happens when you read the three programs. First is the APL program. See how the program uses the T operator. The confusion here lies in the fact that you might not know what T means.

```
     Listing 1.4   Binary representation in APL

  2 2 2 2 2 T n    ⟵——  The unfamiliar T operator is confusing
```

You can't comprehend this program without understanding T. Hence, the confusion here lies in a lack of *knowledge*.

### 1.1.2   Confusion type 2: Lack of information

For the second program, the source of the confusion is different. I assume that with some familiarity with programming, even if you are not an expert in Java, your brain can find the relevant parts of the Java program. The program relies on a specific Java method. Confusion can be caused here by not knowing about the inner workings of toBinaryString().

```
     Listing 1.5   Binary representation in Java

public class BinaryCalculator {
    public static void mian(Integer n) {                         It may be unclear how
        System.out.println(Integer.toBinaryString(n));   ⟵——┐   this method works.
    }
}
```

Even if you can guess the functionality based on the name of the method, you cannot deeply understand what the code does unless you navigate to the definition of toBinaryString() elsewhere in the code and continue reading there. Further, from just this listing, it isn't clear exactly where you would find the definition you need. Thus, the problem here is a lack of *information*.

### 1.1.3   Confusion type 3: Lack of processing power

In the third program, based on the names of variables and the operations, you can make an educated guess about what the code does. But if you really want to follow along, you cannot process the entire execution in your brain. This BASIC program is confusing because you cannot oversee all the small steps being executed. If you need to understand all the steps, you can use a memory aid like intermediate values of variables shown in figure 1.1.

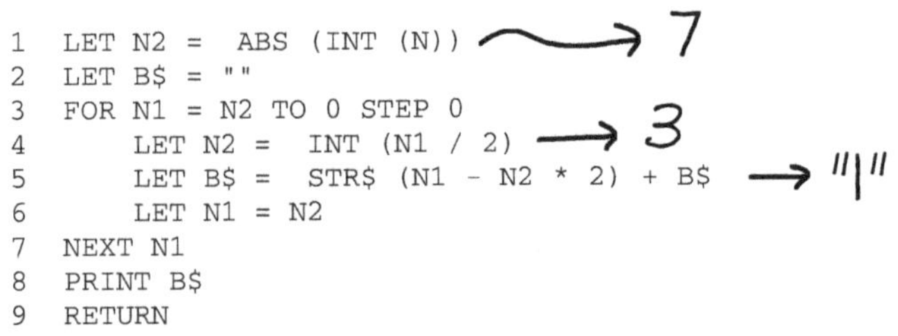

```
1   LET N2 =  ABS (INT (N))         ⟶ 7
2   LET B$ = " "
3   FOR N1 = N2 TO 0 STEP 0
4       LET N2 =  INT (N1 / 2)      ⟶ 3
5       LET B$ =  STR$ (N1 - N2 * 2) + B$   ⟶ "|"
6       LET N1 = N2
7   NEXT N1
8   PRINT B$
9   RETURN
```

**Figure 1.1   Binary representation in BASIC**

The confusion here is related to a lack of *processing power*. It's too hard to hold all the intermediate values of the variables and the corresponding actions in your mind at the same time. If you really want to mentally calculate what this program does, you will likely use a pen and paper to scribble down a few intermediate values, or even write them next to the lines in the code snippet, as shown in this example.

In these three programs we have seen that confusion, while always annoying and uncomfortable, can have three different sources. First, confusion can be caused by a lack of knowledge of the programming language, algorithm, or domain at hand. But confusion can also be caused by not having full access to all the information you need to understand code. Especially because code nowadays often uses various libraries, modules, and packages, understanding code can require extensive navigation in which you have to gather new information while also remembering what you were doing in the first place. Finally, sometimes code is more complicated than your brain can process, and what confuses you is a lack of processing power.

Now let's dive into the different cognitive processes that are associated with each of these three types of confusion.

## 1.2   Different cognitive processes that affect coding

Let's zoom in on the three different cognitive processes that happen in your brain when reading the three example programs. As outlined, different forms of confusion are related to issues with different cognitive processes, all related to memory. These are explained in the remainder of the chapter in more detail.

A lack of knowledge means that not enough relevant facts are present in your *long-term memory* (LTM), the place where all your memories are permanently stored. A lack of information, on the other hand, presents a challenge for your *short-term memory* (STM). Information that you are gathering has to be stored in STM temporarily, but if you have to search in a lot of different places, you might forget some of the things you already read. Finally, when you must process a lot of information, that takes a toll on the *working memory*, which is where your thinking happens. These three cognitive processes are not only in play when reading code, but in all cognitive activities, including (in the context of programming) writing code, designing the architecture of a system, or writing documentation.

### 1.2.1 LTM and programming

The first cognitive process that is used while programming is LTM. This can store your memories for a very long time. Most people can recall events that happened years or even decades ago. Your LTM plays a role in everything that you do, from tying your shoelaces, where your muscles remember what to do almost automatically, to writing a binary search, where you remember the abstract algorithm, the syntax of the programming language, and how to type on a keyboard. Chapter 3 will detail the use of LTM in more detail, including these different forms of remembering and ways to strengthen this cognitive process.

Your LTM stores several types of relevant programming information. It can, for example, store memories of when you successfully applied a certain technique, the meaning of keywords in Java, the meaning of words in English, or the fact that `maxint` in Java is `2147483647`.

The LTM can be compared to the hard drive of a computer, holding facts for long periods of time.

#### APL PROGRAM: LTM

In reading the program in APL, what you use most is your LTM. If you know the meaning of the APL keyword T, you will retrieve that from LTM when reading this program.

The APL program also illustrates the importance of relevant syntax knowledge. If you do not know what T means in APL, you will have a very hard time understanding the program. On the other hand, if you know that it represents the *dyadic encode* function, which is a function that translates a value into a different number representation, reading the program is almost trivial. No words need to be understood, and you do not have to figure out the working of the code step by step either.

### 1.2.2 STM and programming

The second cognitive process involved in programming is STM. Your STM is used to briefly hold incoming information. For example, when someone reads a phone number to you over the phone, it does not go into your LTM straight away. The phone number first goes into your STM, which has a limited size. The estimates differ, but most scientists agree that just a few items fit in STM, and certainly not more than a dozen.

For example, when reading a program, keywords, variable names, and data structures used are temporarily stored in the STM.

**JAVA PROGRAM: STM**

In the Java program, the biggest cognitive process in play is STM. You first process line 1 of listing 1.6, which teaches you that the input parameter n of the function is an integer. At that point, you are not sure what the function will do, but you can continue reading while also remembering that n is a number. The knowledge that n is an integer is stored in your STM for a while. You then continue to line 2, where toBinary-String() indicates to you what the function will return. You might not remember this function in a day, or even in an hour. When your brain has solved the problem at hand—in this case, understanding the function—the STM is emptied.

---

Listing 1.6  A program converting number n into binary representation in Java

```
public static void mian(Int n) {
    System.out.println(Integer.toBinaryString(n));
}
}
```

Even though STM plays a large role in the comprehension of this program, LTM is involved in reading this program too. In fact, our LTM is involved in everything we do. So, when reading the Java program, you use your LTM as well.

For example, if you are familiar with Java, as I assume most readers are, you know that the keywords *public class* and *public static void main* can be disregarded if you are asked to explain what the function does. It is likely you did not even notice that the method is in fact called "mian" and not "main."

Your brain took a shortcut there by assuming a name, showing a blending of the two cognitive processes. It decided to use "main" based on prior experience stored in your LTM rather than using the actual name that you read and that was stored in your STM. This shows that these two cognitive processes are not as separate from each other as I have presented them.

If the LTM is like the hard drive of your brain, storing memories forever, you can think of the STM like the computer's RAM or a cache that can be used to temporarily store values.

### 1.2.3 *Working memory and programming*

The third cognitive process that plays a role in programming is working memory. STM and LTM are mostly storage devices. They hold information, either for a short while after reading or hearing it, in the case of STM, or for a long time, in the case of LTM. The actual thinking, however, happens not in the LTM or STM, but in working memory. This is where new thoughts, ideas, and solutions are formed. If you think of the LTM as a hard drive and the STM as RAM, the working memory is best compared to the processor of the brain.

**BASIC PROGRAM: WORKING MEMORY**

In reading the BASIC program, you use your LTM—for example, when remembering the meaning of keywords like *LET* and *EXIT*. In addition, you use your STM to store some of the information you encounter, like the fact that B$ starts off as an empty string.

However, your brain does a lot more while you are reading the BASIC program. You are mentally trying to execute the code, to understand what is happening. That process is called *tracing*—the mental compiling and executing of code. The part of the brain used to do tracing and other cognitively complex tasks is called the working memory. You can compare it to the processor of a computer, which performs calculations.

When tracing very complex programs, you might feel the need to note the values of variables, either in the code or in a separate table. The fact that your brain feels the need to store information externally can be a sign that your working memory is too full to process more information. We will cover this information overload and how to prevent the brain from overloading in chapter 4.

Here is a quick summary of how the different types of confusion are related to the different cognitive processes:

- Lack of knowledge = Issue in LTM
- Lack of information = Issue in STM
- Lack of processing power = Issue in working memory

## 1.3 Cognitive processes in collaboration

In the previous section, I described in detail three important cognitive processes that are relevant to programming. In summary, your LTM stores information you have acquired for a long time, the STM temporarily stores information you have just read or heard, and the working memory processes information and forms new thoughts. While I described them as separate processes, these cognitive processes have strong relationships with each other. Let's touch on how they relate to one another.

### 1.3.1 A brief dissection of how the cognitive processes interacted

In fact, all three cognitive processes are activated to a certain extent when you do any thinking, as illustrated by figure 1.2. You might have experienced all three processes consciously when you were reading the Java code snippet earlier in this chapter (listing 1.2). Some pieces of information were stored in your STM, for example when you read that n was an integer. At the same time, your brain retrieved the meaning of what an integer is from your LTM, and you were thinking about the meaning of the program using your working memory.

So far in this chapter, we have focused specifically on the cognitive processes that happen when you read code. However, these three cognitive processes are involved in many other programming-related tasks too.

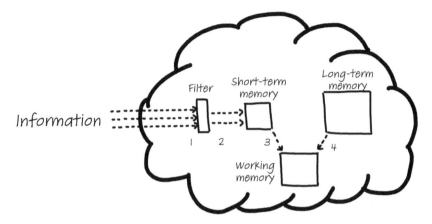

**Figure 1.2**   An overview of the three cognitive processes that this book covers: STM, LTM, and working memory. The arrows labeled 1 represent information coming into your brain. The arrows labeled 2 indicate the information that proceeds into your STM. Arrow 3 represents information traveling from the STM into the working memory, where it's combined with information from the LTM (arrow 4). Working memory is where the information is processed while you think about it.

### 1.3.2   Cognitive processes regarding programming tasks

For example, consider when you read a bug report from a customer. The bug seems to be caused by an off-by-one error. This bug report enters the brain through your senses—your eyes if you are sighted, or your ears if you read with a screen reader. To solve the bug, you must reread code that you wrote a few months ago. While you are rereading the code, your STM stores what you read, while your LTM tells you about what you implemented a few months ago—for example, that you used the actor model then. In addition to memories about your experiences, you also have factual information stored in your LTM, like how you could solve an off-by-one error. All this information—the new information about the bug report from your STM and your personal memories and relevant facts about how to solve similar bugs from your LTM—enters your working memory, where you can think about the problem at hand.

> **EXERCISE 1.1**   To practice your newly gained understanding of the three cognitive processes involved in programming, I've prepared three programs. This time, though, no explanation is given of what the code snippets do. You will, therefore, have to read the programs and decide what they do for yourself. The programs are again written in APL, Java, and BASIC, in that order. However, each of the programs performs a different operation, so you cannot rely on your understanding of the first program to support reading the other programs.
>
> Read the programs carefully and try to determine what they do. While doing this, reflect on the mechanisms that you use. Use the questions in the following table to guide your self-analysis.

|  | Code snippet 1 | Code snippet 2 | Code snippet 3 |
|---|---|---|---|
| Are you retrieving knowledge from LTM? |  |  |  |
| If you are retrieving information from LTM, what information? |  |  |  |
| Are you storing information in your STM? |  |  |  |
| What information are you storing explicitly? |  |  |  |
| What information are you ignoring because it seems irrelevant? |  |  |  |
| Is your working memory processing some parts of the code extensively? |  |  |  |
| Which parts of the code place a heavy load on your working memory? |  |  |  |
| Do you understand why these parts of code make the working memory work? |  |  |  |

### Code snippet 1: An APL program

```
f • {ω≤1:ω ◊ (∇ ω-1)+∇ ω-2}
```

What does this code do? What cognitive processes are involved?

### Code snippet 2: A Java program

```java
public class Luhn {
    public static void main(String[] args) {
        System.out.println(luhnTest("49927398716"));
    }

    public static boolean luhnTest(String number){
        int s1 = 0, s2 = 0;
        String reverse = new StringBuffer(number).reverse().toString();
        for(int i = 0 ;i < reverse.length();i++){
            int digit = Character.digit(reverse.charAt(i), 10);
            if(i % 2 == 0){//this is for odd digits
                s1 += digit;
            }else{//add 2 * digit for 0-4, add 2 * digit - 9 for 5-9
                s2 += 2 * digit;
                if(digit >= 5){
                    s2 -= 9;
                }
            }
        }
        return (s1 + s2) % 10 == 0;
    }
}
```

What does this code do? What cognitive processes are involved?

**Code snippet 3: A BASIC program**

```
100 INPUT PROMPT "String: ":TX$
120 LET RES$=""
130 FOR I=LEN(TX$) TO 1 STEP-1
140    LET RES$=RES$&TX$(I)
150 NEXT
160 PRINT RES$
```

What does this code do? What cognitive processes are involved?

## Summary

- To resolve confusion you must first identify its source. Confusion while coding is usually caused by three issues: a lack of knowledge, a lack of easy-to-access information, or a lack of processing power in the brain.
- Three cognitive processes are involved when you read or write code: long term memory (LTM), short term memory (STM), and working memory.
  - LTM stores knowledge that may need to be accessed after a long period of time. For example, the meaning of keywords is stored in LTM.
  - STM can temporarily hold information like the name of a method or variable.
  - Working memory is where active processing takes place. In code, this may be tasks such as deciding that an index is one too low.
- All three cognitive processes are at work while you're reading code, and the processes complement each other. For example, if your STM encounters a variable name like n, your brain searches your LTM for related programs you've read in the past. And when you read an ambiguous word, your working memory is activated and your brain will try to decide the right meaning in this context.

# Speed reading for code

**This chapter covers**

- Analyzing why reading code quickly is hard even for an experienced developer
- Dissecting how the brain splits up new information into recognizable parts
- Discovering how LTM and STM work together when analyzing information like words or code
- Examining the role of iconic memory when processing code
- Explaining how remembering code can be used as a tool for (self) diagnosis of coding level
- Practicing writing code that is easier for others to read

Chapter 1 introduced three cognitive processes that play a role when programming and reading code. The first cognitive process we covered was LTM, which you can think of as a hard drive that stores memories and facts. The second cognitive process was STM, which is like random-access memory, storing information that comes into the brain for a short time. Finally, there's the working memory, which acts a bit like a processor and processes information from LTM and STM to perform thinking.

The focus of this chapter is on reading code. Reading code is a larger part of a programmer's working life than you might realize. Research indicates that almost 60% of programmers' time is spent *understanding* rather than *writing* code.[1] Thus, improving how quickly you can read code, without losing accuracy, can help you improve your programming skills substantially.

In the previous chapter you learned that STM is where information is stored first when you read code. This chapter will begin by helping you understand why it is so hard to process a lot of information stored in code. If you know what happens in your brain when you are quickly reading code, you can more easily self-monitor your understanding. Next, I'll show you methods to improve your code skills, for example by practicing speed-reading several code snippets. By the end of the chapter, you will know why reading code is so hard. You will also understand how to read code quicker, and you will be aware of techniques you can use to keep improving your code reading skills.

## 2.1 Quickly reading code

The book *Structure and Interpretation of Computer Programs* by Harold Abelson, Gerald Jay Sussman, and Julie Sussman (MIT Press, 1996) contains this well-known sentence: "Programs must be written for people to read and only incidentally for machines to execute." That might be true, but the reality is that programmers practice writing code a lot more than they practice reading code.

This starts early on. When learning to program, there is often a lot of focus on producing code. Most likely, when you learned to program—whether that was in college, at a job, or in a bootcamp—there was a strong focus on creating code. Exercises centered on learning how to solve problems and write code for them. Exercises where you read code were probably nonexistent. Because of this lack of practice, reading code is often harder than it needs to be. This chapter will help you improve your code reading skills.

Reading code is done for a variety of reasons: to add a feature, to find a bug, or to build an understanding of a larger system. What all situations in which you are reading code have in common is that you are looking for specific information present in the code. Examples of information that you could be looking for are the right location to implement a new feature, the location of a certain bug, where you last edited the code, or how a certain method is implemented.

By improving your ability to quickly find relevant information, you can reduce the number of times you have to go back to the code. A higher level of skill in reading code can also reduce how often you have to navigate through the code to find additional information. The time you save on searching through code can then be spent on fixing bugs or adding new features so that you can become a more effective programmer.

In the previous chapter, I asked you to read programs in three different programming languages to get a sense of the three different parts of the brain at work. To dive

---

[1] See "Measuring Program Comprehension: A Large-Scale Field Study with Professionals" by Xin Xia et al. (2017), https://ieeexplore.ieee.org/abstract/document/7997917.

into the role of STM in more depth, look at the following Java program that implements the insertion sort algorithm. You may look at the program for no more than three minutes. Use a clock or stopwatch so you know when the time is up. After the three minutes are up, cover the Java code with a sheet of paper or with your hand.

Keeping the code covered, try to reproduce it as best as you can.

---

**Listing 2.1  A Java program implementing insertion sort**

```java
public class InsertionSort {
  public static void main (String [] args) {
    int [] array = {45,12,85,32,89,39,69,44,42,1,6,8};
    int temp;
    for (int i = 1; i < array.length; i++) {
      for (int j = i; j > 0; j--) {
        if (array[j] < array [j - 1]) {
          temp = array[j];
          array[j] = array[j - 1];
          array[j - 1] = temp;
        }
      }
    }
    for (int i = 0; i < array.length; i++) {
      System.out.println(array[i]);
    }
  }
}
```

### 2.1.1  *What just happened in your brain?*

In reproducing the insertion sort Java program, you used both your STM and LTM. This is illustrated in figure 2.1.

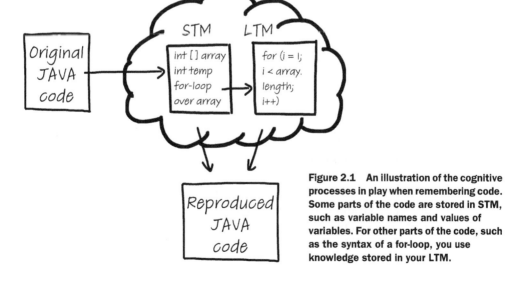

**Figure 2.1  An illustration of the cognitive processes in play when remembering code. Some parts of the code are stored in STM, such as variable names and values of variables. For other parts of the code, such as the syntax of a for-loop, you use knowledge stored in your LTM.**

Your STM was able to hold some of the information you just read. Your LTM added to this knowledge in two ways. First, you were able to rely on syntactic knowledge of Java. Maybe you remembered "a for-loop over the array," which your LTM knows is equivalent to for (int i = 0; i < array.length; i++). Maybe you also remembered "print all elements of the array," which in Java is for (i = 0; i < array.length; i++) {System.out.println(array[i])}.

Second, you could rely on the fact that you knew the code was implementing insertion sort. That might have helped you to fill in some blanks in the program, which you could not remember precisely. For example, maybe you didn't remember from reading the code that two values of the array were swapped, but because you're familiar with insertion sort you knew this was supposed to happen somewhere.

### 2.1.2 *Reexamine your reproduction*

To dive into your cognitive processes, have a second look at your reproduced code. Annotate which parts of the code you think came from your STM directly and which parts were retrieved from LTM. An example of the reproduced code with an annotation of cognitive processes is shown in figure 2.2.

```
public class InsertionSort {
  public static void main (String [] args) {
    int [] array = {45,12,…};
    int temp;
    for (int i = 1; i < array.length; i++) {
      for (int j = i; j > 0; j--) {
        if (array[j] < array [j - 1]) {
        // swap j with j - 1
        temp = array[j];
        array[j] = array[j - 1];
        array[j - 1] = temp;
      }
     }
    }
    //print array
    for (int i = 0; i < array.length; i++) {
      System.out.println(array[i]);
    }
   }
}
```

Figure 2.2   An example of the code from listing 2.1 reproduced by an experienced Java programmer, annotated to indicate the cognitive process in play. The parts of the code that are more darkly shaded are the parts stored in STM, and the lighter shading represents code coming from LTM. Note that more code is reproduced here than was present in the original code listing—for example, some comments were added.

What information is retrieved from your LTM, of course, depends on what you have stored there. Someone less experienced in Java is likely to retrieve a lot less from their LTM, so the image might look very different for you. Also note that in this reproduction some comments are present that were not in the original Java code. In experiments I've conducted with programmers remembering source code, I have found that sometimes people add comments to reproduced code to facilitate remembering. People would, for example, first write down "print the array" and later fill out the actual implementation. Did you do that too?

Comments are, of course, often used to describe code that is already written, but as you can see in this example, they have diverse uses and can also be used as a memory aid for future code. We will discuss the use of comments more extensively in later chapters.

### A SECOND ATTEMPT AT REMEMBERING JAVA

In chapter 1, I explained how LTM and STM collaborate when you're reading code. You've just experienced this collaboration in more depth as you reproduced some parts of the Java insertion sort program from information stored in your LTM.

To deepen your understanding of how extensively you rely on your LTM when reading and understanding code, let's do another exercise. It's the same exercise as the previous one: inspect the program for a maximum of three minutes, then cover the code and try to reproduce it as best as you can without peeking!

The Java code in the next listing is to be used as a memory exercise. Study for three minutes and try to reproduce to your best ability.

---

**Listing 2.2  Java code public**

```java
void execute(int x[]){
    int b = x.length;

    for (int v = b / 2 - 1; v >= 0; v--)
        func(x, b, v);

    // Extract elements one by one
    for (int l = b-1; l > 0; l--)
    {
        // Move current to end
        int temp = x[0];
        x[0] = x[l];
        x[l] = temp;

        func (x, l, 0);
    }
}
```

### 2.1.3  *Reexamining your second attempt at reproducing code*

Without knowing anything about you or your expertise in Java, I feel it's safe to bet that remembering this second program was probably a lot harder. There are a few reasons for this. First, you don't know exactly what this code is doing, which makes it a lot harder to fill in things you forget with knowledge from your LTM.

Second, I intentionally chose "weird" variable names, like b and l for-loop iterators. Unfamiliar names make it harder for you to quickly detect, recognize, and remember patterns. l as loop iterator is especially misleading since it is visually so similar to 1.

### 2.1.4   *Why is reading unfamiliar code hard?*

As the previous example showed, it's not easy to reproduce code you've read. Why is remembering code so hard? The most crucial reason is the limited capacity of your STM.

You cannot physically store all the information that is present in the code you are reading in your STM in order to process it. As you learned in chapter 1, STM stores information that you read or hear for a brief period of time. And when I say brief, I really mean brief! Research indicates it cannot hold information for more than 30 seconds. After 30 seconds, you will have to store the information in your LTM, or it will be lost forever. Imagine someone is reading a phone number to you over the phone, and you lack a place to write it down. If you don't find somewhere to write it down soon (e.g., a physical cache), you will not remember the phone number.

The time for which you can remember information is not the only limitation of STM—the second limitation is size.

Like in a computer, in your brain the long-term storage is a lot bigger than short-term storage. But while for RAM you might be talking about a few gigabytes of memory, your brain's quick storage is a lot smaller. Your STM has just a few slots available for information. George Miller, one of the most influential cognitive science researchers of the previous century, described this phenomenon in his 1956 paper "The Magical Number Seven, Plus or Minus Two: Some Limits on Our Capacity for Processing Information."

More recent research indicates the STM is even smaller, estimating a capacity of between two and six things. This limit holds for almost all people, and scientists so far have not found reliable ways to increase the size of the STM. Isn't it a miracle that humans can do anything with no more than 1 byte of memory?

To cope with these limits, your STM collaborates with your LTM to make sense of what you are reading or remembering. The next section details how the STM collaborates with the LTM in order to overcome its size limitations.

## 2.2   *Overcoming size limits in your memory*

In the previous section you learned about the limits of STM. You experienced them firsthand by trying to remember a piece of code. However, you probably remembered more than six characters from the code snippet. Isn't that a contradiction with having a maximum of just six slots available to store information?

Our ability to store only six things in STM does not only hold for reading code; it holds for any cognitive task. So how is it that people can do anything at all with such a limited memory? How can you read this sentence, for example?

According to Miller's theory, after you've read about six letters, shouldn't you be starting to forget the first letters you read? Clearly you can remember and process more than six letters, but how is that possible? To be able to understand why reading unfamiliar code is so hard, let's look at an important experiment that used chess to teach us more about STM.

### 2.2.1 *The power of chunking*

*Chunks* were first described by the Dutch mathematician Adrian de Groot. (De Groot, by the way, is not pronounced as rhyming with "boot" or "tooth," but sounds more like "growth.") De Groot was a PhD student in mathematics and an avid chess player. He became deeply interested in the question of why one person can become a great chess player while other players are bound to remain "medium" chess players for their entire lives. To investigate the topic of chess ability, de Groot performed two different experiments.

In experiment 1, illustrated in figure 2.3, de Groot showed a chess setup to chess players for a few seconds. After the players had inspected the setup, the pieces were covered and the players had to recreate the setup from memory. De Groot's experiment, in fact, was similar to the exercise you did earlier in this chapter with source code. De Groot was not just interested in everyone's ability to remember the locations of chess pieces. He specifically compared two groups of people. The first group consisted of average chess players, the second of expert players (chess masters). When comparing the performance of average players with chess masters, de Groot found that expert players were much better at recreating the chess setups than average players.

**Figure 2.3** De Groot's first chess experiment in which experts and average chess players were asked to remember a chess setup. Expert players were able to recall more pieces than average players.

De Groot's conclusion from this experiment was that experts outperformed average players because expert chess players simply had an STM with a larger capacity than average players. He also hypothesized that a larger STM could be the reason that the expert players became experts in the first place; expert players could fit more chess pieces in their memories, which allowed them to play better in chess games too.

However, de Groot was not entirely convinced, so he performed another experiment. It was similar to the first experiment: again, average and expert players were asked to remember chess setups after inspecting the setups for a brief period of time. The difference was in the chess setups themselves. Instead of showing the participants a real chess setup like in experiment 1, he showed them chessboards with randomly placed pieces—and not just a little bit random; the chess pieces were set up in entirely unrealistic configurations. De Groot then again compared the performance of the expert players with average players. The results came out differently for the second experiment: both types of players performed equally badly!

The results of experiment 1 and experiment 2 led de Groot to dive deeper into how exactly both groups of chess players remembered the setups. It turned out that in both experiments the average players mostly remembered the setups piece by piece. They would try to recall the setups by saying "a rook at A7, a pawn at B5, a king at C8," and so on.

In the first experiment, however, the expert chess players exhibited a different strategy. The experts very heavily relied on information stored in their LTM. For example, they might remember "a Sicilian opening, but one knight is two squares to the left." Remembering the setup like that, of course, is only possible if you know what pieces are used in the Sicilian opening, which is stored in the LTM. Remembering the setups as the experts did occupies only about four places in working memory (Sicilian opening, knight, 2, left). As you know, the STM is estimated to hold between two and six elements, so four elements could fit.

Some expert players could also connect the setups to their own personal playing history, or the history of games they'd watched or read about. They might remember a setup as "the game I played that one rainy Saturday in March against Betsie, but with castling on the left." This too is information that is stored in the LTM. Remembering a setup by thinking of a previous experience also only occupies just a few slots in STM.

Average players, however, who were trying to remember all the individual pieces would quickly run out of STM. They could not group information in logical ways as experts did. This explained why average players performed worse than experts in experiment 1; when their STM was full, no new locations could be stored.

De Groot called the groups into which people combined information chunks. He considered "Sicilian opening," for example, one chunk, which can fit into one slot in STM. The theory of chunks also adequately explains why both types of players performed equally in experiment 2. In a random chess setup, expert players could no longer rely on the repository of boards in their LTM to quickly divide the pieces into larger groups.

**EXERCISE 2.1**  Maybe you are convinced by de Groot's experiments, but it would be even more powerful to experience chunking yourself!

Look at this sentence for five seconds and try to remember it as best as you can:

$$\text{0|3   0\C<0  b|3)}$$

How much can you remember of that sentence?

**EXERCISE 2.2**   Now try to remember this sentence by inspecting it for five seconds:

*abk  mrtpi  gbar*

I'd guess that second sentence was easier than the first one. That's because this second sentence consists of letters that you recognize. It may be hard to believe, but these two sentences were the same length: 3 words, 12 characters, 9 different characters.

**EXERCISE 2.3**   Let's try one more. This sentence again consists of three words and nine different characters. Look at this sentence for five seconds and try to remember it:

*cat  loves  cake*

The third sentence was a lot easier than the other two, right? You can remember this sentence with great ease. That's because you can chunk the characters in the third sentence into words. You can then remember just three chunks: "cat," "loves," and "cake." The amount of three elements is well below the capacity of your STM, so it's possible to remember all of this sentence easily, while in the first two examples the number of elements likely exceeds the limits of your STM.

**CHUNKING IN CODE**

So far in this chapter, you've seen that the more information you have stored about a specific topic, the easier it is to effectively divide information into chunks. Expert chess players have many different chess setups stored in their LTM, so they can remember a board better. In the previous exercise, in which you were asked to remember characters, letters, and then words, you were able to recall the words with a lot more ease than unfamiliar characters. Words are easier to remember because you can retrieve their meaning from your LTM.

The finding that it is easier to remember when you have a lot of knowledge about something in your LTM also holds in programming. In the remainder of this chapter, we will explore research findings on programming and chunking specifically. After that, we will dive into how to practice chunking code and how to write code that is easy to chunk.

### 2.2.2  *Expert programmers can remember code better than beginners*

De Groot's studies have been widely influential in cognitive science. His experiments also motivated computer science researchers to study whether similar results would hold for programming.

For example, in 1981 Katherine McKeithen, a researcher at Bell Labs, tried to repeat de Groot's experiments on programmers.[2] She and her colleagues showed small, 30-line ALGOL programs to 53 people: beginner, intermediate, and expert programmers. Some of the programs were real programs, inspired by de Groot's first experiment in which he asked participants to remember realistic chess setups. In other programs the lines of code were scrambled, similar to de Groot's second experiment in which the chess pieces were placed in random locations. Participants were allowed to study the ALGOL programs for two minutes, after which they had to reproduce the code to the best of their ability.

McKeithen's results were quite similar to de Groot's: with the unscrambled programs, experts did better than intermediate programmers, and intermediate programmers in turn performed better than beginners. With the scrambled programs there was hardly any difference between the three different groups of programmers, as shown in figure 2.4.

The biggest takeaway from this research is that beginners will be able to process a lot less code than experts. This can be important to remember when you are onboarding a new team member or when you are learning a new programming language yourself.

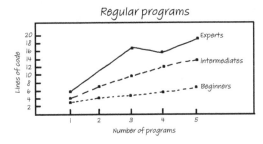

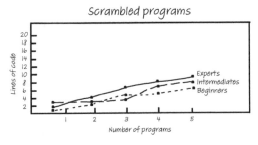

**Figure 2.4  The number of lines of code that beginners, intermediates, and experts could recall in McKeithen et al.'s experiments. The top image shows participants' performance on regular programs, where experts clearly excel. The bottom image shows performance on scrambled, nonsensical programs; here, the performance of experts, intermediates, and beginners is very similar.**

---

2 "Knowledge Organization and Skill Differences in Computer Programmers" by Katherine B. McKeithen et al. (1981), http://mng.bz/YA5a.

Even a smart person capable of programming well in a different programming language or context will struggle with unfamiliar keywords, structures, and domain concepts when these aren't yet stored in their LTM. You'll learn strategies for doing this quickly and reliably in the next chapter.

## 2.3    *You see more code than you can read*

Before we dive deeper into the details of STM, I first want to spend some time on what happens when information enters the brain. There is a stage that information passes through before it reaches STM, called *sensory memory*.

In our computer metaphor, you can think of sensory memory as an I/O buffer communicating with an input device like a mouse or a keyboard. Information sent from peripheral devices is briefly stored in the I/O buffer. This is true for our sensory memory too; it briefly holds visual, auditory, or haptic input. Each of the five senses—sight, hearing, taste, smell, touch—has its own cache in the sensory memory. Not all of these are interesting to discuss in the context of programming, so in this chapter we will limit ourselves to the one for sight, called the *iconic memory*.

### 2.3.1    *Iconic memory*

Before information reaches your STM, it first enters the sensory memory through your senses. When reading code, information comes in through your eyes, after which it is briefly stored in the iconic memory.

The best way to illustrate the iconic memory is to imagine that it is New Year's Eve, and you are holding a sparkler. If you move the sparkler quickly enough, you can form a letter in the air. You've probably never thought about what makes that possible, but your iconic memory is what enables you to see patterns in light. The iconic memory can store visual stimuli, which are created by an image you just saw, for a little while. You can experience another example if you close your eyes after reading this sentence. With your eyes closed, you still "see" the shape of the page. That too is iconic memory.

Before we investigate how we can use the iconic memory in reading code, let's examine what we know about it. One of the pioneers of research on iconic memory was American cognitive psychologist George Sperling, who researched sensory memory in the 1960s. In his most famous study,[3] participants were shown a 3×3- or 3×4-letter grid. This grid was similar to those you might see at an eye exam, but with all the letters being the same size, as shown in figure 2.5.

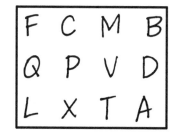

**Figure 2.5   An example of Sperling's letter grid, which participants had to remember**

Participants were shown the images for a twentieth of a second (0.05 seconds or 50 milliseconds), after which they were asked to recall a randomly selected line of the grid, such as the top row or the left column.

---

[3] "The Information Available in Brief Visual Presentations" by George Sperling (1960), http://mng.bz/O1ao.

In 50 milliseconds they would never be able to really read the letters, because the reaction time of a human eye is around 200 milliseconds (one-fifth of a second)—which is quick, but not quick enough. Yet in this experiment, participants could remember all letters in a random line or column from the grid in about 75% of the cases. Because the participants were recalling a random line, the fact that they succeeded 75% of the time meant that they had stored many or all of the 9 or 12 letters in the grid, which is more than would fit in STM.

It was not the case that these participants had excellent memories. When participants were asked to reproduce all the letters, they did a lot worse than when they were asked to name a specific set of letters. Typically participants could remember about half of the letters. That second finding fits with what we already know about the STM, which was also known when Sperling conducted his experiments: it can store up to about six items. The fact that many of the participants were able to remember all the letters when asked for only three or four at a time, however, showed that the letter grid in its entirety was stored somewhere, and that "somewhere" needed to be different than the STM with its limited capacity. Sperling called the location of information coming from the visual sense the iconic memory. As shown in his experiments, not all information that is stored in the iconic memory can be processed in the STM.

### ICONIC MEMORY AND CODE

As you just learned, everything you read is first stored in your iconic memory. But not everything that your iconic memory stores can be processed by your STM, so when you read code in detail, you have to make choices about what you can process. These choices, however, do not happen consciously—overlooking certain details in code often happens by accident. This means that you can theoretically remember more information about code than you can process in your STM.

You can use this knowledge to try to read code more efficiently by first looking at it for a brief period of time and then reflecting on what you have seen. This "code at a glance" exercise will help you gain an initial image of the code.

### EXERCISE 2.4

Select a piece of code that is somewhat familiar to you. It can be something from your own codebase, or a small and simple piece of code from GitHub. It doesn't matter all that much what code you select, or the programming language used. Something the size of half a page works best, and if possible, printing it on paper is encouraged.

Look at the code for a few seconds, then remove it from sight and try to answer the following questions:

- What is the structure of the code?
  - Is the code nested deeply or it is flat?
  - Are there any lines that stand out?
- How is whitespace used to structure the code?
  - Are there gaps in the code?
  - Are there large blobs of code?

### 2.3.2 *It's not what you remember; it's the way you remember it*

When you try to reproduce code you just read, studying the lines of code that you can reproduce can be a great diagnostic tool that helps you understand your own (mis)understanding. However, it's not just *what* you can remember—the *order* in which you remember the code can also be a tool for understanding.

The researchers who repeated de Groot's chess studies using ALGOL programs performed another experiment that provided more insights into chunking.[4] In the second experiment, beginner, intermediate, and expert programmers were trained to remember 21 ALGOL keywords, such as *IF, TRUE*, and *END*.

The keywords used in the study are shown in figure 2.6. If you want to, you can try to remember all the keywords yourself.

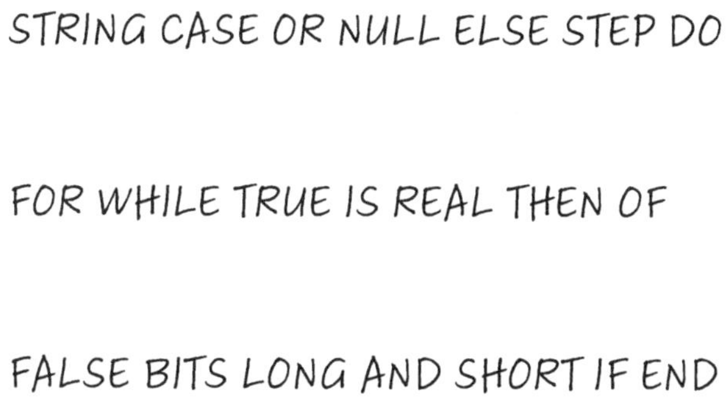

STRING CASE OR NULL ELSE STEP DO

FOR WHILE TRUE IS REAL THEN OF

Figure 2.6   The 21 ALGOL keywords that McKeithen et al. used in their study. Beginners, intermediate programmers, and experts were trained to learn all 21 keywords.

FALSE BITS LONG AND SHORT IF END

When the participants could repeat all 21 keywords reliably the researchers asked them to list all the keywords. If you have memorized them too, try to write them down now, so you can compare yourself with the people in the study.

From the order in which participants repeated the keywords, McKeithen et al. were able to gain insight into the connections they had created between keywords. The results of the study showed that beginners grouped the ALGOL keywords in different ways than experts. Beginners, for example, often used sentences as memory aids, such as "TRUE IS REAL THEN FALSE." Experts, however, would use their prior knowledge of programming to group the keywords; for example, they combined TRUE and FALSE, and IF, THEN, and ELSE. This study again confirmed that experts think about code in a different way than beginners do.

#### HOW TO WRITE CHUNKABLE CODE

Once you have done the earlier remember-and-chunk exercise several times, you will start to develop an intuition about what types of code are chunkable. From de Groot's study with chess players, we know that situations that are usual or predictable, like famous openings, ease chunking. So, if your goal is to create chess boards that are easy

---

[4] The results of this experiment were reported in the same paper, "Knowledge Organization and Skill Differences in Computer Programmers" by Katherine B. McKeithen et al.

to remember, use a well-known opening. But what can we do in code to make it easier to read? Several researchers have studied ways to write code in such a way that it is easier to chunk, and thus easier to process.

#### USE DESIGN PATTERNS

If you want to write code that is easy to chunk, make use of design patterns. Those were the findings of Walter Tichy, professor of computer science at the Karlsruhe Institute of Technology in Germany. Tichy has investigated chunking in code, but this happened somewhat by accident. He was not studying code memory skills, but instead was looking into design patterns. He was especially interested in the question of whether design patterns help programmers when they are *maintaining* code (adding new features or fixing bugs).

Tichy started small, with a group of students, testing whether giving them information on design patterns helped them understand code.[5] He divided the students into two groups: one group received code with documentation, while the other group received the same code but without documentation on design patterns. The results of Tichy's study showed that having a design pattern present in the code was more helpful for performing maintenance tasks when the programmers knew that the pattern was present in the code.

Tichy performed a similar study on professionals, too.[6] In this case the participants started with the code modification exercise, then subsequently took a course on design patterns. After the course, they again modified code, with or without a design pattern. The results of this study on professionals are shown in figure 2.7. It should be noted that the participants in this study maintained different code after the test, so they were not familiar with the code used after the course. The study used two codebases: participants who saw codebase A before the course used codebase B afterward, and vice versa.

This figure presents the results of Tichy's study with box-and-whisker plots.[7] It shows that after taking a course on design patterns (as seen in the righthand graphs labeled "posttest"), the time participants needed to maintain code was lower for the code with patterns but not for the code without patterns. The results of this study indicate that gaining knowledge about design patterns, which is likely going to improve your chunking ability, helps you process code faster. You can also see in the graphs that there is a difference in effect for different design patterns: the decrease in time is bigger for the observer pattern than for the decorator pattern.

---

[5] See "Two Controlled Experiments Assessing the Usefulness of Design Pattern Information During Program Maintenance," by Lutz Prechelt, Barbara Unger, and Walter Tichy (1998), http://mng.bz/YA9K.

[6] "A Controlled Experiment Comparing the Maintainability of Programs Designed with and without Design Patterns—A Replication in a Real Programming Environment," by Marek Vokáč, Walter Tichy, Dag I. K. Sjøberg, Erik Arisholm, Magne Aldrin (2004), http://mng.bz/G6oR.

[7] The box represents half of the data, with the top line the median of the third quartile and the bottom line the median of the first quartile. The line within the box represents the median and the "whiskers" show the minimum and maximum values.

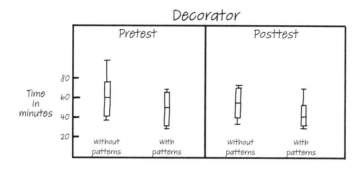

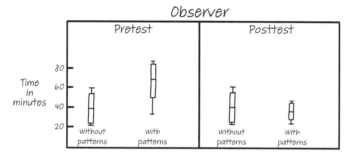

Figure 2.7 These graphs show the results of Walter Tichy's study on design patterns with professionals. "Without patterns" indicates the time participants took to modify the original code without design patterns, while "with patterns" shows the time they took on the code that included design patterns. "Pretest" is the time that participants took before the course on design patterns; "posttest" is the time after the design patterns course. The results show that after the course maintenance time was significantly lower for code that contains design patterns.

## WRITE COMMENTS

Should you write comments or should code "document itself"? This is a question that often sparks debate among programmers. Researchers have studied this question too and have found several interesting directions to dive into.

Research has shown that when code contains comments, programmers will take more time to read it. You might think that is a bad thing—that comments slow you down—but in fact, this is a sign that comments are being read when programmers read code. At the very least this is showing that you are not adding comments to your code for nothing. Martha Elizabeth Crosby, a researcher at the University of Hawaii, studied how programmers read code and what role comments play in their reading behavior.[8] Crosby's work shows that beginners focus a lot more on comments than experienced programmers do. Part 4 of this book will cover the process of onboarding junior colleagues into your team in more depth, but Crosby's findings suggest that adding comments to code can be a good way to make it easier for new programmers to understand your codebase.

In addition to supporting novice programmers, comments also play a role in how developers chunk code. Quiyin Fan's 2010 dissertation at the University of Maryland, "The Effects of Beacons, Comments, and Tasks on Program Comprehension Process in Software Maintenance," showed that developers depend heavily on comments

---

[8] "How Do We Read Algorithms? A Case Study" by Martha E. Crosby and Jan Stelovsky, https://ieeexplore.ieee .org/document/48797.

when reading code. In particular, high-level comments like "This function prints a given binary tree in order" can help programmers chunk larger pieces of code. Low-level comments, on the other hand, such as "Increment i (by one)" after a line that reads i++;, can create a burden on the chunking process.

## LEAVE BEACONS

A final thing you can do to make the process of chunking code easier is to include *beacons*. Beacons are parts of a program that help a programmer understand what the code does. You can think of a beacon like a line of code, or even part of a line of code, that your eye falls on which makes you think, "Aha, now I see."

Beacons typically indicate that a piece of code contains certain data structures, algorithms, or approaches. As an example of beacons, consider the following Python code that traverses a binary tree.

---

**Listing 2.3   In-order tree traversal in Python**

```python
# A class that represents a node in a tree

class Node:
    def __init__(self, key):
        self.left = None
        self.right = None
        self.val = key


# A function to do in-order tree traversal

def print_in_order(root):
    if root:

        # First recur on left child
        print_in_order(root.left)

        # then print the data of node
        print(root.val)

        # now recur on right child
        print_in_order(root.right)


print("Contents of the tree are")
print_in_order(tree)
```

This Python code contains several beacons from which a reader can deduce that this code uses a binary tree as the data structure:

- Comments using the word "tree"
- Variables called root and tree
- Fields called left and right
- String contents in the code that concern trees ("Contents of the tree are")

Beacons provide an important signaling service for programmers during the comprehension process because they often act as a trigger for programmers to confirm or refute hypotheses about the source. For example, when you start to read the Python code in the previous listing, you might not have any idea what this code is doing. When you read the first comment and the class `Node`, you get the sense that this code concerns trees. The fields `left` and `right` then further narrow your hypothesis, indicating that this code works on a binary tree.

We typically distinguish two different types of beacons: *simple beacons* and *compound beacons*.

Simple beacons are self-explaining syntactic code elements, such as meaningful variable names. In the preceding Python code, `root` and `tree` are simple beacons. In some code, operators such as `+`, `>`, and `&&` and structural statements such as `if`, `else`, and so on can be considered simple beacons too because they are simple enough to process and can help a reader unlock the functionality of code by themselves.

Compound beacons are larger code structures comprised of simple beacons. Compound beacons provide semantic meaning for functions that simple beacons execute together. In the Python code in listing 2.3, `self.left` and `self.right` together form a compound beacon. Separately, they do not offer much insight into the code, but together they do. Code elements can also serve as compound beacons. For instance, a for-loop can be a compound beacon because it contains the variable, the initial assignment, and the increment and the boundary values.

Beacons can take many forms; we have already seen that variable and class names can serve as beacons, and other identifiers such as method names can be beacons too. In addition to names, specific programming constructs like a swap or initialization to an empty list can also be beacons.

Beacons have a relationship to the chunks, but most researchers see them as different concepts. Beacons are usually seen as smaller parts of code than chunks. Crosby, whose work on the use of comments I summarized earlier, also studied the role of beacons. She found that expert programmers, but not novices, make heavy use of beacons when they are reading and comprehending code.[9] The following exercise will help you recognize useful beacons.

### EXERCISE 2.5

Selecting the right kinds of beacons to use in code can take some practice. Use this exercise to deliberately practice using beacons in code.

### Step 1: Select code

For this exercise select an unfamiliar codebase, but do select one in a programming language that you are familiar with. If possible, it would be great to do this exercise on a codebase where you know someone familiar with the details. You can then use that person as a judge of your understanding. In the codebase, select one method or function.

---

[9] See "The Roles Beacons Play in Comprehension for Novice and Expert Programmers" by Martha E. Crosby, Jean Scholtz, and Susan Wiedenbeck, http://mng.bz/zGKX.

**Step 2: Study code**
Study the selected code and try to summarize the meaning of the code.

**Step 3: Actively notice beacons that you use**
Whenever you have an "aha" moment where you get a bit closer to the functionality of the code, stop and write down what it was that led you to that conclusion. This could be a comment, a variable name, a method name, or an intermediate value—all of those can be beacons.

**Step 4: Reflect**
When you have a thorough understanding of the code and a list of beacons, reflect using these questions:

- What beacons have you collected?
- Are these code elements or natural language information?
- What knowledge do they represent?
- Do they represent knowledge about the domain of the code?
- Do they represent knowledge about the functionality of the code?

**Step 5: Contribute back to the code (optional)**
Sometimes, but not always, the beacons you have selected could be improved or extended. Or the code might be in need of additional beacons that aren't there yet. This is a great moment to enrich the code with the new or improved beacons. Because you weren't familiar with the code before this exercise, you have a good perspective on what would help someone else who is new to the codebase too.

**Step 6: Compare with someone else (optional)**
If you have a coworker or friend who wants to improve their beacon use too, you can do this exercise together. It can be interesting to reflect on the differences both of you had in reproducing code. Because we know there are large differences between beginners and experts, this exercise might also help you understand your level of skill in a programming language relative to someone else's.

### 2.3.3 *Practice chunking*

The studies described earlier in this chapter showed that people with more experience can remember more chess pieces or words or lines of code. While knowing more programming concepts comes with experience, there are several things you can do to practice chunking code deliberately.

In many places in this book, you will see the phrase *deliberate practice*. Deliberate practice is using small exercises to improve a certain skill. Push-ups are deliberate practice for your arm muscles; tone ladders are deliberate practice for musicians; spelling words is deliberate practice for new readers. In programming, for many different reasons, deliberate practice is not all that commonly used. Many people have learned programming mainly by programming a lot. While that works, it might not work as effectively as possible. To deliberately practice chunking, actively trying to remember code is a great exercise.

**EXERCISE 2.6**

This exercise helps you recognize what concepts you are familiar with and what concepts are harder for you by testing your code reading memory. The underlying assumption is that, as shown by the experiments outlined, familiar concepts are easier to remember. What you can remember is what you know, so these exercises can be used for (self) diagnosis of your code knowledge.

**Step 1: Select code**

Select a codebase you are somewhat familiar with—maybe something you work with regularly, but not mainly. It can also be something you personally wrote a while ago. Make sure you have at least some knowledge of the programming language the code is written in. You have to know more or less what the code does, but not know it intimately. You want to be in a situation similar to the chess players; they know the board and the pieces but not the setup.

In the codebase, select a method or function, or another coherent piece of code roughly the size of half a page, with a maximum of 50 lines of code.

**Step 2: Study code**

Study the selected code for a bit, for a maximum of two minutes. Set a timer so you don't lose track of the time. After the timer runs out, close or cover the code.

**Step 3: Reproduce the code**

Take a piece of paper, or open a new file in your IDE, and try to recreate the code as best as you can.

**Step 4: Reflect**

When you are sure you have reproduced all the code you possibly can, open the original code and compare. Reflect using these questions:

- Which parts did you produce correctly with ease?
- Are there any parts of the code that you reproduced partly?
- Are there parts of the code that you missed entirely?
- Do you understand why you missed the lines that you did?
- Do the lines of code that you missed contain programming concepts that are unfamiliar to you?
- Do the lines of code that you missed contain domain concepts that are unfamiliar to you?

**Step 5: Compare with someone else (optional)**

If you have a coworker who wants to improve their chunking abilities too, you can do this exercise together. It can be very interesting to reflect on the differences in the code you reproduce. Because we know there are large differences between beginners and experts, this exercise might also help you understand your level of skill in a programming language relative to someone else's.

## Summary

- The STM has a capacity of two to six elements.
- To overcome the size limitation, your STM collaborates with your LTM when you remember information.
- When you read new information, your brain tries to divide the information into recognizable parts called chunks.
- When you lack enough knowledge in your LTM, you have to rely on low-level reading of code, like letters and keywords. When doing that, you will quickly run out of space in your STM.
- When your LTM stores enough relevant information, you can remember abstract concepts like "a for-loop in Java" or "selection sort in Python" instead of the code at a lower level, occupying less space in your STM.
- When you read code, it is first stored in the iconic memory. Only a bit of the code is subsequently sent to the STM.
- Remembering code can be used as a tool for (self) diagnosis of your knowledge of coding. Because you can most easily remember what you already know, the parts of code that you remember can reveal the design patterns, programming constructs, and domain concepts you are most familiar with.
- Code can contain characteristics that make it easier to process, such as design patterns, comments, and explicit beacons.

# How to learn programming syntax quickly

## This chapter covers

- Examining why extensive syntax knowledge is important
- Selecting techniques to remember programming syntax
- Organizing what you can do to prevent forgetting syntax
- Deducing when to study syntax and programming concepts for the most effective results
- Discovering how syntax and programming concepts are stored in LTM
- Practicing elaboration to strengthen memories and better remember programming concepts

This chapter focuses on how people learn to remember things. This chapter will help you to understand why certain knowledge sticks, while other knowledge is forgotten. For example, at one point you probably learned that System.out.print()

is the method that prints in Java. However, you do not have all of Java's methods memorized. I'm sure you have sometimes felt the need to look up specific syntax. For example, would you know whether to use addDays(), addTimespan(), or plusDays() to add a day to a DateTime?

You might not care that much about knowing syntax by heart—after all, we can all look up information online, right? However, as the previous chapter showed, what you already know influences how efficiently you process code. Therefore, memorizing programming syntax, concepts, and data structures will help you to process code faster.

This chapter introduces four important techniques that will help you memorize programming concepts better and more easily. This will strengthen your long-term storage of programming concepts, which in turn will allow for better chunking and reading of code. If you have ever struggled with remembering the syntax of Flexbox in CSS, the order of parameters in matplotlib's boxplot() method, or the syntax of anonymous functions in JavaScript, this chapter has you covered!

## 3.1    *Tips for remembering syntax*

In previous chapters, you saw that trying to remember code line by line is hard. Remembering what syntax to use when producing code can also be challenging. For example, can you write code from memory for the following situations?

- Reading a hello.txt file and writing all lines to the command line
- Formatting a date in the order of day-month-year
- A regular expression matching words that start with "s" or "season"

Even though you are a professional programmer, you might have needed to look up some of the specific syntax for these exercises. In this chapter, we will explore not only why it's hard to remember the right syntax, but also how to get better at it. First, though, we will take a deeper look at why it is so important that you can remember code.

Many programmers believe that if you do not know a certain piece of syntax, you can just look it up on the internet and that therefore syntax knowledge is not all that important. There are two reasons why "just looking things up" might not be a great solution. The first reason was covered in chapter 2: what you already know impacts to a large extent how efficiently you can read and understand code. The more concepts, data structures, and syntax you know, the more code you can easily chunk and thus remember and process.

### 3.1.1    *Disruptions play havoc with your workflow*

The second reason is that an interruption of your work can be more disruptive than you think. Just opening a browser to search for information might tempt you to check your email or read a bit of news, which may not be relevant to the task at hand. You might also lose yourself in reading detailed discussions on programming websites when you are searching for related information.

Chris Parnin, a professor at North Carolina State University, has extensively studied what happens when programmers are interrupted at work.[1] Parnin recorded 10,000 programming sessions by 85 programmers. He looked at how often developers were interrupted by emails and colleagues (which was a lot!), but he also examined what happens after an interruption. Parnin determined that interruptions are, unsurprisingly, quite disruptive to productivity. The study showed that it typically takes about a quarter of an hour to get back to editing code after an interruption. When interrupted during an edit of a method, programmers were able to resume their work in less than a minute in only 10% of cases.

Parnin's results showed that programmers often forgot vital information about the code they were working on while they were away from the code. You might recognize that "What was I doing again?" feeling after returning to code from a search. Programmers in Parnin's study also often needed to put in deliberate effort to rebuild the context. For example, they might navigate to several locations in the codebase to recall details before actually continuing the programming work.

Now that you know why remembering syntax is important, we'll dive into how to learn syntax quickly.

## 3.2 *How to learn syntax quickly with flashcards*

A great way to learn anything quickly, including syntax, is to use *flashcards*. Flashcards are simply paper cards or Post-Its. One side has a prompt on it—the thing that you want to learn. The other side has the corresponding knowledge on it.

When using flashcards for programming, you can write the concept on one side and the corresponding code on the other. A set of flashcards for list comprehensions in Python might look like this:

1 Basic comprehension <-> `numbers = [x for x in numbers]`
2 Comprehension with filter <-> `odd_numbers = [x for x in numbers if x % 2 == 1]`
3 Comprehension with calculation <-> `[x*x for x in numbers]`
4 Comprehension with filter and calculation <-> `squares = [x*x for x in numbers if x > 25]`

You use flashcards by reading the side of the card with the prompt on it and trying your best to remember the corresponding syntax. Write the syntax on a separate piece of paper or type the code in an editor. When you're finished, flip the card over and compare the code to see if you got it right.

Flashcards are commonly used in learning a second language and are tremendously useful for that. However, learning French using flashcards can be a cumbersome task because there are so many words. Even the big programming languages like C++ are much smaller than any natural human language. Learning a good chunk of the basic syntactic elements of a programming language therefore is doable with relatively low effort.

---

[1] See "Resumption Strategies for Interrupted Programming Tasks" by Chris Parnin and Spencer Rugaber (2011), http://mng.bz/0rpl.

**EXERCISE 3.1**  Think of the top 10 programming concepts you always have trouble remembering.

Make a set of flashcards for each of the concepts and try using them. You can also do this collaboratively in a group or team, where you might discover that you are not the only one who struggles with certain concepts.

### 3.2.1  When to use the flashcards

The trick to learning syntax is to use the flashcards often to practice. There are, however, also plenty of apps, like Cerego, Anki, and Quizlet, that allow you to create your own digital flashcards. The benefit of these apps is that they remind you when to practice again. If you use the paper flashcards or an app regularly, you will see that after a few weeks your syntactic vocabulary will have increased significantly. That will save you a lot of time on Googling, limit distractions, and help you to chunk better.

### 3.2.2  Expanding the set of flashcards

There are good times to add flashcards to your set. First, when you're learning a new programming language, framework, or library, you can add a card each time you encounter a new concept. For example, if you've just started learning the syntax of list comprehensions, create the corresponding card or cards right away.

   A second great time to expand your set of cards is when you're about to Google a certain concept. That is a signal that you do not yet know that concept by heart. Write the concept you decided to look up on one side of a card and the code you found on the other side.

   Of course, you'll need to use your judgment. Modern programming languages, libraries, and APIs are huge, and there's no need to memorize all of their syntax. Looking things up online is totally fine for fringe syntactic elements or concepts.

### 3.2.3  Thinning the set of flashcards

When you use your flashcards regularly, after a while you might start to feel that you know some of the cards well. When this happens, you might want to thin out your set of cards a bit. To keep track of how well you know certain concepts, you can keep a little tally on each card of your right and wrong answers, as shown in figure 3.1.

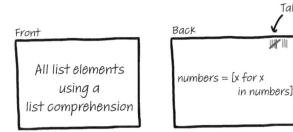

Figure 3.1  Example of a flashcard with a tally of right and wrong answers. Using a tally, you can keep track of what knowledge is already reliably stored in your LTM.

If you get a card right a bunch of times in a row, you can discard it. Of course, if you find yourself struggling again, you can always put the card back in. If you use an app to make flashcards, the apps will typically thin the set for you by not showing you cards that you already know well.

## 3.3     *How to not forget things*

The previous section showed how you can use flashcards to quickly learn and easily remember syntax. But how long should you practice? When will you finally know the entirety of Java 8? This section will shine a light on how often you will have to revisit knowledge before your memory is perfect.

Before we can turn our attention to how to *not* forget things, we need to dive into how and why people forget. You already know that the STM has limitations—it cannot store a lot of information at once, and the information it stores is not retained for very long. The LTM also has limitations, but they are different.

The big problem with your LTM is that you cannot remember things for a long time without extra practice. After you read, hear, or see something, the information is transferred from your STM to your LTM—but that doesn't mean it is stored in the LTM forever. In that sense, a human's LTM differs significantly from a computer's hard drive, on which information is stored relatively safely and durably.

The decay for LTM is not seconds, like that of the STM, but it is still a lot shorter than you might think. The forgetting curve is illustrated in figure 3.2. As you can see, in an hour you will typically already have lost half of what you read. After two days, just 25% of what you learned remains. But that's not the entire picture—the graph in figure 3.2 represents how much you remember if you do not revisit the information at all.

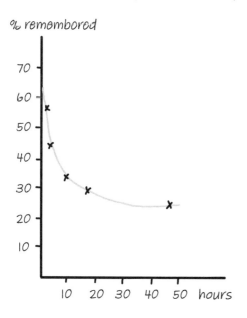

Figure 3.2   **A graph illustrating how much information you remember after being exposed to it. After two days, just 25% of the knowledge remains in your LTM.**

### 3.3.1   *Why do we forget memories?*

To understand why some memories are forgotten so quickly, we need to take a deep dive into the workings of the LTM—starting with how things are remembered.

Storage of memories in the brain is not based on zeros and ones, but it does share a name with how we store information to disk: *encoding.* When they talk about encoding, however, cognitive scientists aren't precisely referring to the translation of thoughts to storage—the exact workings of this process are still largely unknown—but rather to the changes that happen in the brain when memories are formed by neurons.

#### HIERARCHY VERSUS NETWORKS

We have compared the LTM to a hard drive, but storage in the brain does not actually work hierarchically, in the way that files are arranged in folders with subfolders. As figure 3.3 shows, memories in the brain are organized more in a network structure. That's because facts are connected to large numbers of other facts. An awareness of these connections between different facts and memories is important to understand why people forget information, which is the topic we are going to discuss next.

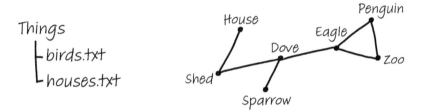

**Figure 3.3   Two ways of organizing data: on the left, a hierarchical filesystem; on the right, memories organized as a network**

#### THE FORGETTING CURVE

Hermann Ebbinghaus was a German philosopher and psychologist who became interested in studying the capabilities of the human mind in the 1870s. At that time, the idea of measuring people's mental capacities was relatively unheard of.

Ebbinghaus wanted to understand the limits of human memory using his own memory as a test. He wanted to push himself as far as possible. He realized that trying to remember known words or concepts was not a true test because memories are stored with associations, or relationships to each other. For example, if you try to remember the syntax of a list comprehension, knowing the syntax of a for-loop might help you.

To create a fairer means of assessment, Ebbinghaus constructed a large set of short nonsense words, such as *wix, maf, kel,* and *jos.* He then conducted an extensive set of experiments, using himself as a test subject. For years he studied lists of these nonsense words by reading them aloud, with the help of a metronome to keep up the pace, and kept track of how much practice was needed to be able to recall each list perfectly.

In 1880, after a decade, he estimated that he had spent almost 1,000 hours practicing, and he could recite 150 a minute. By testing himself at different intervals, Ebbinghaus was able to estimate the time span of his memory. He summarized his findings in his 1885 publication *Über das Gedächtnis* (*Memory: A Contribution to Experimental Psychology*). His book contained the formula for forgetting shown in figure 3.4, which lies at the base of the concept of the forgetting curve.

$$b = 100 \times \frac{1.84}{(\log_{10} t)^{1.25} + 1.84}$$

**Figure 3.4   Ebbinghaus's formula to estimate how long a memory will last**

A recent study by Dutch professor Jaap Murre of the University of Amsterdam confirmed that Ebbinghaus's formula is largely correct.[2]

### 3.3.2   *Spaced repetition*

We know now how quickly people forget things, but how will that help us not forget the syntax of `boxplot()` in matplotlib or list comprehensions in Python? In turns out that Ebbinghaus's experiments in remembering nonsense words not only allowed him to predict how long it would take him to forget things, but also shed light on how to prevent forgetting. Ebbinghaus observed that he could reliably learn a set of 12 meaningless words with 68 repetitions on day 1 followed by 7 the next day (total times: 75), or he could study the set of words just 38 times spaced out over the course of 3 days, which is half the study time.

Extensive research has been done on the forgetting curve, from research on simple mathematical procedures like addition with young kids to biological facts for high schoolers. One study that shed more light on the optimal distance between repetitions was conducted by Harry Bahrick of Ohio Wesleyan University, who again used himself as a test subject but also included his wife and two adult children, who were also scientists and interested in the topic.[3]

They all set themselves the goal of learning 300 foreign words; his wife and daughters studied French words, and Bahrick himself studied German. They divided the words into 6 groups of 50 and used different spacing for the repetitions of each group. Each group of words was studied either 13 or 26 times at a set interval of 2, 4, or 8 weeks. Retention was then tested after 1, 2, 3, or 5 years.

One year after the end of the study period, Bahrick and his family found that they remembered the most words in the group of 50 that they had studied the most and with the longest intervals between practices—26 sessions, each 8 weeks apart. They were able to recall 76% of the words from that group a year later versus 56% in the

---

[2] See "Replication and Analysis of Ebbinghaus' Forgetting Curve" by Jaap Murre (2015), https://journals.plos.org/plosone/article?id=10.1371/journal.pone.0120644.

[3] See "Maintenance of Foreign Language Vocabulary and the Spacing Effect" by Harry Bahrick et al. (1993), www.gwern.net/docs/spacedrepetition/1993-bahrick.pdf.

group studied at an interval of two weeks. Recall diminished over the following years but remained consistently higher for the same group of words they studied for the longest period.

In summary, you remember the longest if you study over a longer period. That doesn't mean you need to spend more time studying; it means you should study at more spaced-out intervals. Revisiting your set of flashcards once a month will be enough to help your memory in the long run, and it's also relatively doable! This is, of course, in stark contrast with formal education, where we try to cram all the knowledge into one semester, or with bootcamps that seek to educate people in three months. Knowledge learned in such a way only sticks if you continue to repeat what you've learned frequently afterward.

> **TIP**  The biggest takeaway from this section is that the best way science knows to prevent forgetting is to practice regularly. Each repetition strengthens your memory. After several repetitions spaced out over a long period, the knowledge should remain in your LTM forever. If you were ever wondering why you've forgotten a lot of what you learned in college, this is why! Unless you revisit knowledge, or are forced to think about it, you will lose memories.

## 3.4    *How to remember syntax longer*

You now know that practicing syntax is important because it helps you to chunk code and will save you a lot of time on searching. We have also covered how often you should practice; don't try to memorize all your flashcards in a day, but spread your study out over a longer period. The remainder of the chapter will talk about how to practice. We will cover two techniques to strengthen memories: retrieval practice (actively trying to remember something) and elaboration (actively connecting new knowledge to existing memories).

You might have noticed earlier that I didn't tell you to simply read both sides of the flashcards. Rather, I asked you to read the side containing the prompt, which is the thing that makes you remember the syntax.

That's because research has shown that actively trying to remember makes memories stronger. Even if you do not know the full answer, memories are easier to find when you have often tried to find them before. The remainder of this chapter will explore this finding in more depth and help you to apply it to learning programming.

### 3.4.1    *Two forms of remembering information*

Before we dive into how remembering can strengthen memories, we first need to understand the problem in more depth. You might think that a memory either is stored in your brain or isn't, but the reality is a bit more complex. Robert and Elizabeth Bjork, professors of psychology at the University of California, distinguished two different mechanisms in retrieving information from LTM: storage strength and retrieval strength.

### STORAGE STRENGTH

Storage strength indicates how well something is stored in LTM. The more you study something, the stronger the memory of it is, until it becomes virtually impossible to forget it. Can you imagine forgetting that 4 times 3 is 12? However, not all information you have stored in your brain is as easy to access as the tables of multiplication.

### RETRIEVAL STRENGTH

Retrieval strength indicates how easy it is to remember something. I'm sure you've had that feeling where you're sure you know something (a name, a song, a phone number, the syntax of the `filter()` function in JavaScript), but you can't quite recall it; the answer is on the tip of your tongue; you just can't reach it. That is information for which the storage strength is high—when you finally remember it, you can't believe you ever couldn't recall it—but the retrieval strength is low.

It is generally agreed that storage strength can only increase—recent research indicates that people never really forget memories[4]—and that it is the retrieval strength of memories that decays over the years. When you repeatedly study some piece of information, you strengthen the storage strength of that fact. When you try to remember a fact that you know you know, without extra study, you improve retrieval strength ability.

## 3.4.2 *Just seeing information is not enough*

When you're looking for a particular piece of syntax, the problem often lies with your retrieval strength, not with your storage strength. For example, can you find the right code to traverse a list in C++ in reverse from the options in the following listing?

> Listing 3.1   Six options to traverse a list in C++

```
1. rit = s.rbegin(); rit != s.rend(); rit++
2. rit = s.revbegin(); rit != s.end(); rit++
3. rit = s.beginr(); rit != s.endr(); rit++
4. rit = s.beginr(); rit != s.end(); rit++
5. rit = s.rbegin(); rit != s.end(); rit++
6. rit = s.revbeginr(); rit != s.revend(); rit++
```

All these options look quite similar, and even for an experienced C++ programmer it can be tricky to remember the right version, despite having seen this code several times. When you are told the right answer, it will feel like you knew it all along: "Of *course* it's `rit = s.rbegin(); rit != s.rend(); rit++`!"

Hence, the issue here is not the strength with which the knowledge is stored in your LTM (the storage strength) but the ease with which you can find it (the retrieval strength). This example shows that even if you've seen code a dozen times before, simply being exposed to the code may not be enough for you to be able to remember it. The information is stored somewhere in your LTM but not readily available when you need it.

---

[4] "Recollection, Familiarity, and Cortical Reinstatement: A Multivoxel Pattern Analysis," by Jeffrey D. Johnson, Susan G. R. McDuff, Michael D. Rugg, and Kenneth A. Norman. *Neuron*, vol. 63, no. 5, September 8, 2009.

### 3.4.3 *Remembering information strengthens memories*

The exercise in the previous section showed that it's not enough to simply store information in your LTM. You also need to be able to retrieve it with ease. Like many things in life, retrieving information gets easier when you practice it a lot. Because you have never really tried to remember syntax, it is hard to recall it when you do need it. We know that actively trying to remember something strengthens memory—this is a technique that goes back as far as Aristotle.

One of the first studies on retrieval practice was done by a schoolteacher called Philip Boswood Ballard, who published a paper on the topic called "Obliviscence and Reminiscence" in 1913. Ballard trained a group of students to memorize 16 lines from the poem "The Wreck of the Hesperus," which recounts the story of a vain skipper who causes the death of his daughter. When he examined their recall performance, he observed something interesting. Without telling the students that they would be tested again, Ballard had them reproduce the poem again after two days. Because they did not know another test was coming, the students had not studied the poem any further. During the second test, the students on average remembered 10% more of the poem. After another two days, their recall scores were higher again. Suspicious of the outcome, Ballard repeated such studies several times—but he found similar results each time: when you actively try to recall information without additional study, you will remember more of what you learned.

Now that you're familiar with the forgetting curve and the effects of retrieval practice, it should be even more clear why simply looking up syntax you don't know each time you need it is not a great idea. Because looking it up is so easy and is such a common task, our brains feel like they don't really need to remember syntax. Therefore, the retrieval strength of programming syntax remains weak.

The fact that we do not remember syntax, of course, leads to a vicious cycle. Because we don't remember it, we need to look it up. But because we keep looking it up instead of trying to remember it, we never improve the retrieval strength of these programming concepts—so we must keep looking them up, ad infinitum.

So next time you're about to Google something, it might be worth first actively trying to remember the syntax. Even though it might not work that time, the act of trying to remember can strengthen your memory and might help you remember next time. If that doesn't work, make a flashcard and actively practice.

### 3.4.4 *Strengthen memories by actively thinking*

In the previous section you learned that actively trying to remember information, with retrieval practice, makes information stick in your memory better. You also know that practicing memorizing information over an extended period works best. But there is a second way you can strengthen memories: by actively thinking about and reflecting on the information. The process of thinking about information you just learned is called *elaboration*. Elaboration works especially well for learning complex programming concepts.

Before we can dig into the process of elaboration and how you can use it to better learn new programming concepts, we need to take a closer look at how storage in the brain works.

## SCHEMATA

You've seen that memories in your brain are stored in a networked form, with relationships to other memories and facts. The ways in which thoughts and the relationships between them are organized in our minds are called *schemas*, or *schemata*.

When you learn new information, you will try to fit the information into a schema in your brain before storing it in LTM. Information that fits an existing schema better will be easier to remember. For example, if I ask you to remember the numbers 5, 12, 91, 54, 102, and 87 and then list three of them for a nice prize of your choice, that will be hard to do, because there are no "hooks" to connect the information to. This list will be stored in a new schema: "Things I am remembering to win a nice prize."

However, if I ask you to remember 1, 3, 15, 127, 63, and 31, that may be easier to do. If you think about it for a little bit, you can see that these numbers fit into a category of numbers: numbers that, when transformed into a binary representation, consist of only ones. Not only can you remember these numbers more easily, but you might also be more motivated to remember the numbers because this is a sensible thing to do. You know that if you know the upper bound of numbers in bits, that can help in solving certain problems.

Remember that when the working memory processes information, it also searches the LTM for related facts and memories. When your memories are connected to each other, finding the memories is easier. In other words, retrieval strength is higher for memories that relate to other memories.

When we save memories, the memories can even be changed to adapt themselves to existing schemata. In the 1930s, British psychologist Frederic Bartlett conducted an experiment where he asked people to study a short Native American tale called *The War of the Ghosts* and then try to recall the story weeks or even months later.[5] From their descriptions, Bartlett could see that the participants had changed the story to fit their existing beliefs and knowledge. For example, some participants omitted details they considered irrelevant. Other participants had made the story more "Western" and in line with their cultural norms; for example, by replacing a bow with a gun. This experiment showed that people do not remember bare words and facts but that they adapt memories to fit with their existing memories and beliefs.

The fact that memories can be altered as soon as we store them can have downsides. Two people involved in the same situation might remember it entirely differently afterward because their own thoughts and ideas will affect how they store the memories. But we can also use the fact that memories can be changed or saved to our advantage by storing relevant known information along with the added information.

---

[5] See his book *Remembering: A Study in Experimental and Social Psychology* (Cambridge University Press, 1932).

## USING ELABORATION TO LEARN NEW PROGRAMMING CONCEPTS

As you saw earlier in this chapter, memories can be forgotten when the retrieval strength—the ease with which you can recollect information—is not strong enough. Bartlett's experiment shows that even on the first save, when a memory is initially stored in LTM, some details of the memory can be altered or forgotten.

For example, if I tell you that James Monroe was the fifth president of the United States, you might remember that Monroe is a former president but forget that he was the fifth one before storing the memory. The fact that you do not remember the number can be caused by many factors; for example, you might think it is irrelevant, or too complex, or you might have been distracted. There are a lot of factors that impact how much is stored, including your emotional state. For example, you are more likely to remember a certain bug that kept you at your desk overnight a year ago than a random bug you fixed in a few minutes today.

While you cannot change your emotional state, there are many things you can do to save as much as possible of a new memory. One thing you can do to strengthen the initial encoding of memories is called *elaboration*. Elaboration means thinking about what you want to remember, relating it to existing memories, and making the new memories fit into schemata already stored in your LTM.

Elaboration might have been one of the reasons the pupils in Ballard's study were better able to remember the words of the poem over time. Repeatedly recalling the poem forced the students to fill in missing words, each time committing them back to memory. They also likely connected parts of the poem to other things they remembered.

If you want to remember new information better, it helps to explicitly elaborate on the information. The act of elaboration strengthens the network of related memories, and when a new memory has more connections it's easier to retrieve it. Imagine you are learning a new programming concept, such as list comprehensions in Python. A list comprehension is a way to create a list based on an existing list. For example, if you want to create a list of the squares of numbers you already have stored in a list called `numbers`, you can do that with this list comprehension:

```
squares = [x*x for x in numbers]
```

Imagine you are learning this concept for the first time. If you want to help yourself remember it better, it helps a great deal to elaborate deliberately by thinking of related concepts. For example, you might try thinking of related concepts in other programming languages, of alternative concepts in Python or other programming languages, or of how this concept relates to other paradigms.

**EXERCISE 3.2**  Use this exercise the next time you learn a new programming concept. Answering the following questions will help you elaborate and strengthen the new memory:

- What concepts does this new concept make you think of? Write down all the related concepts.
- Then, for each of the related concepts you can think of, answer these questions:
  - Why does the new concept make me think of this concept that I already know?
  - Does it share syntax?
  - Is it used in a similar context?
  - Is this new concept an alternative to one I already know?
- What other ways do you know to write code to achieve the same goal? Try to create as many variants of this code snippet as you can.
- Do other programming languages also have this concept? Can you write down examples of other languages that support similar operations? How do they differ from the concept at hand?
- Does this concept fit a certain paradigm, domain, library, or framework?

## Summary

- It's important to know quite a bit of syntax by heart because more syntax knowledge will ease chunking. Also, looking up syntax can interrupt your work.
- You can use flashcards to practice and remember new syntax, with a prompt on one side and code on the other side.
- It's important to practice new information regularly to fight memory decay.
- The best kind of practice is retrieval practice, where you try to remember information before looking it up.
- To maximize the amount of knowledge you remember, spread your practice over time.
- Information in your LTM is stored as a connected network of related facts.
- Active elaboration of new information helps strengthen the network of memories the new memory will connect to, easing retrieval.

# How to read complex code

4

**This chapter covers:**

- Analyzing what happens when your working memory is overloaded by complex code
- Comparing two different types of working memory overload when programming
- Refactoring code for readability to compensate for an overloaded working memory
- Creating a state table and a dependency graph to support your working memory when reading complex code

Chapter 1 introduced the different ways in which code can be confusing. We've seen that confusion can be caused by a lack of information, which must be acquired and stored in your STM, or by a lack of knowledge, which requires storing information in your LTM. This chapter covers the third source of confusion: a lack of processing power in the brain.

Sometimes the code you are reading is just too complex for you to fully understand. Because reading code is not an activity that most programmers practice often, you might find that you lack strategies to deal with reading code you do not understand. Common techniques such as "read it again" and "give up" are not helpful.

In the previous chapters, we covered techniques to help you read code better. In chapter 2 you learned about techniques for more effective chunking of code, and chapter 3 provided tips for storing more syntax knowledge in your LTM, which also aids in reading code. However, sometimes code is so complex that even with a lot of syntax knowledge and efficient chunking strategies it's still too hard to process.

This chapter dives into the cognitive processes that underlie the processing power of the brain, which we commonly call the *working memory*. We will explore what working memory is and how code can be so confusing that it overloads your working memory. After we've covered the basics, I'll show you three techniques to support your working memory so you can process complex code with more ease.

## 4.1 *Why it's hard to understand complex code*

In chapter 1, I showed you an example of a BASIC program whose execution was complicated enough that you probably couldn't process it all just by reading the code. In such a case you might be tempted to scribble intermediate values next to the code, as shown in figure 4.1.

```
1   LET N2 =  ABS (INT (N))        7
2   LET B$ = ""
3   FOR N1 = N2 TO 0 STEP 0
4       LET N2 =  INT (N1 / 2)       3
5       LET B$ = STR$ (N1 - N2 * 2) + B$     "|"
6       LET N1 = N2
7   NEXT N1
8   PRINT B$
9   RETURN
```

**Figure 4.1  A program converting the number N into a binary representation in BASIC. The program is confusing because you cannot see all the small steps that are being executed. If you need to understand all the steps, you may use a memory aid like writing down the intermediate values of the variables.**

The fact that you feel the need to do this means that your brain lacks the capacity to process the code. Let's compare the BASIC code to the second example from chapter 1, a Java program that calculates the binary representation of an integer n. While interpreting this code might also take some mental energy, and it's possible that unfamiliarity with the inner workings of the toBinaryString() method may cause you some confusion, it is unlikely you'll feel the need to make notes while reading it.

**Listing 4.1  A Java program to convert n to a binary representation**

```
public class BinaryCalculator {
    public static void main(Integer n) {
        System.out.println(Integer.toBinaryString(n));
    }
}
```

Not knowing about the inner workings of `toBinaryString()` can cause confusion. In previous chapters we delved into two of the cognitive processes at play when you read complex code: STM and LTM. To understand why you sometimes need to offload information, you need to understand the third cognitive process introduced in chapter 1, which we have not yet discussed in detail. The *working memory* represents the brain's capacity to think, to form new ideas, and to solve problems. Earlier, we compared the STM to the RAM of a computer and the LTM to the hard drive. Following that analogy, the working memory is like the brain's processor.

### 4.1.1  *What's the difference between working memory and STM?*

Some people use working memory as a synonym for STM, and you might have seen the two terms used interchangeably. Others, however, distinguish between the two concepts, and we will do that in this book. The role of the STM is to *remember* information. The role of the working memory, on the other hand, is to *process* information. We will treat these processes as separate.

> **DEFINITION**  The definition of *working memory* that we will use in the remainder of this book is "STM applied to a problem."

Figure 4.2 shows an example of the difference between the two processes: if you are remembering a phone number you use your STM, whereas if you are adding integers you use your working memory.

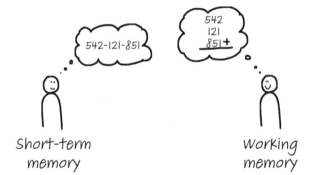

**Figure 4.2  The STM briefly stores information (like a phone number, as shown on the left), while the working memory processes information (like when performing a calculation, as shown on the right).**

As you saw in chapter 2, the STM can typically only hold two to six items at a time. More information can be processed when the information is divided into recognizable chunks, like words, chess openings, or design patterns. Because the working memory is the STM applied to a certain problem, it has the same limitation.

Like the STM, the working memory is only capable of processing two to six things at a time. In the context of working memory, this capacity is known as the *cognitive load*. When you are trying to solve a problem that involves too many elements that cannot be divided efficiently into chunks, your working memory will become "overloaded."

### 4.1.2   *Types of cognitive load as they relate to programming*

This chapter will introduce methods to systematically address cognitive load, but before we can cover these techniques, we need to explore the different types that exist. The researcher who first proposed cognitive load theory was the Australian professor John Sweller. Sweller distinguished three different types of cognitive load: intrinsic, extraneous, and germane. Table 4.1 provides a quick summary of how cognitive load varies.

**Table 4.1   Types of cognitive load**

| Load type | Brief explanations |
|-----------|--------------------|
| Intrinsic load | How complex the problem is in itself |
| Extraneous load | What outside distractions add to the problem |
| Germane load | Cognitive load created by having to store your thought to LTM |

We will focus on the first two types of cognitive load here; we discuss germane load in more depth in a later chapter.

#### INTRINSIC COGNITIVE LOAD WHEN READING CODE

*Intrinsic cognitive load* is cognitive load caused by features of a problem that the problem contains by nature. For example, imagine that you have to calculate the hypotenuse of a triangle, as illustrated in figure 4.3.

Solving this calculation has certain characteristics that are inherent to the problem. For example, you need to know Pythagoras's theorem ($a^2 + b^2 = c^2$) to solve it, and you have to be able to calculate first the squares of 8 and 6 and then the square root of the sum of the results. Because there is no other way to solve the problem or to simplify these steps, this load is *intrinsic* to the problem. In programming, we often use the term *inherent complexity* to describe these intrinsic aspects of a problem. In cognitive science, we say that these aspects cause cognitive load of the intrinsic type.

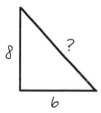

**Figure 4.3   A geometry problem in which the lengths of two sides of a triangle are given and the third needs to be calculated. This can be a problem that is hard to solve, depending on your prior knowledge. However, the problem itself cannot be made any simpler without changing it.**

#### EXTRANEOUS COGNITIVE LOAD WHEN READING CODE

In addition to the natural, intrinsic load that problems can cause in the brain, there is also cognitive load that is *added* to problems, often by accident. For example, in figure 4.4, the same question about finding the length of the hypotenuse is formulated in a different way, requiring us to make a mental connection between the labels for the two sides of the triangle, whose lengths and values are known. This additional work results in a higher *extraneous cognitive load*.

Consider these values for a and b:

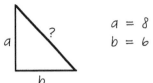

a = 8
b = 6

**Figure 4.4**  **This way of finding the length of the third side of a triangle incurs a higher extraneous cognitive load in this form.**

Solving the problem has not really been made harder—we still need to remember and apply Pythagoras's theorem. However, our brains do need to work harder on extraneous tasks: connecting a to the value 8 and b to the value 6. In programming, we think of this type of extraneous load as similar to accidental complexity: aspects of a program that make a problem harder than it needs to be.

What creates extraneous load is not the same for every programmer. The more experience you have using a certain concept, the less cognitive load it creates for you. For example, the two Python code examples in the following listing are computationally equivalent.

**Listing 4.2   Two versions of a Python program to select all items above 10**

```
above_ten = [a for a in items if a > 10]

above_ten = []
for a in items:
    if a > 10: new_items.append(a)
```

Because the two code snippets both solve the same problem, they share the same intrinsic cognitive load. However, whether they represent the same extraneous cognitive load for you depends on your prior knowledge: if you're not familiar with list comprehensions, then the extraneous load caused by the first example will be much higher than for someone who is experienced in using them.

> **EXERCISE 4.1**  The next time you read unfamiliar code, try to monitor your own cognitive load. When the code is hard to process and you feel the need to make notes or follow the execution step by step, it is likely you are experiencing a high cognitive load.

When you experience high cognitive load, it is worthwhile to examine which parts of the code are creating the different types of cognitive load. You can use the following table to analyze this.

| Lines of code | Intrinsic cognitive load | Extraneous cognitive load |
|---|---|---|
|  |  |  |

## 4.2 Techniques to reduce cognitive load

Now that you know the diverse ways in which code can overload the working memory, it's time to direct our attention to ways of lowering cognitive load. The remainder of this chapter discusses three methods that will make it easier for you to read complex code. The first technique is one you might already be familiar with, albeit in a different context: refactoring.

### 4.2.1 Refactoring

A *refactoring* is a transformation of code that improves its internal structure but does not change the code's external behavior. For example, if a certain block of code is very long, you might want to split the logic into multiple functions, or if the codebase exhibits duplication, you might want to refactor it to gather all the duplicated code in one place for easy reuse. In the following Python code listing, for example, the repeated calculation could be placed into a method.

**Listing 4.3   Python code that repeats the same calculation twice**

```
vat_1 = Vat(waterlevel = 10, radius = 1)
volume_vat_1 = math.pi * vat_1.radius **2 * vat_1. water_level
print(volume_vat_1)

vat_1 = Vat(waterlevel = 25, radius = 3)
volume_vat_2 = math.pi * vat_2. radius **2 * vat_2. water_level
print(volume_vat_2)
```

In most cases, refactoring is done to make it easier to maintain the resulting code. For example, eliminating duplicate code means changes to that code only have to be made in one location.

But code that is more maintainable overall is not always more readable now. For example, consider a piece of code that contains many method calls and thus depends on code spread out over many different places in a file or even in multiple files. That architecture might be more maintainable because all the logic has its own method. However, such *delocalized* code can also be harder on your working memory because you will have to scroll or search for function definitions in different locations.

Therefore, sometimes you might want to refactor code not to make it more maintainable in the long run but more readable for you at that point in time. We define such a refactoring as a *cognitive refactoring*. A cognitive refactoring is a change to a code base that does not change its external behavior, similar to a regular refactoring. However, the goal of a cognitive refactoring is not to make the code more maintainable, but to make it more readable for the current reader at the current point in time.

A cognitive refactoring can sometimes involve *reverse refactoring*, which decreases maintainability, such as *inlining*—taking the implementation of a method and copying the body of the function directly at the call site. Some IDEs can perform this refactoring automatically. Inlining code can be especially helpful when a method's name is not very revealing, such as calculate() or transform(). When reading a call to a method with a vague name, you will need to spend some time up front to understand what the method does—and it will likely take several exposures before the functionality of the method is stored in your LTM.

Inlining the method lowers your extraneous cognitive load and might help you comprehend the code that calls the method. Additionally, studying the code of the method itself might help you understand the code, which can be easier with more context. Within the new context, you might also be able to choose a better name for the method.

Alternatively, you might want to reorder methods within the code—for example, code may be easier to read if a method's definition appears close to the first method call. Of course, many IDEs nowadays have shortcuts to navigate to method and function definitions, but using such a function also takes up a bit of working memory and might thus cause additional extraneous cognitive load.

Cognitive refactorings are often meant for one person, because what is understandable depends on your own prior knowledge. In many cases, cognitive refactorings are temporary, only meant to allow you understand the code, and can be rolled back once your understanding is solidified.

While this process might have been a big hassle a few years ago, version control systems are now used for most codebases and are integrated into most IDEs, which makes it relatively easy to start a local "understanding" branch where you execute the changes needed to comprehend the code. And if some of your refactorings turn out to be valuable in a broader sense, they can be merged with relative ease.

### 4.2.2    *Replacing unfamiliar language constructs*

The remainder of this chapter covers techniques that can help you combat the three possible sources of confusion when reading code (lack of knowledge, information, and processing power). If the code you are reading contains programming concepts you are not familiar with, you are dealing with a lack of knowledge. We'll start with a technique that can be helpful in these cases.

In some situations, the unfamiliar constructs you are working with could be expressed in a different, more familiar way. For example, many modern programming languages (like Java and C#) support *anonymous functions*, often referred to as *lambdas*. Lambdas are functions that do not need to be given a name (hence "anonymous"). Another example is a list comprehension in Python. Lambdas and list comprehensions are great ways to make code shorter and more readable, but many programmers are not familiar with them and read them with less ease than they would read a for- or while-loop.

If the code you are reading or writing is simple and straightforward, lambdas or list comprehensions might not pose a problem, but if you are working with more complex code, such advanced structures might cause your working memory to become overloaded. Less familiar language constructs increase the extraneous cognitive load on your working memory, so when you are reading complex code, it can be beneficial for your working memory to not have to deal with these.

While the precise language constructs you might want to replace are, of course, dependent on your own prior knowledge, there typically are two reasons to replace code to lower your cognitive load: first because these constructs are known to be confusing, and second because they have a clear equivalent that is more basic. Both conditions apply to lambdas and list comprehensions, so these are good examples to use to demonstrate this technique. It can be useful to translate these to a for- or while-loop to lower the cognitive load until you gain more understanding of what the code is doing. Ternary operators are also a good candidate for such a refactoring.

### LAMBDAS

The Java code in the following listing is an example of an anonymous function used as a parameter for a `filter()` function. If you are familiar with the use of lambdas, this code will be easy enough to follow.

**Listing 4.4** A `filter()` function in Java that takes an anonymous function as an argument

```
Optional<Product> product = productList.stream().
            filter(p -> p.getId() == id).
            findFirst();
```

However, if lambdas are new to you, this code might cause too much extraneous cognitive load. If you feel you are struggling with the lambda expression, you can simply rewrite the code to use a regular function temporarily, as in the following example.

**Listing 4.5** A `filter()` function in Java that uses a traditional function as an argument

```
public static class Toetsie implements Predicate <Product> {
    private int id;

    Toetsie(int id){
        this.id = id;
    }

    boolean test(Product p){
```

```
                return p.getID() == this.id;
    }
}

Optional<Product> product = productList.stream().
        filter(new Toetsie(id)).
        findFirst();
```

## LIST COMPREHENSIONS

Python supports a syntactic structure called *list comprehensions,* which can create lists based on other lists. For example, you can use the following code to create a list of first names based on a list of customers.

> **Listing 4.6   A list comprehension in Python transforming one list into another list**

```
customer_names - [c.first_name for c in customers]
```

List comprehensions can also use filters that make them a bit more complex—for example, to create a list of the names of customers over 50 years of age, as shown in the next listing.

> **Listing 4.7   A list comprehension in Python using a filter**

```
customer_names =
    [c.first_name for c in customers if c.age > 50]
```

While this code might be easy enough to read for someone who is used to list comprehensions, for someone who isn't (or even someone who is, if it's embedded in a complex piece of code), it might cause too much strain on the working memory. When that happens, you can transform the list comprehension to a for-loop to ease understanding.

> **Listing 4.8   A for-loop in Python transforming one list into another list using a filter**

```
customer_names = []

for c in customers:
    if c.age > 50:
        customer_names.append(c.first_name)
```

## TERNARY OPERATORS

Many languages support *ternary operators,* which are shorthand for if statements. They typically have the form of a condition followed by the result when the condition is true and then the result when the condition is false. For example, listing 4.9 is a line of JavaScript code that checks whether the Boolean variable isMember is true using a ternary operator. If isMember is true, the ternary operator returns $2.00; if not, it returns $10.00.

**Listing 4.9   JavaScript code using a ternary operator**

```
isMember ? '$2.00' : '$10.00'
```

Some languages, such as Python, support ternary operations in a different order, giving first the result when the condition is true, followed by the condition and then the result when the condition is false. The following example is a line of Python code that checks whether the Boolean variable isMember is true using a ternary operator. As in the JavaScript example, if isMember is true, the ternary operator returns $2.00, and if it isn't, it returns $10.00.

**Listing 4.10   Python code using a ternary operator**

```
'$2.00' if is_member else '$10.00'
```

Conceptually, a ternary operator is not hard to understand; as a professional programmer, you're probably familiar with conditional code. However, the fact that the operation is placed on one line or that the order of the arguments is different from a traditional if statement might cause the code to create too much extraneous cognitive load for you.

To some people, the refactorings described in the previous sections might feel weird or wrong. You might believe that shortening code with a lambda or a ternary is always preferable because it's more readable, and you might object to the idea of refactoring code to a worse state. However, as you've seen in this chapter and earlier in this book, "readable" is really in the eye of the beholder. If you're familiar with chess openings, it's easy to remember them; likewise, if you're familiar with using ternaries, it's easy to read code that contains them. What is easy to read depends on your prior knowledge, and there is no shame in helping yourself understand code by translating it to a more familiar form.

Depending on your codebase, however, you might want to revert the changes you've made to the code for readability purposes once you're sure you understand it. If you are new to a team and you're the only one unfamiliar with list comprehensions, you'll want to leave them in place and roll back your refactorings.

### 4.2.3   *Code synonyms are great additions to a flashcard deck*

While there's no shame in changing code temporarily to aid comprehension, this does point to a limitation in your understanding. In chapter 3, you learned about creating a deck of flashcards to use as a learning and memory aid, with code on one side and a textual prompt on the other. For example, a card on for-loops could have "print all numbers between 0 and 10 in C++" on one side and the corresponding C++ code (shown in the following listing) on the other.

**Listing 4.11    C++ code for printing the numbers between 0 and 10**

```cpp
for (int i = 0; i <= 10; i = i + 1) {
  cout << i << "\n";
}
```

If you often struggle with, for example, list comprehensions, you can consider adding a few cards on that programming construct to your deck. For more advanced programming concepts like these, it can work better to have code on both sides of the flashcard rather than a text explanation—that is, you can have the vanilla code on one side, and on the other the equivalent code using the advanced concept, such as a ternary or lambda.

## 4.3    *Memory aids to use when your working memory is overloaded*

The previous section introduced a technique to reduce the cognitive load that code can create, refactoring it to a more familiar form. However, even in its refactored state, code might still overload your working memory if its structure is too complex. There are two ways code with a complicated structure can overload the working memory.

First, you may not know exactly which parts of the code you need to read. This causes you to read more of the code than is needed, which may be more than your working memory is able to process.

Second, with code that is highly connected, your brain is trying to do two things at the same time: understand individual lines of code and understand the structure of the code to decide where to continue reading. For example, when you encounter a method call for which you do not know the exact functionality, you might need to locate and read the method before you can continue reading the code at the call site.

If you have ever read the same piece of code five times in a row without making progress, you probably didn't know what parts of the code to focus on, or in what order. You may have been able to understand each line of code individually, but lacked an understanding of the bigger picture. When you reach the limits of your working memory, you can use a memory aid to help you focus on the right parts of the code.

### 4.3.1    *Creating a dependency graph*

Creating a dependency graph on top of your code can help you to understand the flow and to read the code by following the logical flow. For this technique, I would advise you to print out the code, or convert it to a PDF and open it on a tablet so you can make annotations digitally. Follow these steps to annotate the code to support your memory in processing it:

1    Circle all the variables.

Once you have the code in a form you can annotate, start by finding all the variables and circling them, as shown in figure 4.5.

```
from itertools import islice

digits = "0123456789abcdefghijklmnopqrstuvwxyz"

def baseN(num,b):
    if num == 0: return "0"
    result = ""
    while num != 0:
        num, d = divmod(num, b)
        result += digits[d]
    return result[::-1] # reverse

def pal2(num):
    if num == 0 or num == 1: return True
    based = bin(num)[2:]
    return based == based[::-1]

def pal_23():
    yield 0
    yield 1
    n = 1
    while True:
        n += 1
        b = baseN(n, 3)
        revb = b[::-1]
        #if len(b) > 12: break
        for trial in ('{0}{1}'.format(b, revb), '{0}0{1}'.format(b, revb),
                      '{0}1{1}'.format(b, revb), '{0}2{1}'.format(b, revb)):
            t = int(trial, 3)
            if pal2(t):
                yield t

for pal23 in islice(pal_23(), 6):
    print(pal23, baseN(pal23, 3), baseN(pal23, 2))
```

**Figure 4.5  Code in which all variables are circled to support understanding**

2  Link similar variables.

Once you have located all the variables, draw lines between occurrences of the same variable, as illustrated in figure 4.6. This helps you to understand where data is used in the program. Depending on the code, you may also want to link similar variables (for example, accesses into a list, as in customers[0] and customers[i]).

Linking all the variables will help you read the code, because instead of searching for other occurrences, you can simply follow the lines. This lowers your cognitive load and thus frees up working memory for you to focus on the code's functionality.

3  Circle all method/function calls.

Once you have located all the variables, focus on the methods and functions in the code. Circle them in a different color.

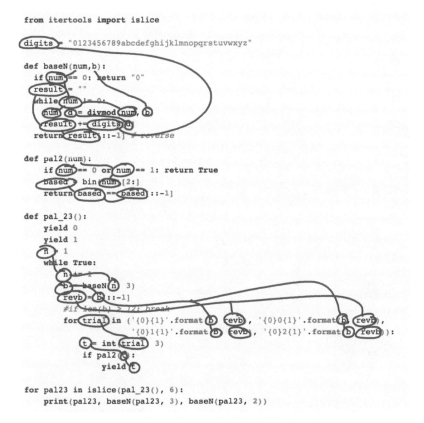

**Figure 4.6   Code in which all variables are circled and linked to their other occurrences to support understanding**

4  Link methods/functions to their definitions.

    Draw a line between each function or method definition and the locations where they are invoked. Focus special attention on methods with just one invocation, because these methods are candidates to be inlined with a refactoring, as explained earlier in this chapter.

5  Circle all instances of classes.

    Once you have located the variables and functions, focus on classes. Circle all instances of classes in a third color.

6  Draw a link between classes and their instances.

    As a final step in examining the code, link instances of the same class to their definition if that definition is present in the code. If the definition is not present, you can link the instances of the same class to each other.

The colored pattern you have created using the previous six steps indicates the flow of the code and can be used as an aid in reading it. You now have a reference you can refer to for information about the code's structure, saving you the effort of, for example, having to search for definitions while also deciphering the meaning of the code, which can overload your working memory. You can start at an entry point of the code, such as the main() method, and read it from there. Whenever you encounter a link to a method call or class instantiation, you can follow the line you drew and continue reading at the right place straight away, avoiding wasting time searching or reading more code than needed.

### 4.3.2 Using a state table

Even when code is refactored to the easiest possible form aligned with your prior knowledge and with all dependencies marked, it can still be confusing. Sometimes the cause of the confusion is not the structure of the code but the calculations it performs. This is an issue of a lack of processing power.

For example, let's revisit a the BASIC code from chapter 1 that converts the number N into a binary representation. In this program the variables influence each other heavily, so a detailed examination of their values is required to understand it. You can use a memory aid, like a dependency graph for code like this that performs complicated calculations, but there's another tool that can help with calculation-heavy code: a *state table*.

A state table focuses on the values of variables rather than the structure of the code. It has columns for each variable and lines for each step in the code. Take another look at our example BASIC program in the next listing. It's confusing because you cannot see all the intermediate calculations and their effects on the different variables.

---

**Listing 4.12  BASIC code that converts a number N to its binary representation**

```
1   LET N2 =  ABS (INT (N))
2   LET B$ = ""
3   FOR N1 = N2 TO 0 STEP 0
4       LET N2 =  INT (N1 / 2)
5       LET B$ =  STR$ (N1 - N2 * 2) + B$
6       LET N1 = N2
7   NEXT N1
8   PRINT B$
9   RETURN
```

|        | N | N2 | B$ | N1 |
|--------|---|----|----|----|
| Init   | 7 | 7  | —  | 7  |
| Loop 1 |   | 3  |    | 3  |
| Loop 2 |   |    |    |    |

Figure 4.7  An example of a partial state table of the BASIC code for calculating the binary representation of a number

If you need to understand code like this with many interconnected calculations, you can use a memory aid like the partial state table shown in figure 4.7.

Follow these steps to create a state table:

1  Make a list of all the variables.

   If you have already created a dependency graph for this program, as described in the previous section, it will be easy to list the variables because you'll have circled all of them in the same color.

2  Create a table and give each variable its own column.

   In the state table, each variable will get one column in which its intermediate values can be recorded, as shown in figure 4.7.

3  Add one row to the table for each distinct part of the execution of the code.

Code that contains complex calculations will most likely also contain some complex dependencies, such as a loop depending on a calculation, or a complicated if statement. Rows in the state table represent separate parts of the dependencies. For example, as shown in figure 4.7, a row can represent one iteration in a loop, preceded by the initialization code. Alternatively, a row could represent a branch in a large if statement, or simply a group of coherent lines of code. In extremely complex and terse code, one row in the table might even represent one line of code.

4  Execute each part of the code and then write down the value each variable has in the correct row and column.

Once you've prepared the table, work your way through the code and calculate the new value of each variable for each row in the state table. The process of mentally executing code is called *tracing* or *cognitive compiling*. When tracing the code using a state table, it can be tempting to skip a few variables and only fill in part of the table, but try to resist that temptation. Working through it meticulously will help you gain a deeper understanding of the code, and the resulting table will support your overloaded working memory. On a second read of the program you can use the table as a reference, allowing you to concentrate on the coherence of the program rather than on the detailed calculations.

## An app to support the working memory

Manual creation of visualizations to support your working memory has a lot of value because it forces you to examine the code in detail. However, these visualizations can also be created automatically. An elegant program for this purpose is Python Tutor, created by Philip Guo, professor of cognitive science at the University of California, San Diego. PythonTutor, which is now available for many programming languages in addition to Python, visualizes the execution of a program. For example, the following figure shows that Python stores integers and lists differently; for an integer, the value is stored, whereas for a list, a pointer-like system is used.

**Figure 4.8   Python Tutor showing the difference between storing the integer** x **and its value directly and storing a list** fruit **with a pointer**

Research exploring the use of Python Tutor in education[1] has shown that it takes students a while to get used to working with the program, but that it is helpful, especially when debugging.

### 4.3.3   *Combining dependency graphs and state tables*

This section and section 4.2 describe two techniques to support your working memory when reading code by offloading some information about the code onto paper: drawing a dependency graph and creating a state table. These techniques focus on different parts of the code: while the dependency graph draws your attention to how the code is organized, the state table captures the calculations in the code. When exploring unfamiliar code, you can use both exercises to gain a full picture of its inner workings and to use as memory aids when reading the code after completing them.

**EXERCISE 4.2**   Following the steps outlined in the previous sections, create both a dependency graph and a state table for each of the following Java programs.

**Program 1**

```
public class Calculations {
    public static void main(String[] args) {
        char[] chars = {'a', 'b', 'c', 'd'};
        // looking for bba
        calculate(chars, 3, i -> i[0] == 1 && i[1] == 1 && i[2] == 0);
    }
    static void calculate(char[] a, int k, Predicate<int[]> decider) {
        int n = a.length;
        if (k < 1 || k > n)
            throw new IllegalArgumentException("Forbidden");

        int[] indexes = new int[n];
        int total = (int) Math.pow(n, k);

        while (total-- > 0) {
            for (int i = 0; i < n - (n - k); i++)
                System.out.print(a[indexes[i]]);
            System.out.println();

            if (decider.test(indexes))
                break;

            for (int i = 0; i < n; i++) {
                if (indexes[i] >= n - 1) {
                    indexes[i] = 0;
                } else {
                    indexes[i]++;
```

---

[1] See "The Use of Python Tutor on Programming Laboratory Session: Student Perspectives" by Oscar Karnalim and Mewati Ayub (2017), https://kinetik.umm.ac.id/index.php/kinetik/article/view/442.

```
                            break;
                    }
                }
            }
        }
    }
}
```

```
public class App {
    private static final int WIDTH = 81;
    private static final int HEIGHT = 5;

    private static char[][] lines;
    static {
        lines = new char[HEIGHT][WIDTH];
        for (int i = 0; i < HEIGHT; i++) {
            for (int j = 0; j < WIDTH; j++) {
                lines[i][j] = '*';
            }
        }
    }

    private static void show(int start, int len, int index) {
        int seg = len / 3;
        if (seg == 0) return;
        for (int i = index; i < HEIGHT; i++) {
            for (int j = start + seg; j < start + seg * 2; j++) {
                lines[i][j] = ' ';
            }
        }
        show(start, seg, index + 1);
        show(start + seg * 2, seg, index + 1);
    }

    public static void main(String[] args) {
        show(0, WIDTH, 1);
        for (int i = 0; i < HEIGHT; i++) {
            for (int j = 0; j < WIDTH; j++) {
                System.out.print(lines[i][j]);
            }
            System.out.println();
        }
    }
}
```

## Summary

- Cognitive load represents the limit of what the working memory can process. When you experience too much cognitive load, you cannot properly process code.
- There are two types of cognitive load that are relevant in programming: intrinsic cognitive load is created by the inherent complexity of a piece of code, while

extraneous cognitive load is added to code either accidentally (by the way it is presented) or because of gaps in the knowledge of the person reading the code.

- Refactoring is a way to reduce extraneous cognitive load by transforming code to align better with your prior knowledge.
- Creating a dependency graph can help you understand a piece of complex and interconnected code.
- Creating a state table containing the intermediate values of variables can aid in reading code that is heavy on calculations.

# Part 2

# On thinking about code

In part 1, we examined the roles of the STM, the LTM, and the working memory when processing code. We also looked at what we know about learning programming syntax and concepts and how to support your brain when reading code.

In part 2, we will focus not so much on reading code but on thinking about code: how to deeply understand programs and avoid bugs in thinking.

# Reaching a deeper understanding of code

## This chapter covers

- Examining the different roles that variables can play in programs
- Comparing surface knowledge of code and understanding of the intent of the creator
- Comparing reading and learning natural language to reading and learning code
- Exploring different strategies to gain a deeper understanding of code

Earlier in this book we discussed using flashcards and repeated practice as techniques to learn syntax, and we covered strategies to quickly familiarize yourself with new code, such as highlighting variables and their relationships. While knowing syntax and understanding the relationships between variables is an important step to understanding code, there are deeper issues that play a role when thinking about code.

When you read an unfamiliar piece of code, it can be hard to see what the code is doing. To use a cognitive term introduced earlier in this book, you might say that when reading unfamiliar code, your cognitive load is high. We have seen that cognitive load can be lowered substantially by learning syntax and new programming concepts and by rewriting code.

Once you have a good understanding of what the code is doing, the next step is to think about the code at hand in more depth. How was it created? Where might you add a new feature? What are some possible design alternatives?

In earlier chapters we talked about schemata, or how memories are organized in the brain. Memories are not stored separately but have links to other memories. You can take advantage of these connections when reasoning about code because memories stored in your LTM help you create chunks in your working memory that can help you think about code.

Thinking about code is the topic of this chapter, in which we will dive into gaining a deeper understanding of code. We will cover three strategies to reflect on code at a deeper level, including methods to reason about the ideas, thoughts, and decisions of the code's creator. First, we will examine a framework that will help you reason about code. Then we'll discuss different levels of understanding and some techniques for going deeper. Finally, we'll dig into some strategies originating from reading natural language that can help with reading code. Recent research indicates that the skills we need for reading code and the skills we use for reading natural language are strongly related, which means that we programmers can learn a lot from how natural language is read for deeper understanding.

## 5.1   *Roles of variables framework*

When reasoning about code, it is clear that variables play a central role. Understanding what types of information variables hold is key to being able to reason about and make changes to code. If you don't understand what a certain variable is supposed to represent, thinking about the code will be tremendously hard. This is why good variable names can serve as beacons, helping us gain a deeper understanding of the code that we are reading.

According to professor Jorma Sajaniemi at the University of Eastern Finland, the reason variables are hard to understand is that most programmers do not have a good schema in their LTM to relate variables to. Sajaniemi argues that we tend to use chunks that either encompass too much, like "variable" or "integer," or are too small, such as a specific variable name like number_of_customers. Instead, programmers need something in between, which motivated him to design the *roles of variables* framework. A variable's role indicates what it does within the program.

### 5.1.1   *Different variables do different things*

As an example of the different roles variables can play, consider the following Python program. The function prime_factors(n) in the code returns the number of prime factors into which n can be separated:

```
upperbound = int(input('Upper bound?'))
max_prime_factors = 0
for counter in range(upperbound):
    factors = prime_factors(counter)
    if factors > max_prime_factors:
        max_prime_factors = factors
```

This program contains four variables: upperbound, counter, factors, and max_prime_factors. However, if we simply describe this program as having four variables, it's not going to be all that helpful for comprehending the program; that is too abstract. Looking at the variable names might help a bit but does not explain everything. counter, for example, is still very generic. Is this a static number of things, or does it change in the program? Examining the roles that each of the four variables plays might help.

In this program, the user is asked for a value, which is stored in the variable upperbound. After this a loop will run until it reaches this upper bound in the variable counter. The variable factors temporarily holds the number of prime factors for the current value of counter. Finally, the variable max_prime_factors represents the highest number encountered in the execution of the loop.

The roles of variables framework captures this difference in the behavior of these variables. The variable upperbound plays the role of a *most recent holder*: it stores the most recently entered upper bound. counter, on the other hand, is a *stepper*, which iterates through a loop. max_prime_factors is a *most wanted holder*; it stores a value that is being searched for. The variable factors is a most recent holder; it stores the most recent number of prime factors. In the following section, I will explain these roles, and the others in the framework, in more detail.

### 5.1.2   *Eleven roles to cover almost all variables*

As the previous example shows, the roles that variables play are common. Many programs have a variable that is a stepper or a most wanted holder. In fact, Sajaniemi argues that with just 11 roles, you can describe almost all variables:

- *Fixed value*—A variable whose value does not change after initialization plays the role of a fixed value. This can be a constant value if the programming language you are using allows for values to be fixed, or it can be a variable that is initialized once and afterward is not changed. Examples of fixed-value variables include mathematical constants like pi, or data read from a file or database.
- *Stepper*—When iterating in a loop, there is always a variable stepping through a list of values. That is the role of the stepper, whose value can be predicted as soon as the succession starts. This can be an integer, like the canonical i iterating in a for-loop, but more complicated steppers are also possible, like size = size / 2 in a binary search, where the size of the array to be searched is cut in half on every iteration.

- *Flag*[1]—A variable used to indicate that something has happened or is the case. Typical examples are is_set, is_available, or is_error. Flags are often Booleans, but they can be integers or even strings.

- *Walker*—A walker traverses a data structure, similar to a stepper. The difference lies in the way the data structure is traversed. A stepper always iterates over a list of values that are known beforehand, like in a for-loop in Python: for i in range(0, n). A walker, on the other hand, is a variable that traverses a data structure in a way that is unknown before the loop starts. Depending on the programming language, walkers can be pointers or integer indices. Walkers can traverse lists, for example in binary search, but more often traverse data structures like a stack or a tree. Examples of a walker are a variable that is traversing a linked list to find the position where a new element should be added or a search index in a binary tree.

- *Most recent holder*—A variable that holds the latest value encountered in going through a series of values is a most recent holder. For example, it might store the latest line read from a file (line = file.readline()), or a copy of the array element last referenced by a stepper (element = list[i]).

- *Most wanted holder*—Often when you are iterating over a list of values, you are doing that to search for a certain value. The variable that holds that value, or the best value found so far, is what we call a most wanted holder. Canonical examples of a most wanted holder are a variable that stores a minimum value, a maximum value, or the first value meeting a certain condition.

- *Gatherer*—A gatherer is a variable that collects data and aggregates it into one value. This can be a variable that starts at zero and collects values while iterating through a loop, like this:

```
sum = 0
for i in range(list):
    sum += list[i]
```

Its value can, however, also be calculated directly in functional languages or languages that encompass certain functional aspects: functional_total = sum(list).

- *Container*—A container is any data structure that holds multiple elements that can be added and removed. Examples of containers are lists, arrays, stacks, and trees.

- *Follower*—Some algorithms require you to keep track of a previous or subsequent value. A variable in this role is called a follower and is always coupled to another variable. Examples of follower variables are a pointer that points to a previous element in a linked list when traversing the list, or the lower index in a binary search.

---

[1] Sajaniemi's framework specifically names this a "one-way flag," but I think that specific role is too narrow.

- *Organizer*—Sometimes a variable has to be transformed in some way for further processing. For example, in some languages, you cannot access individual characters in a string without converting the string to a character array first, or you may want to store a sorted version of a given list. These are examples of organizers, which are variables that are only used for rearranging or storing values differently. Often, they are temporary variables.
- *Temporary*—Temporary variables are variables that are used only briefly and are often called `temp` or `t`. These variables may be used to swap data or to store the result of a computation that is used multiple times in a method or function.

Figure 5.1 presents an overview of Sajaniemi's 11 roles and helps you figure out what role a variable might play.

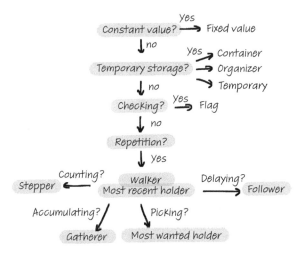

**Figure 5.1** You can use this flowchart to help you determine the role of a variable in a piece of code.

## 5.2    Roles and paradigms

Roles are not restricted to a specific programming paradigm, but they occur in all paradigms. We have already seen in the example of the gatherer that gatherers also occur in functional languages. You'll see the variables playing the roles outlined in the previous section in object-oriented programming too. For example, consider the following Java class:

```java
public class Dog {
  String name;
  int age;
  public Dog (String n) {
    name = n;
    age = 0;
  }
  public void birthday () {
    age++;
  }
}
```

Instances of Dog have two attributes: name and age. The value of the attribute name does not change after initialization; it is a *fixed value*. The attribute age behaves similarly to the variable counter in the Python program we looked at earlier: it steps through a known sequence starting at 0 and increasing on each birthday, so as such, its role is *stepper*.

### 5.2.1   Benefits of roles

For most professional programmers, the roles in Sajaniemi's framework will be somewhat familiar (maybe by other names). Rather than introducing new concepts, the purpose of this list is to give you a new vocabulary to use when discussing variables. Especially when shared among a team, the framework can be a great way to improve understanding and communication about code.

Being familiar with these roles can have benefits for newcomers too. Studies have shown that this framework can help students to mentally process source code and that students who use the roles of variables framework outperform those who do not.[2] One reason it's so effective is that often a group of roles together characterizes a certain type of program. For example, a program with a stepper and a most wanted holder value is a search program.

**EXERCISE 5.1** This is a great time to practice using the roles of variables framework. Find some code that you are unfamiliar with and examine the variables taking note of the following for each:

- The name of the variable
- The type of the variable
- The operations in which the variable plays a role
- The role of the variable according to Sajaniemi's roles of variables framework

Fill out this table for each variable you find in the code.

| Variable name | Type | Operations | Role |
|---|---|---|---|
|  |  |  |  |

Once you have filled out the table, reflect on your decisions about the role of each variable. How did you determine the role? Which of the other aspects played a part in your decision? Was it influenced by the name of the variable, its operations, comments in the code, or maybe your own experience with the code?

---

[2] See, for example, "An Experiment on Using Roles of Variables in Teaching Introductory Programming" by Jorma Sajaniemi and Marja Kuittinen (2007), www.tandfonline.com/doi/full/10.1080/08993400500056563.

## PRACTICAL TIPS FOR WORKING WITH ROLES OF VARIABLES

When reading entirely unfamiliar code, I find that it helps to print out the code on paper or save it as a PDF that I can annotate. I realize it may feel weird to read code outside of the IDE, and you will certainly miss some features, like being able to search through the code. However, being able to write notes can deepen your thinking about the code, enabling you to interact with it on a different level.

I have done code on paper exercises with many professional programmers, and once they get past their first inhibitions, they have all found it tremendously valuable. Of course, for larger projects you may not be able to print all the relevant source code, but you can start with one class or part of the program. If printing out the code is not feasible because of its size or for other practical reasons, many of the note-taking techniques described here can also be done in an IDE using comments.

When working through exercise 5.1, I like to print the code out and mark the role of each variable with a little icon, as shown in figure 5.2.

Once you have memorized the icons, they quickly become a strong memory aid. To make memorizing them easier, you can create a deck of flashcards.

| Fixed value | ⊗ |
| Stepper | ⌐ |
| Flag | ⊩ |
| Walker | ⟟ |
| Most recent holder | ▣ |
| Most wanted holder | ▽ |
| Gatherer | ♨ |
| Container | ⬠ |
| Follower | ↶ |
| Organizer | ▤ |
| Temporary | ◔ |

**Figure 5.2  You can create a set of icons corresponding to the 11 roles a variable can play according to Sajaniemi's framework and use them to mark the roles of variables in unfamiliar code. These are the icons I use.**

Figure 5.3 shows the earlier Python code example with the roles of variables annotated.

```
        ⊗
        /
upperbound = int(input('Upper bound?'))
max_prime_factors = 0
for counter in range(upperbound):
  ⌐    factors = prime_factors(counter)
       if factors > max_prime_factors:
           max_prime_factors = factors ⟋ 5
                            ▽
```

**Figure 5.3  A code snippet in Python, annotated with icons that indicate the roles of the variables in the program. The upperbound variable is a most recent holder, counter is a stepper, and max_prime_factors is a most wanted holder.**

When writing code, it can be very valuable to put the name of the role into the variable name, especially when all people working with the code are familiar with the concept of roles. While it might make the name of the variable longer, it does convey important information and saves the reader the effort of figuring out the role for themselves.

### 5.2.2  *Hungarian notation*

The roles of variables framework may have reminded you of something called *Hungarian notation*. The idea of Hungarian notation is to encode the type of a variable into its name—for example, strName is a string that represents a name and lDistance is a long that represents a distance. This convention stems from languages lacking a type system for encoding the types of variables.

Hungarian notation was described by Charles Simonyi in his 1976 PhD thesis "Meta-Programming: A Software Production Method"—which still makes for a good read. Simonyi went on to work for Microsoft, where he led the development of Word and Excel. His naming convention became the standard for software developed by Microsoft, and later for software developed in Microsoft languages like Visual Basic.

Hungarian notation was first used extensively in the Basic Combined Programming Language (BCPL), seen by many as an ancestor of C, back in the 1970s. In the days when there were no IDEs with IntelliSense, you could not easily see the type of a variable in the editor. Therefore, adding information about a variable's type to its name could improve the readability of a codebase. The trade-off was that it made the names longer and thus harder to read, and when a type had to change, many variable names could potentially be impacted. Nowadays, because most editors can easily show the type of a variable, Hungarian notation is not seen as adding value in a language with types, because it just makes variable names longer. Encoding types in a variable's name like this is thus not common practice anymore, and today the use of Hungarian notation is generally frowned upon.

### APPS HUNGARIAN VS. SYSTEM HUNGARIAN

However, simply encoding types in variable names is in fact not what Simonyi proposes in his thesis. Encoding the types of variables in their names is what we now call *systems Hungarian notation*.

Simonyi's proposal was far more semantic in nature. Today, it's referred to as *Apps Hungarian notation*. In Apps Hungarian, prefixes have a more specific meaning than just indicating the types of variables. For example, in his thesis, Simonyi suggests using cX to count instances of X (so cColors could be the number of colors in a UI) and lX to indicate the length of an array, as in lCustomers. The reason this form of the convention is called Apps Hungarian is because of Simonyi's involvement with Word and Excel at Microsoft. The Excel codebase contains many variables prefixed rw or col, which are excellent examples of the convention put to good use. Row and column values will both be integers, but for readability purposes, it is great to be able to tell from the name which one is meant.

For reasons that are not entirely clear, the Windows team also adopted the convention, but only for data types, not semantic. Joel Spolsky, who worked on Excel before founding Stack Overflow, has attributed the misinterpretation of Hungarian notation to the fact that Simonyi uses the word "type" instead of "kind" to explain the role of the prefix.[3]

---

[3] "Making Wrong Code Look Wrong," by Joel Sprosky, May 11, 2005, www.joelonsoftware.com/2005/05/11/making-wrong-code-look-wrong/.

If you look at Simonyi's original work, however, his explanation of types appears on the same page as concrete, non-type examples like c*X* for counting. I think it is more likely that a small group of people, or maybe just one, simply started to use the system in the wrong way, and that usage spread. As we will see in more detail in chapter 10, people often stick with conventions once they are in the code. However it came to be, the wrong form of Hungarian notation was popularized in the Windows world—largely by Charles Petzold's influential book *Programming Windows* (Microsoft Press, 1998)—and then came people saying, "Hungarian notation is considered harmful," and the rest is history.

However, I think there is still a lot of value in Simonyi's ideas. Some of the proposals advocated by Apps Hungarian are very much like the roles in Sajamieni's framework. For example, Simonyi used the prefix t to denote a temporary value, and also proposed min and max as prefixes for the minimal and maximal values in an array, which are typical examples of most wanted values from the roles of variables framework. It's a pity that the main benefit of the original Hungarian notation—making it easier to read code because less mental effort is needed to reason about the role of a variable—seems to have been lost because of a misunderstanding of the goal of the naming convention.

## 5.3 Gaining a deeper knowledge of programs

So far in this chapter, we have seen that determining the roles of variables can help us reason about code. In chapter 4, I introduced another technique to quickly gain knowledge about code: circling the variables and determining the relationships between them. These techniques are tremendously useful but are relatively *local*: they help us to understand individual pieces of code. We will now focus on methods to seek a deeper understanding of the code. What was the goal of its creator? What were they trying to achieve, and what decisions were made in that process?

### 5.3.1 Text knowledge vs. plan knowledge

Dissecting different levels of understanding was the goal of Nancy Pennington, a professor of psychology at the University of Colorado. She created a model of two different levels at which a programmer can understand source code: *text structure knowledge* and *plan knowledge*.

According to Pennington's model, text structure knowledge relates to surface-level understanding of parts of the program, such as knowing what a keyword does or knowing the role of a variable. Plan knowledge, on the other hand, represents understanding what a programmer planned when they created the program or what they were aiming to achieve. The goals of the programmer who created the code are not only hidden in variables and their roles but become more apparent when we examine how code is structured and connected. The next subsections will teach you how to dig more deeply into the intentions of code.

### 5.3.2    *Different stages of program understanding*

Having plan knowledge of a program means understanding what parts of the code relate to other parts and how. The goal of this subsection is to describe the theory behind comprehension of code in detail, as well as suggest exercises to help you practice quickly seeing the flow.

Jonathan Sillito, a professor at Brigham Young University, has defined four different stages at which a person can understand code.[4] According to Sillito, who observed 25 programmers while they were reading code, programmers typically start by searching for a *focal point* in the code. This can be the entry point in the code, such as a `main()` method in a Java program or an `onLoad()` method in a web application. It may also be a line that is interesting for another reason, like a line at which an error has just occurred or a line a profiler has flagged as consuming many resources.

From this focal point, programmers can build their knowledge. This can be done by executing the code and placing a breakpoint on that line or by inspecting the code, for example, by searching the codebase for other occurrences of the variables involved or using IDE features to jump to other places in the code using that line.

The understanding of the programmer grows from there, developing into an understanding of a larger concept—for example, understanding the results of one function on input or knowing which fields a class has. In the final stage, the programmer has a full understanding of the entire program, like seeing that the focal line of code is part of a certain algorithm or understanding all the different subclasses of a class.

To summarize, the four steps commonly taken when moving from superficial knowledge of a program to deeper understanding are as follows:

1 Find a focal point.
2 Expand knowledge from the focal point.
3 Understand a concept from a set of related entities.
4 Understand concepts across multiple entities.

The focal point of code is an important notion when reading code. Simply put, you have to know where to start reading. Some frameworks and techniques, like dependency injection frameworks, can fragment focal points so that they are far apart and hard to link together. To be able to know where to start, you need to understand how the framework links code together.

Such a situation can leave a reader of the code (and oftentimes even the writer) unsure of the actual structure of the running system, even if each line of code is quite understandable. This is an example of a situation in which the programmer has *text knowledge* but lacks *plan knowledge*. This can be frustrating because you have the feeling that you should know what the code does (as it doesn't look complicated), but the underlying structure is hard to see.

---

[4] See "Questions Programmers Ask During Software Evolution Tasks" by Jonathan Sillito, Gail C. Murphy, and Kris De Volder (2006), www.cs.ubc.ca/~murphy/papers/other/asking-answering-fse06.pdf.

## APPLYING THE STAGES FOR DEEP UNDERSTANDING TO CODE

Now that you understand the difference between plan knowledge and text knowledge, let's revisit the technique demonstrated in chapter 4 as a way to relieve cognitive load when reading complex code:

1  Circle all the variables.
2  Link similar variables.
3  Circle all method/function calls.
4  Link methods/functions to their definitions.
5  Circle all instances of classes.
6  Draw a link between classes and their instances.

Maybe you realized that these six steps are an instantiation of Sillito's abstract model. The difference is that in the steps in chapter 4 there was no specific entry point; the model was applied to all variables, methods, and instances. When you want to gain a deeper understanding of a specific part of code, follow these steps, but for a specific entry point.

These steps again are best executed by printing out the code on paper and manually highlighting parts of it. Alternatively, you can work through the steps in an IDE, where you add comments to the relevant lines of code. Just as we did with the six-step process in chapter 4, let's walk through the four-step process for gaining plan knowledge of code in a little more detail:

1  Find a focal point.

    Start your exploration of the code at a certain focal point. This may be the `main()` method, but it can also be a certain part of the code that warrants a deeper understanding, such as the location of a runtime error or a line of code that a profiler has flagged as slow.

2  Expand knowledge from the focal point.

    Look for relationships in the code. Starting at the focal point, circle all the relevant entities (variables, methods, and classes) that play a role. You might want to link similar variables, for example, accesses into one list, like `customers[0]` and `customers[i]`. Expand your search by looking at what methods and functions the lines of code at the first level themselves link to.

    What you are highlighting now is called a *slice* of code. The slice of a line of code *X* is defined as all lines of code that transitively relate to line *X*.

    Focusing on a slice helps you understand where data is used in the program. For example, you can now ask yourself whether there is a certain line or method heavily connected to the focal point. Where do these relationships occur? Those locations might be a great starting point for exploring the code in more depth. What parts of code are heavy on method calls? Those too might be good focus points for further investigation.

3  Understand a concept from a set of related entities.

You now have several lines highlighted that relate to the focal point. There are several lessons that can be learned from the *call patterns* in a piece of code. For example, is there a method called in several places within the slice you've highlighted? That method likely plays a large role in the codebase and warrants further investigation. Similarly, any methods that are not being used in the code you are studying can be disregarded for now. When you are editing code in the IDE, you might want to reformat the code so that the methods being called are close to the focal point and methods not in use are placed outside of your view. That saves you a bit of cognitive load in scrolling through the code.

We can also look at what parts within the slice are heavy on method calls. Heavily connected parts of code are likely to represent key concepts, so these can also be good focus points for further study. Once you have investigated the important locations further, you can create a list of all related classes. Write the list of relationships down and reflect on it in depth. Do the entities you've identified and the relationships between them help you form an initial idea of the concept behind the code?

4  Understand concepts across multiple entities.

As a final step, you want to get a high-level understanding of the different concepts in the code. For example, you want to understand not only the data structures contained in the code, but also the operations applied to them and the constraints on them. What are you allowed to do, and what is forbidden? For example, is a tree a binary tree or can a node have an arbitrary number of children? Are there constraints on the tree? For example, will an error be thrown if you add a third node, or is that up to the user?

In the final step, you can create a list of concepts present in the code to document your understanding. Both the list of entities resulting from step 3 and this list of concepts might be valuable to add back to the code as documentation.

**EXERCISE 5.2**  Find another piece of unfamiliar code in your own codebase. Alternatively, you can search for some code on GitHub. It doesn't really matter what code you use, but it should be something you're not familiar with. Now follow these steps to gain a deep understanding of this code:

1  Find a focal point in the code. Since you are not fixing a bug or adding a feature, your entry point into the code will likely be the start of the code—for example, a main() method.

2  Determine the slice of code related to the focal point, either on paper or within the IDE. This might require some refactoring of the code to move the code involved in the slice closer together.

3  Based on your exploration in step 2, write down what you learned about the code. For example, what entities and concepts are present in the code, and how do they related to each other?

## 5.4   *Reading text is similar to reading code*

Even though programmers have to read a lot of code—as mentioned earlier in this book, it's estimated that the average programmer spends nearly 60% of their workday reading code rather than writing it[5]—we developers do not practice reading code much. For his book *Coders at Work* (Apress, 2009), Peter Seibel interviewed developers about their habits, including code reading. While most people Seibel interviewed said that reading code was important and that programmers should do it more, very few of them could name code that they had read recently. Donald Knuth was a notable exception.

Because we lack practice, good strategies, and good schemata, we often must rely on the much slower praxis of reading the code line by line or stepping through the code with a debugger. This in turn leads to a situation where people prefer to write their own code rather than reuse or adapt existing code because "It's just easier to build it myself." What if it were as easy to read code as it is to read natural language? In the remainder of this chapter, we will first explore how reading code and reading language are similar, and then dive into techniques for reading natural language that can be applied to reading code to make it easier.

### 5.4.1   *What happens in the brain when we read code?*

Researchers have tried to understand what happens in someone's brain when they've been programming for a very long time. We saw some early examples of this earlier in the book, such as the experiments conducted in the 1980s by Bell Labs researcher Katherine McKeithen, whose work we covered in chapter 2, where she asked people to remember ALGOL programs in order to form an initial understanding of chunking in programming.[6]

Early experiments involving programming and the brain often used techniques common at the time, like having participants remember words or keywords. While these research methods are still commonly used today, researchers also employ more modern—and arguably much cooler—techniques. These include the use of brain imaging techniques to gain a deeper understanding of what brain areas, and corresponding cognitive processes, programming triggers.

#### BRODMANN AREAS

Even though a lot about the brain is not yet known, we have a pretty decent understanding of what parts of the brain are related to what types of cognitive functions. This is mainly thanks to German neurologist Korbinian Brodmann. As early as 1909, he published a book, *Vergleichende Lokalisationslehre der Großhirnrinde*, detailing the locations of 52 different regions in the brain, now known as *Brodmann areas*. For each area,

---

[5] See "Measuring Program Comprehension: A Large-Scale Field Study with Professionals" by Xin Xia et al. (2017), https://ieeexplore.ieee.org/abstract/document/7997917.

[6] "Knowledge Organization and Skill Differences in Computer Programmers" by Katherine B. McKeithen et al. (1981), http://spider.sci.brooklyn.cuny.edu/~kopec/research/sdarticle11.pdf.

Brodmann detailed the mental functions that reside primarily in that region, such as reading words or remembering. The amount of detail in the map he produced is continuously increasing, thanks to numerous studies in the ensuing years.[7]

Because of Brodmann's work and subsequent studies on the regions of the brain, we now have a reasonable idea of where cognitive functions "live" in the human brain. Knowing which parts of the brain are associated with reading or the working memory has helped us understand the essence of larger tasks.

These types of studies can be done using a *functional magnetic resonance imaging (fMRI)* machine. An fMRI machine can detect which Brodmann areas are active by measuring blood flow in the brain. In fMRI studies, participants are commonly asked to perform a complex task, such as solving a mental puzzle. By measuring increases in blood flow to different Brodmann areas, we can determine what cognitive processes are involved in solving that task, such as the working memory. A limitation of the fMRI machine, however, is that people are not allowed to move while the machine is scanning. As such, the range of tasks participants can do is limited and does not include tasks that involve making notes or producing code.

### EVIDENCE FROM FMRI ABOUT WHAT CODE DOES IN THE BRAIN

The existence of the Brodmann map (and fMRI machines, of course) also made scientists curious about programming. What brain areas and cognitive functions might be involved? In 2014, the first study on programming in an fMRI machine was done by German computer science professor Janet Siegmund.[8] Participants were asked to read Java code that represented well-known algorithms, including sorting or searching in a list and computing the power of two numbers. Meaningful variable names in the code snippets were replaced by obfuscated names, so participants would spend cognitive effort comprehending the program's flow rather than guessing at the functionality of the code based on variable names.

Siegmund's findings reliably showed that program comprehension activates five Brodmann areas, all located in the left hemisphere of the brain: BA6, BA21, BA40, BA44, and BA4.

The fact that Brodmann areas BA6 and BA40 are involved in programming is not surprising. These areas are related to working memory (the brain's processor) and attention. The involvement of BA21, BA44, and BA47, however, might be a bit more surprising to programmers. These areas are related to natural language processing. This finding is interesting because Siegmund obfuscated all variable names in the programs.

This suggests that, even though the variable names were obfuscated, the participants were reading other elements of the code (for example, keywords) and attempting to draw meaning from them, just as we do when reading words in a natural language text.

---

[7] If you're interested, you can visit www.cognitiveatlas.org for a recent map.

[8] See "Understanding Programmers' Brains with fMRI" by Janet Siegmund et al. (2014), www.frontiersin .org/10.3389/conf.fninf.2014.18.00040/event_abstract.

### 5.4.2   *If you can learn French, you can learn Python*

We've seen that fMRI scans have shown that areas of the brain related to both working memory and language processing are involved in programming. Does that imply that people with a larger working memory capacity and better natural language skills will be better programmers?

Recent research sheds more light on the question of what cognitive abilities play a role in programming. Associate Professor Chantel Prat of the University of Washington led a study on the connection between cognitive skills and programming that assessed the performance of its participants (36 students who took a Python course on Code Academy) in a range of areas, including mathematics, language, and reasoning, as well as programming ability.[9] The tests Prat used to measure the non-programming cognitive abilities of the participants in this study were commonly used and known to reliably test these skills. For example, for mathematical skills, an example question reads: "If it takes five machines 5 minutes to make five widgets, how long would it take 100 machines to make 100 widgets?" The test for fluid reasoning resembled an IQ test; students, for example, had to finish a sequence of abstract images.

For programming ability, the researchers looked at three factors: the scores of the students on the Code Academy quizzes; an end project in which the students had to create a Rock, Paper, Scissors game; and a multiple-choice exam. Python experts created the exam and the grading scheme for the end project.

Because the researchers had access to both programming ability scores and scores for other cognitive abilities for each student, they were able to create a predictive model to see what cognitive abilities predicted programming ability. What Prat and her colleagues found might be surprising to some programmers. Numeracy—the knowledge and skills people need to apply mathematics—had only a minor predictive effect, predicting just 2% of the variance between participants. Language abilities were a better predictor, accounting for 17% of the variance. This is interesting because we as a field typically stress the fact that mathematical skills are important, and many programmers I know insist they are bad at learning natural languages. The best predictor for all three tests was working memory capacity and reasoning skills, accounting for 34% of the variance between participants.

In this study, the researchers not only measured the cognitive abilities of the 36 participants, but also brain activity during testing, using an electroencephalography (EEG) device. Unlike an fMRI machine, this is a relatively simple device that measures brain activity with electrodes placed on the head. The EEG data was taken into account when examining the three programming tasks.

For learning rate—that is, how quickly students passed through the Code Academy course—language ability was a particularly large factor. Learning rate and other programming skills were correlated, so it wasn't as though the quick students were simply

---

[9] "Relating Natural Language Aptitude to Individual Differences in Learning Programming Languages" by Chantal S. Prat et al. (2020), www.nature.com/articles/s41598-020-60661-8.

rushing through the course without understanding anything. Of course, the underlying factor here might be that students who read well learn a lot in general, while students who struggle with reading do not learn as quickly or easily, independent of the domain of programming they were taught in this study.

For programming accuracy, measured by performance on the Rock, Paper, Scissors task, general cognitive skills (including working memory and reasoning) mattered most. For declarative knowledge, measured by a multiple-choice test, EEG activity was an important factor too. As shown in figure 5.4, the results of this study seem to indicate that how well you can learn a programming language is predicted by your skill at learning natural languages.

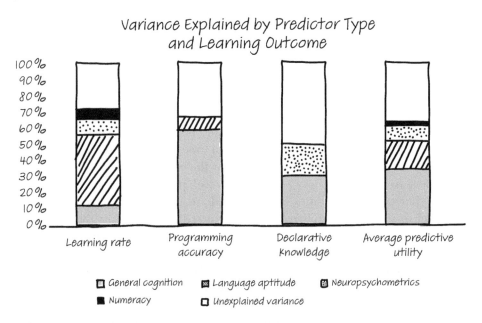

Figure 5.4   The results of Prat's study, which show that numeracy skills (in light blue) are only a minor predictor of programming ability. Language aptitude (in pink) is a much stronger predictor, especially of how quickly one can learn a programming language. Source: www.nature.com/articles/s41598-020-60661-8.pdf. Source: Chantal S. Prat et al. (2020).

This is a result that may be somewhat unexpected to many programmers. Computer science is often seen as a STEM (science, technology, engineering, and mathematics) field and grouped with those subjects at universities (including mine). In the culture of programming, mathematics skills are sought after as helpful or even required skills. These new findings might require us to update our thinking on what predicts programming ability.

### HOW DO PEOPLE READ CODE?

Before we dive into reading code, let's reflect on how we read a (nonfiction) text, such as a newspaper. What do you do when you read a newspaper article?

There are a lot of strategies people commonly use when reading text. For example, you might scan the text before reading it in depth to determine if it's worth your time. You might also consciously look at images that appear alongside the text as you read to help support your understanding of the text and its context or make notes to summarize what you're reading or to highlight the most important parts. Scanning text and looking at accompanying images are *text comprehension strategies.* Many of these strategies are actively taught and practiced in school, so it's likely that they're automatic and you use them without thinking.

We'll dive into improving your code-reading skills shortly, but first let's look at what scientific research has found about how people read code.

> **EXERCISE 5.3** Think of a time when you were reading a nonfiction text. What strategies did you employ before, during, and after reading the text?

#### WHEN PROGRAMMERS READ CODE, THEY SCAN IT FIRST

When researchers want to understand what people look at, they use *eye trackers.* Eye trackers are devices that can be used to determine where on a screen or page people are focusing their attention. They're used extensively in marketing research to determine what kinds of advertisements catch people's eyes the longest. Eye trackers can be physical devices and were used as early as the 1920s, when they still occupied an entire room. Modern eye trackers are a lot smaller. They can work with hardware, like a Microsoft Kinect tracking depth, or even be entirely software-based and track the user's gaze with image recognition.

Eye trackers have enabled researchers to better understand how people read code. For example, a team of researchers at the Nara Institute of Science and Technology, led by professor Hidetake Uwano, observed that programmers scan code to get an idea of what the program does.[10] They found that in the first 30% of the time spent reviewing the code, the participants viewed over 70% of the lines. Performing this type of quick scan is common behavior when reading natural language to get an overview of the structure of the text, and it appears that people transfer this strategy to reading code.

#### BEGINNERS AND EXPERTS READ CODE DIFFERENTLY

To compare how developers read code and how people read natural language, Teresa Busjahn, a researcher at Freie Universität Berlin, led a study involving 14 novice programmers and 6 experts.[11] Busjahn and her colleagues first studied the difference between text reading and natural language reading. She found that code is read less linearly than natural language: novice programmers followed a linear path on text with approximately 80% of their eye movements, while they read linearly in 75% of

---

[10] See "Analyzing Individual Performance of Source Code Review Using Reviewers' Eye Movement" by Hidetake Uwano et al. (2006), www.cs.kent.edu/~jmaletic/cs69995-PC/papers/Uwano06.pdf.

[11] See "Eye Movements in Code Reading: Relaxing the Linear Order" by Teresa Busjahn et al. (2015), https://ieeexplore.ieee.org/document/7181454.

eye movements for code. In the cases where the novice programmers did not read linearly, they often followed the call stack rather than reading from top to bottom.

Busjahn not only compared code to text, she also compared novice programmers with expert programmers. Comparing the code-reading practices of the novices with those of the experts revealed a difference in the two groups' code reading practices: novices read more linearly and follow the call stack more frequently than expert programmers. Learning to follow the call stack while reading code, apparently, is a practice that comes with experience.

## 5.5    *Text comprehension strategies applied to code*

As the previous section showed, the cognitive skills used for reading code are similar to those used for reading natural language. This means we may be able to apply insights gained from studying how people read texts in natural language to reading code.

There has been a lot of research into effective reading strategies and how to learn them. Strategies for reading comprehension can be roughly divided into these seven categories:[12]

- *Activating*—Actively thinking of related things to activate prior knowledge
- *Monitoring*—Keeping track of your understanding of a text
- *Determining importance*—Deciding what parts of a text are most relevant
- *Inferring*—Filling in facts that are not explicitly given in the text
- *Visualizing*—Drawing diagrams of the read text to deepen understanding
- *Questioning*—Asking questions about the text at hand
- *Summarizing*—Creating a short summary of a text

Because there are cognitive similarities between reading code and reading text, it's feasible that strategies for reading natural language will also be useful in code reading. This section explores each of the seven known strategies for reading text in the context of reading code.

### 5.5.1    *Activating prior knowledge*

We know that programmers scan new code before diving in. But why would scanning code be helpful? One reason is that it will give you an initial sense of the concepts and syntactic elements that are present in the code.

In previous chapters, we saw that when you think about things, your working memory will search your LTM for related memories. Actively thinking about code elements will help your working memory to find relevant information stored in the LTM that might be helpful in comprehending the code at hand. A good strategy for deliberately activating prior knowledge is to give yourself a fixed amount of time— say, 10 minutes—to study code and get a sense of what it's about.

---

[12]"The Seven Habits of Highly Effective Readers," by Kathy Ann Mills, 2008, https://www.researchgate.net/publication/27474121_The_Seven_Habits_of_Highly_Effective_Readers.

**EXERCISE 5.4**  Study a piece of unfamiliar code for a fixed amount of time (say, 5 or 10 minutes, depending on the length). After studying the code for this fixed amount of time, try to answer the following concrete questions about it:

- What was the first element (variable, class, programming concept, and so on) that caught your eye?
- Why is that?
- What was the second thing you noticed?
- Why?
- Are these two things (variables, classes, programming concepts) related?
- What concepts are present in the code? Do you know all of them?
- What syntactic elements are present in the code? Do you know all of them?
- What domain concepts are present in the code? Do you know all of them?

The result of this exercise might motivate you to look up more information about unfamiliar programming or domain concepts in the code. When you encounter an unfamiliar concept, it is best to try to study it before diving into the code again. Learning about a new concept at the same time as reading new code will likely cause excessive cognitive load, making both the concept and the code less effective.

## 5.5.2    *Monitoring*

When reading code, it is important to keep track of what you are reading and whether you understand it. Keep a mental note not only of what you understand, but also of what you find confusing. A good strategy is to print out the code and mark the lines you understand and the ones that confuse you. You can do this with icons like the ones you used to mark the roles of variables.

Figure 5.5 shows a piece of JavaScript code that I've annotated this way—I use a tick mark for code that I understand and a question mark for lines or parts of lines that confuse me. Monitoring your understanding like this will help you when you read the code for a second time, as you can then focus on the confusing lines in more depth.

Annotations marking what confuses you can be very helpful in monitoring your own understanding, but they can also be an aid in seeking help. If you can clearly communicate which parts of the code are confusing, you can ask the author for an explanation about certain lines. This will be more effective than if you say, "I have no idea what this does."

```
✓ import { handlerCheckTodo } from '../handlers/checkedTask.js';
✓ import { handlerDeleteTodo } from '../handlers/deletetask.js';
✓ import { restFulMethods } from '../restful/restful.js';

✓ export class app {
  ✓ state = [];
  ✓ nexId = 0;

  ✓ renderTodos(todosArray) {
    ✓ const Tbody = document.createElement('tbody');

    ✓ for (const todo of todosArray) {
      ? const trEl = document.createElement('tr');
      ✓ trEl.className = 'today-row';
      ? const DivEl = document.createElement('div');
      ✓ DivEl.className = 'row';
      ✓ const divElSecond = document.createElement('div');
      ✓ divElSecond.className = 'col-1';

      ✓ const TdEl = document.createElement('td');
      ✓ const checkBoxEl = document.createElement('input');
      ✓ checkBoxEl.type = 'checkbox';
      ✓ checkBoxEl.addEventListener('click', handlerCheckTodo);

      ✓ checkBoxEl.dataset.index = todo.id;
```

Figure 5.5   A code snippet in JavaScript annotated with icons that indicate understanding. A check mark means the line is understood, and a question mark indicates a certain line is confusing.

### 5.5.3   Determining the importance of different lines of code

When reading code, it can be very useful to reflect on which lines are important. You can do this as a deliberate exercise. It doesn't matter all that much how many important lines you choose—it could be 10 for a short snippet or 25 for a larger program. What matters is that you think about which parts of the code are likely to have the most influence on the program's execution.

If you are using printed code, you can mark important lines with an exclamation mark.

**EXERCISE 5.5**   Select a piece of unfamiliar code and give yourself a few minutes to decide on the most important lines in the program. Once you have selected the lines, answer these questions:

- Why did you select those lines?
- What role do those lines have? For example, are they lines that perform initialization, or input/output, or data processing?
- How are these lines connected to the overall goal of the program?

**WHAT IS AN IMPORTANT LINE OF CODE?**   You might wonder what an important line of code is, and that's a great question! I have often done the exercise of marking important lines of code with a development team, where each team member individually marks what they think are the most important lines and the team compares notes afterward.

It's not uncommon for people in a team to disagree about which lines are important. Some people argue that the lines where the most intensive calculations happen are the most important lines, while other people select an import statement for a relevant library or an explanatory comment. People with backgrounds in different programming languages or domains might have different ideas about the importance of particular lines of code, and that's OK. Don't think of it as a disagreement to be solved but an opportunity to learn.

The nice thing about doing this exercise with your team is that it doesn't just teach you about the code, but also about yourself and your teammates (priorities, experience, and so on).

### 5.5.4 *Inferring the meaning of variable names*

A lot of the meaning of a program is contained in the structure of the code itself—for example, in the use of loops and conditional statements. There is also meaning in the names of program elements such as variables, and some of that meaning might need to be inferred. If code contains a variable called shipment, it can be valuable to gain an understanding of what a shipment means within the domain of the code. Is a shipment the same as an order, a group of products meant for one customer? Or is a shipment a set of products to be shipped to a factory?

As you've seen already, variable names can serve as important *beacons*: hints as to what the code is about. When reading code, it can thus be valuable to consciously pay attention to them.

An exercise for this is to go through the code line by line and create a list of all the identifier names (variables, classes, methods, functions). This is something you can do even when you are totally confused about what the code does. It may feel a bit weird to analyze code so mechanically, but reading all the identifiers will help your working memory. Once you focus on the names, you can then search your LTM for related information. The information that is found supports the working memory to process the code with more ease.

Once you've created the list of identifiers, you can use it to gain a deeper understanding of the code. For example, you can divide the variable names into two different categories: names of variables that are related to the domain of the code, such as Customer or  Package, and variable names that are related to programming concepts, such as Tree or List. Some variable names combine both categories, such as CustomerList or FactorySet. Others cannot be understood without context, which means you will need to spend more effort to investigate their meaning—for example, by trying to decide which role they play using Sajaniemi's framework, discussed earlier in this chapter.

> **EXERCISE 5.6** Select a piece of source code and meticulously create a list of all the variable names present in the program.

Fill out the following table for all of the variable names.

| Name | Domain? | Concept? | Is the name understandable without looking at the code? |
|------|---------|----------|-------------------------------------------------------|
|      |         |          |                                                       |

Using the table of variable names, you can answer these questions:

- What is the domain or topic of the code?
- What programming concepts are used?
- What can you learn from these names?
- Which names are related to each other?
- Are there names that are ambiguous when looked at without context?
- What meaning could ambiguous names have in this codebase?

### 5.5.5   *Visualizing*

In previous chapters you saw several techniques for visualizing code to gain a deeper understanding, including creating a state table and tracing the flow of a piece of code.

There are several other visualization strategies that can be used for understanding code. One technique that can be helpful for very complex code of which a deeper understanding is needed is to list all operations in which variables are involved.

#### OPERATION TABLES

When working with unfamiliar code, it can sometimes be difficult to predict how the values of variables will change as the code is executed. When code is too hard to process right away, it can help to create an operation table. For example, the following JavaScript code snippet may be hard to understand if you do not know that a zip function merges two lists.

Listing 5.1   JavaScript code that zips lists `as` and `bs` using a given function `f`

```javascript
zipWith: function (f, as, bs) {
  var length = Math.min(as.length, bs.length);
  var zs = [];
  for (var i = 0; i < length; i++) {
    zs[i] = f(as[i], bs[i]);
  }
  return zs;
}
```

In such a case it can help to inspect the variables, methods, and functions and determine what operations they are involved in. For example, `f` is applied to `as[i]` and bs[i], so it is a function. Inspecting as and bs, we see that they are being indexed, so these variables must be lists or dictionaries. Once you have determined the types of variables in a complex piece of code through their operations, it can be easier to determine their roles.

**EXERCISE 5.7** Select a piece of unfamiliar code and write down the names of all the variables, functions, and classes in the code. Then list all the operations associated with each identifier.

| Identifier name | Operation(s) |
| --- | --- |
|  |  |

Once you've created this table, read through the code again. Has filling in the table helped you gain a deeper understanding of the roles of the variables and the meaning of the problem as a whole?

## 5.5.6 Questioning

Asking yourself questions while reading code will help you understand the code's goals and functionality. In the previous sections, you saw numerous examples of questions you can ask about code. A few more valuable questions are as follows:

- What are the five most central concepts of the code? These could be identifier names, themes, classes, or information found in comments.
- What strategies did you use to identify the central concepts? For example, did you look at method names, documentation, or variable names or draw on your prior knowledge of a system?
- What are the five most central computer science concepts in the code? These could be algorithms, data structures, assumptions, or techniques.
- What can you determine about the decisions made by the creator(s) of the code—for example, the decision to implement a certain version of an algorithm, use a certain design pattern, or use a certain library or API?
- What assumptions do these decisions rely on?
- What are the benefits of these decisions?
- What are some potential downsides of these decisions?
- Can you think of alternative solutions?

These questions go deeper than text structure knowledge and can help you reach a plan to understand the code.

### 5.5.7   *Summarizing code*

A final strategy from text comprehension that we can apply to code comprehension is summarizing what you have just read. Writing a summary of code in natural language will help you gain a deeper understanding of what's happening in that code. This summary might also serve as additional documentation, either for yourself personally or even as actual documentation of the code if it was lacking beforehand.

Some of the techniques we covered earlier in this chapter can be a great aid in summarizing code. For example, looking at the most important lines, listing all the variables and their related operations, and reflecting on the decisions that were made by the creator of the code are great ways to get started on a summary.

EXERCISE 5.8   Summarize a piece of code by filling in the following table. Of course, you can add more information to the summary than I've suggested in this exercise.

| Origin | |
|---|---|
| Goal of the code: What is the code trying to achieve? | |
| Most important lines of code | |
| Most relevant domain concepts | |
| Most relevant programming constructs | |
| Decisions made in the creation of the code | |

## *Summary*

- When reading unfamiliar code, figuring out what roles the variables play, such as stepper or most wanted value, can help deepen your understanding.
- When it comes to understanding code, there is a difference between *text structure knowledge,* which means knowing the syntactic concepts used in code, and *plan knowledge,* which means understanding the intentions of the code's creator.
- There are many similarities between reading code and reading natural language, and your ability to learn a natural language can be a predictor of your ability to learn to program.
- Strategies that are commonly used to aid deep understanding of natural language texts, such as visualizing and summarizing, can also be applied to gain a deeper understanding of code.

# Getting better at solving programming problems

In the previous chapters, you learned about different cognitive processes active in the brain when programming. We explored how information is stored briefly in the STM while reading code and how information is retrieved from the LTM when it needs to be applied. We also discussed the working memory, which is active when we think about code. Then, in chapter 5, we discussed strategies for deeply engaging with unfamiliar code.

The focus of this chapter is how we solve problems. As a professional programmer, you will often weigh different solutions to problems. Will you model all the customers of a company as a simple list or as a tree, organized by their default branch? Will you use an architecture based on microservices or should all the logic be in one place?

When you're considering different solutions to problems, you'll often find that different alternatives all have value. Deciding which solution to use can be hard because there are so many factors to take into account. For example, will you prioritize ease of use or performance? Will you consider potential changes you expect to the code in the future or will you just look at the current task?

This chapter presents two frameworks that can help you gain more insight into how to make decisions about different software designs. We will first study the mental representations that the brain creates while problem solving and programming. Being aware of the representations you use to think about code will enable you to solve more types of problems and to reason about code and solve problems more effectively. This chapter covers two techniques involving models that will help you strengthen your LTM and support your working memory to achieve these goals.

Second, we will look at how we think about computers when solving problems. When programming, we don't always consider all aspects of the machines we're working on. Sometimes we can abstract many of the details—for example, when you're creating a user interface, most of the specifics of the operating system are not that relevant. However, when implementing a machine learning model or when creating a phone app, the specifications of the machine that the code will run on matter. The second framework that we will look at in this chapter helps you think about problems at the right level of abstraction.

## 6.1 Using models to think about code

When people solve problems, they almost always create models. Models are simplified representations of reality, and the main goal of a model is to support you in thinking about a problem and ultimately solving it. Models can have various shapes and levels of formality. A rough calculation on the back of a beer mat is a model, but an entity-relationship diagram of a software system is also a model.

### 6.1.1 The benefits of using models

In previous chapters, we created various types of models that supported thinking about code. For example, we created a state diagram to show the values of variables, as shown in figure 6.1. We also created a dependency graph, which is another kind of model of code.

Using explicit models of code when you solve a problem has two benefits. First, models can help communicate information about programs to others. If I have created a state diagram, I can show someone else all the intermediate values of the variables to

```
1    LET N2 =  ABS (INT (N))
2    LET B$ = ""
3    FOR N1 = N2 TO 0 STEP 0
4        LET N2 =  INT (N1 / 2)
5        LET B$ =  STR$ (N1 - N2 * 2) + B$
6        LET N1 = N2
7    NEXT N1
8    PRINT B$
9    RETURN
```

| | N | N2 | B$ | NI |
|---|---|---|---|---|
| Init | 7 | 7 | — | 7 |
| Loop 1 | | 3 | 1 | 3 |
| Loop 2 | | | | |

**Figure 6.1   A BASIC program that converts the number N into a binary representation. You can use a memory aid like the partial state table shown here to help you understand how the program works.**

help them understand how the code works. This is especially helpful with larger systems. For example, if we look at an architectural diagram of code together, I can point out classes and the relationships between them and objects that would otherwise be invisible or hidden in code.

A second benefit of models is that they can help you solve problems. When you are close to the limit of items you can process at once, making a model can be a useful way to lower cognitive load. Just as a child might add 3+5 using a number line (a kind of model) rather than doing the calculation in their head, programmers might map out the architecture of a system on a whiteboard because it is too hard to hold all the elements of a large codebase in the working memory.

Models can be a big help in solving problems because they help the LTM identify relevant memories. Often models have constraints; for example, a state diagram only shows the values of variables and an entity relationship diagram only shows classes and their relationships. Focusing on a certain part of a problem can support your thinking about a solution, and these constraints force you to do just that. Thinking of the number line while adding helps to put the focus on the activity of counting, and an entity relationship diagram forces you to think about what entities or classes your system will consist of and how they relate to each other.

### NOT ALL MODELS ARE EQUALLY HELPFUL

Not all models that we can use to think about problems are equal, however. As programmers, we know the importance of representation and its effects on solving problems. For example, dividing a number by two is trivial when we have converted the number to a binary representation—we simply need to shift the bits right by one. While this is a relatively simple example, there are numerous problems where the representation influences the solution strategy.

The importance of representation can be nicely illustrated in more depth by the following problem concerning a bird and two trains. A bird is sitting on a train about to leave Cambridge, England, heading to London. Just as that train departs, a second train departs from London, 50 miles away. The bird takes off and flies toward the second train at a speed of 75 miles per hour. Both trains are traveling at 50 miles per hour. When the bird gets to the second train, it turns around and flies back toward the first one, and it keeps doing this until the two trains meet. How far has the bird flown when the trains meet?

Many people's first intuition is to think of the trains and how the bird moves between them (figure 6.2).

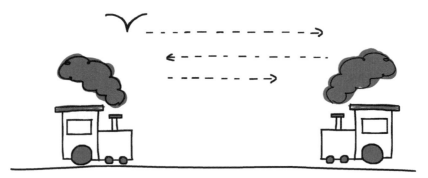

**Figure 6.2   Modeling the distance a bird travels between two moving trains, from the view of the bird. This leads to a correct but very complex solution involving calculating the locations of both trains.**

Modeling the trajectory of the bird is a correct solution, but it involves a complicated set of equations that most people would prefer to avoid. An easier solution focuses on the bird itself and goes as follows. The trains will meet in the middle between London and Cambridge after 30 minutes. At that point, both trains have traveled 25 miles. Since the bird flies at a speed of 75 miles per hour, after half an hour, the bird has flown 37.5 miles. This is a nice illustration of the fact that the way in which you think about a problem can heavily impact how you solve it and the effort it takes to do so.

In programming, we also work with different representations of problems. Some programming languages limit the number of possible representations, which can be both helpful and harmful in solving problems. For example, a language like APL is perfect for modeling solutions that involve matrices but can be hard to use for problems that need a different representation. Java, on the other hand, has the option of creating classes to represent all sorts of problems, so you can use Java for problems involving matrices, but you'll need to do the extra work of creating a matrix class. In Java, it is more likely that you would reach for a solution involving two nested for-loops instead, because these are built in and commonly used.

## 6.2   *Mental models*

So far we've worked with models that are explicitly created outside our brains. State tables, dependency graphs, and entity relationship diagrams are models that are constructed on paper or a whiteboard. You can choose to make such a model when you need to communicate with others or think more deeply about a problem. But there are also models you can use when thinking about a problem that are not made explicit outside of your brain. These are called *mental models*.

In the previous section you saw that the representation you use to solve a problem influences how you think about the problem. The same is true for mental models: some support thinking better than others. In this section we'll explore what mental models are and how you can use them explicitly when solving problems.

An example of a mental model we use for code is thinking about traversing a tree. In the code and the computer, of course, there isn't a real tree that we traverse; there are just values in memory that we think of as a tree structure. This model helps us reason about the code. It is easier to think about "the children of that node" than it is to think about "the elements that that element refers to."

Mental models were initially described by Scottish philosopher Kenneth Craik in his 1943 book *The Nature of Explanation*. Craik described mental models as mental "scale models" of phenomena in nature. According to Craik, people use mental models to predict, reason about, and explain the world around them.

The definition of a mental model that I like best is this one: a mental model creates an abstraction in your working memory that you can use to reason about the problem at hand.

While interacting with computers, we create many types of mental models. For example, when thinking of a filesystem, you might think of a group of files in a folder together. Of course, when you think about it a bit more deeply, you know that there are not really files or folders on your hard drive; a hard drive only contains zeros and ones. But when we think about those zeros and ones, we think of them as being organized into those structures.

We also use mental models when thinking about code. An example of a mental model we use when thinking about programming is the idea that a specific line of code is being executed. Even for compiled languages that is the way we reason about programs, while of course what's executed is not the line of Java or C itself, but the generated bytecode corresponding to that line. Even though the execution of lines of code is not a correct or complete representation of how program execution works, it can be a helpful model to use when reasoning about programs.

Models can also fail us, though—for example, when you step through highly optimized code in a debugger and find that the compiler's optimizer transformed the code underneath enough that the debugger moves in ways that seem unrelated to how you think the source code will be executed.

**EXERCISE 6.1** Consider a piece of code you used in the last few days. What mental models of that code did you use while programming? Did those mental models concern the computer or code execution or other aspects of programming?

## 6.2.1    *Examining mental models in detail*

Mental models share an important characteristic with models expressed outside the brain: the model adequately represents the problem but is simpler and more abstract than reality. Mental models also have other important characteristics, which are outlined in table 6.1.

Table 6.1    **Key characteristics of mental models, paired with examples in programming**

| Characteristic | Example |
|---|---|
| Mental models are incomplete. A mental model does not have to be a complete model of the target system, much like a scale model simplifies the physical object it models in some ways. An incomplete mental model can be useful for its holder if it abstracts the irrelevant details. | Thinking of a variable as a box that holds a value does not adequately support thinking about reassignment. Will the second value fit in the box with the first value? Or will the first value be pushed out? |
| Mental models are unstable. Mental models do not have to stay the same forever; in fact, they very often change over the period that they are in use. For example, if you create a mental model of electricity as the flow of water, you might picture it as a straight river initially, but as a widening and narrowing river when you learn more about how electricity flows. Holders of a mental model might also forget parts of the model when they do not engage with it enough. | When we learn to program, thinking of a variable like a box that holds a value is helpful. However, after a while, we realize that a variable cannot hold more than one value, so a name tag becomes a better analogy. |
| Multiple mental models can coexist, even if they are inconsistent with each other. Novices in particular often have "locally coherent but globally inconsistent" mental models, which tend to be closely tied to the details of the particular case they're considering.[a] | You can think of a variable like a box holding a value. Alternatively, you might think of a variable like a name tag you attach to a value. Both mental models can exist at the same time and might have benefits in different situations. |
| Mental models can be "weird" and even feel like superstitions. Often people believe things that do not really make sense. | Have you ever asked a computer to do something, like "Please work this time?" Even though you know a computer is not a sentient being and cannot listen to you, you might still hold a mental model of a computer as an entity that can decide to act in your favor. |
| People are frugal when using mental models. Because the brain consumes lots of energy, people will typically prefer to do extra physical work if that saves mental effort. | For example, when debugging, many programmers prefer to make small changes to their code (tweaks) and run it again to see if the bug is fixed rather than spending the energy to create a good mental model of the problem. |

[a] Gentner, Dedre. (2002). Psychology of mental models. In N. J. Smelser & P. B. Bates (Eds.), *International Encyclopedia of the Social and Behavioral Sciences* (pp. 9683–9687), Elsevier.

### 6.2.2 *Learning new mental models*

As is shown in table 6.1, people can hold different, competing mental models in their minds at the same time. You can superficially think of a file as being "in" a folder, while also knowing that, in fact, a file is a reference to a location on the hard drive where information is stored.

When learning to program, people often learn new mental models gradually. For example, initially you might think of a document on the hard drive as an actual physical sheet of paper with words on it that's stored somewhere, while later you learn that the hard drive can only store zeros and ones. Or you might first think of a variable and its value as a name and telephone number in an address book, then update that model when you learn more about how the computer's memory works. You might think that when you learn how something works in more depth, the old, "wrong" mental model is removed from your brain and replaced by a better one. However, in previous chapters we have seen that it is not likely that that information disappears completely from the LTM. That means there is always a risk that you will fall back on incorrect or incomplete mental models you learned previously. Multiple mental models can remain active simultaneously, and the boundaries between the models are not always clear. So, especially in a situation of high cognitive load, you might suddenly use an old model.

As an example of competing mental models, consider this riddle: What happens to a snowman if you dress it in a nice, warm sweater? Will it melt faster or slower than it would without a sweater?

Your first thought might be that the snowman will melt faster, since your brain immediately fetches the mental model of a sweater being a thing that provides warmth. But upon further consideration, you will conclude that a sweater does not give warmth but rather helps keep our body warmth in. Because the sweater insulates, it will keep the cold that the snowman loses in, so the snowman will actually melt slower, not faster.

Similarly, you might fall back on simple mental models when reading complex code. For example, when reading code that heavily uses pointers, you might confuse values and memory addresses, mixing mental models of variables and pointers. Or, when debugging complex code making use of asynchronous calls, you might use an old, incomplete mental model of synchronous code.

> **EXERCISE 6.2** Think of two mental models that you know for a single programming concept, such as variables, loops, file storage, or memory management. What are the similarities and differences between the two mental models?

### 6.2.3 *How to use mental models efficiently when thinking about code*

In previous chapters, we discussed different cognitive processes in the brain. We talked about the LTM, where not only memories about life events but also abstract representations of knowledge, called schemata, are stored. We've also covered the working memory, which is where thinking happens.

You might wonder what cognitive process mental models are associated with. Are these models stored in the LTM and retrieved when needed? Or does the working memory form them when thinking about code? Understanding how mental models are processed is important because that knowledge can help us improve our use of these models. If they are mainly located in the LTM, we can train ourselves to remember them with flashcards, while if they are created in the working memory, we might want to use visualizations to support that cognitive process in its use of mental models.

Curiously enough, after Kenneth Craik's initial book on mental models, the topic was not studied further for almost 40 years. Then, in 1983, two books, both called *Mental Models*, were published by different authors. The authors of these books held different views on how mental models are processed in the brain, as you'll see in the following sections.

### MENTAL MODELS IN WORKING MEMORY

The first book on mental models that came out in 1983 was by Philip Johnson-Laird, a professor of psychology at Princeton. Johnson-Laird argued that mental models are used while reasoning and thus live in the working memory. In his book, he describes a study where he and a colleague investigated the use of these models. Participants were given sets of sentences describing a table setting: for example, "The spoon is to the right of the fork" and "The plate is to the right of the knife." After hearing the descriptions, the participants were asked to do some unrelated tasks. They were then given four descriptions of table settings and asked which of the descriptions was most similar to the one they had been given.

Of the descriptions participants were allowed to choose from, two were completely bogus, one was the real one they had heard, and one was a description that could be inferred from the layout. For example, from "The knife is to the left of the fork" and "The fork is to the left of the plate" one can infer that the plate is to the right of the knife without explicitly being told. Participants were then asked to rank the four descriptions, starting with the one best representing the description they'd been given.

They generally ranked both the real and the inferred descriptions higher than the two bogus ones, from which the researchers concluded that participants had made a model in their minds of the table setting, which they used to select the right answer.

What we can learn from Johnson-Laird's work to improve thinking about programming is that having an abstract model of code is helpful: it allows you to reason about the model itself rather than relying on referring back to the code, which would be less efficient.

### CONCRETE MODELS WORK BETTER

Later in this chapter we will explore how to deliberately create mental models when reasoning about code. But first we need to discuss one aspect of Johnson-Laird's study we have not covered yet. His experiment had an interesting twist!

Participants received different types of descriptions. In some cases, the original descriptions they were given matched only one table setting. However, sometimes the original descriptions could match different realistic arrangements. For example, in figure 6.3 the statements "The fork is to the left of the spoon" and "The spoon is to the right of the fork" fit both table settings. On the other hand, the statement "The plate is between the spoon and the fork" only fits the left table setting in figure 6.3.

**Figure 6.3  Example table settings that participants were asked to match with the provided descriptions. Here, "The fork is to the left of the spoon" fits both table settings.**

When Johnson-Laird compared the performance of participants on both types of descriptions—determinate and indeterminate—he found that those who had been given determinate descriptions selected the correct answers more often than those who had been given descriptions that could match multiple table settings. The difference was large: 88% correct answers for the first group versus 58% for the second. These results indicate that creating a more concrete model of a situation strongly supports reasoning.

Bringing these results back to programming indicates that the more details a mental model has, the easier it is to reason about the system at hand and to answer questions about the system correctly.

### CREATING MENTAL MODELS OF SOURCE CODE IN THE WORKING MEMORY

We have seen in this chapter that mental models, when they are correct and concrete, can support thinking about complex systems. That leads to the question of how to create such mental models. When code is simple, you might be able to create a mental model without a lot of effort. However, when code is more complex, or you have less knowledge about the codebase or the domain, creating an accurate mental model will take more work. It's worth it, though, because that model can be a great asset.

Following these steps can help you form a mental model of complex code in your working memory:

1  Begin by creating local models.

In earlier chapters, you learned about using hand-drawn models to support your working memory, such as creating state tables and dependency graphs. While these methods are local, representing only a small part of a codebase, they can help you create a mental model of a larger piece of code too, in two ways. First, by supporting the working memory, these local models lower cognitive load, so you can focus on creating a larger mental model with more ease. Second, these smaller models can be the building blocks for a larger mental model. For example, a dependency graph can point to a few strongly connected lines of code that might play an important role in the formation of a mental model.

2   List all relevant objects in the codebase and the relationships between objects.

When forming a mental model of code, you want to be able to reason about elements in it. A mental model of a program that creates invoices, for example, might include the constraint that a person can have multiple invoices but an invoice just belongs to one person. To understand the interactions between the different elements in the code, first list the elements using a whiteboard or digital tool, then map out the relationships. This will help give you a clearer picture of the overall system.

3   Answer questions about the system and use the answers to refine your model.

You can now try to answer questions about the system you're working with using the mental model you constructed in steps 1 and 2 and verify them in code. What the right questions are depends on the system at hand, but a few generic questions that often work are the following:

a   What are the most important elements (classes, objects, pages) of the system? Are they present in the model?

b   What are the relationships between these important elements?

c   What are the main goals of the program?

d   How does the goal relate to the core elements and their relationships?

e   What is a typical use case? Is it covered in the model?

## MENTAL MODELS IN LTM

So far in this section we've talked about using mental models for reasoning, which Johnson-Laird described as situated in the working memory. However, there is a different view on mental models, which describes them as being stored in the LTM.

The second book on mental models that appeared in 1983 was written by Dedre Gentner and Albert Stevens, researchers at the R&D firm Bolt, Beranek, and Newman Inc. (BBN). Unlike Johnson-Laird, they argued that generic mental models are stored in the LTM and can be recalled when needed.

For example, a person might store a mental model of how liquids flow, which is used when pouring milk into a glass. Because the model is generic, people will know that when pouring pancake batter into a bowl, the liquid might behave a bit differently from milk, because it's thicker, but will still fit the mental model of how liquid flows.

How does this apply to programming? In programming, you might store an abstract representation of how tree traversal works: there is a root at which you start, and then you can either explore breadth first, by looking at all the children of a given node, or depth first, where you choose one child and explore its children until you cannot proceed any further. When you encounter a program that works with trees, you can invoke the generic mental model of trees.

Gentner and Stevens's description of mental models is somewhat similar to schemata in the LTM: mental models stored in the LTM help you organize data and can be used when you encounter new situations similar to ones you have seen before. For example, you can probably understand tree traversal in a programming language you have never seen before using your previously stored mental model.

### CREATING MENTAL MODELS OF SOURCE CODE IN THE LTM

Thinking of mental models in this way would lead to a different way of improving your use of mental models. Rather than creating concrete instances of mental models when reading complex source code, Gentner and Steven's view would indicate that to make better use of them you need to build up a larger vocabulary of potential mental models. In earlier chapters, you learned about ways of expanding the information stored in LTM too.

One way that we covered of expanding the knowledge stored in your LTM is the use of flashcards. The flashcards we discussed in chapter 3 had a programming concept on one side and corresponding code on the other. If you want to store more mental models to use when reasoning about code, you can also use flashcards. However, they will contain different information now. The goal of this second form of flashcards is not to extend your knowledge of syntactic concepts but to extend your vocabulary of mental models, or ways to think about code. Place the name of a mental model on one side of the card (the prompt) and a brief explanation or visualization of the mental model on the other side.

What mental models you will use to think about code partly depends on the domain, the programming language, and the architecture of the code. However, some things are generally worth using:

- Data structures, such as directed and undirected graphs and different forms of lists
- Design patterns, such as the observer pattern
- Architectural patterns, such as Model–View–Controller
- Diagrams, such as entity relationship diagrams or sequence diagrams
- Modeling tools, such as state diagrams or Petri nets

There are two ways you can use a set of flashcards of mental models. You can use them to test your knowledge, in the same way as the syntax flash cards: read a prompt and then verify that you know the corresponding explanation. As explained previously, whenever you encounter a pattern you are not familiar with, you can add a card to your deck of mental models.

A second way to use the deck is when reading code you are struggling with. Go through your deck of mental models and decide for each one whether it might apply to the code at hand.

For example, if you pick a card about trees, ask yourself, "Can I think of this code in the form of a tree?" If that pattern might apply, you can start to create an initial model based on this card. For a tree, that will mean deciding what nodes, leaves, and edges would be present in the model and what they might represent.

**EXERCISE 6.3** Create an initial deck of flashcards with mental models that might be useful for code you are working on. Write the name of the mental model on one side as a prompt and an explanation of the model on the other side. Append the explanation with questions to ask when applying this mental model. For example, for a tree you will model nodes, leaves, and edges, so a starting question could be "What pieces of code can be represented as leaves?" Similarly, to use the mental model of a state table you will need to create a list of variables, so a starter question could be "What are the variables?"

You can do this exercise together as a team too and learn from each other's models. Having a shared vocabulary of mental models can greatly ease communication about code.

#### MENTAL MODELS LIVE BOTH IN THE LTM AND IN THE WORKING MEMORY

Both views of mental models—that they are used in the working memory and that they are stored in LTM—are still commonly held. While the two competing opinions on mental models might seem contradictory, as we have seen in this chapter, both theories have their value, and in fact they complement each other nicely. In the 1990s studies showed that both are true to a certain extent: mental models stored in LTM can influence the construction of mental models in the working memory.[1]

## 6.3   *Notional machines*

In the previous section we discussed mental models, representations that we form in our brains when reasoning about problems. Mental models are generic and found in all domains. However, research on programming languages also uses the concept of a *notional machine*. While a mental model can be a model of anything in the world in general, a notional machine is a model we use when reasoning about how a computer executes code. To be more precise, a notional machine is an abstract representation of the computer we use to think about what it's doing.

When attempting to understand how a program or programming language works, most of the time we are not interested in all the details about how the physical computer works. We don't care about how bits are stored using electricity. Instead, we care about the effect of the programming language at a higher conceptual level, such as swapping two values or finding the largest element in a list. To indicate the difference between the real physical machine and what the machine does at a more abstract level, we use the term "notional machine."

For example, a notional machine for Java or Python might include the concept of references but can omit memory addresses. Memory addresses can be considered an implementation detail you do not need to be aware of when programming in Java or Python.

---

[1] For an overview, see "Toward a Unified Theory of Reasoning" by Johnson-Laird and Khemlani, https://www.sciencedirect.com/science/article/pii/B9780124071872000010.

A notional machine is a consistent and correct abstraction of the execution of a programming language, even though it might be incomplete, as we just saw. Notional machines, therefore, differ from a programmer's mental models, which can be wrong or inconsistent.

The clearest way I have found to understand the difference between a notional machine and a mental model is that a notional machine is an explanation of how a computer works. When you have internalized the notional machine and can use it with ease, the notional machine becomes your mental model. The more you learn about a programming language, the closer your mental model gets to the notional machine.

### 6.3.1 *What is a notional machine?*

The term is a bit cryptic, so before we look at examples of notional machines and how we use them in programming, I want to unpack the term itself. The first point to make is that a notional machine represents a *machine*, something that can be interacted with at will. That is an important difference from the mental models we form about, for example, physics or chemistry. While we can certainly use scientific experiments to build an understanding of the world around us, there are also many things we cannot experiment with, or at least not safely. For example, when we are forming mental models of the behavior of electrons or radioactivity, it is hard to have an experimental setup at home or work that we can safely learn from. In programming, we have a machine we can interact with at any time. Notional machines are designed to build a correct understanding of a machine that executes code.

The other part of the term is *notional*, which according to the Oxford dictionary means "existing as or based on a suggestion, estimate, or theory; not existing in reality." When we are considering how a computer does what it does, we are not interested in all the details. We are mostly interested in a hypothesized, idealized version of how a computer works. For example, when we think of a variable x getting a value 12, in most of the cases we do not care about the memory address where the value is stored and the pointer that connects x to that memory address. It is enough to think of x as an entity with a current value that lives somewhere. A notional machine is the abstraction we use to reason about the computer's functioning at the level of abstraction needed at a given time.

### 6.3.2 *Examples of notional machines*

The idea of the notional machine was conceived by Ben du Boulay, a professor at the University of Sussex, while he was working on Logo in the 1970s. Logo was an educational programming language designed by Seymour Papert and Cynthia Solomon. It was the first language to introduce the *turtle*: an entity that can draw lines and be controlled by code. The name comes from the Greek word *logos*, meaning word or thought.

du Boulay first used the term "notional machine" to describe his strategy for teaching Logo to children and teachers. He described it as "the idealized model of the computer implied by the constructs of the programming language." du Boulay's explanations included handmade visualizations, but mainly used analogies.

For example, du Boulay used a factory worker as an analogy for the language execution model. The worker is capable of executing commands and functions, and it has ears with which it can hear parameter values, a mouth that speaks outputs, and hands that carry out the actions described by the code. This representation of programming concepts started simple but was gradually built up to explain the entirety of the Logo language, including built-in commands, user-defined procedures and functions, subprocedure calls, and recursion.

As you have seen, notional machines are designed to explain the workings of a machine executing code, and therefore they also share some characteristics with machines. For example, like a physical machine, a notional machine has the notion of "state." When we think of a variable as a box, this virtual, notional box can be empty or have a value "in" it.

There are also other forms of notional machines that are not as tied to hardware. You likely use abstract representations of the machine that executes when you read and write code. For example, when thinking about how calculations work in programming languages, we often analogize the working of the computer to that of a mathematician. Consider this expression in Java as an example:

```
double celsius = 10;
double fahrenheit = (9.0/5.0) * celsius + 32;
```

When you have to predict the value of `fahrenheit`, you will likely use a form of substitution: you replace the variable `celsius` on the second line by its value, `10`. As a next step, you might mentally add brackets to indicate operator precedence:

```
double fahrenheit = ((9.0/5.0) * 10) + 32;
```

Performing a mental calculation based on transformation is a perfect model of what will be calculated, but it does not represent the calculation that a machine performs. What happens in the actual computer is quite different, of course. The machine most likely uses a stack for evaluation. It will transform the expression to reverse Polish notation and push the result of `9.0/5.0` onto the stack, before popping it off to multiply it by 10 and pushing the results back for further calculation. This is a perfect example of a notional machine that is partly wrong but useful. We could call this the "substitution notional machine," and it's likely closer to the mental model of most programmers than the stack-based model.

### 6.3.3 *Different levels of notional machines*

You've seen a few examples of notional machines now. Some operate at the level of the programming language and abstract all the details of the underlying machine, such as the substitution notional machine.

Other notional machines, such as representing a stack as a physical stack of papers, are more representative of how the physical machine executes the program. In using notional machines as a way of explaining and understanding programming concepts, it can be useful to purposefully think of what details the notional machine hides and exposes. Figure 6.4 shows an overview of four different levels of abstraction at which a notional machine can operate, including an example per level. For example, "variables as boxes" plays a role at the programming language level and at the level of the compiler/interpreter but abstracts details about the compiled code and the operating system.

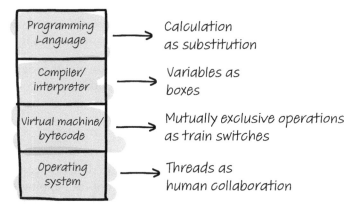

**Figure 6.4   Different levels at which a notional machine can use abstractions. For example, the "calculation as substitution" notional machine we have seen abstracts everything apart from the programming language, while representing threads as human collaboration focuses on the workings of the operating system.**

It can be important to realize what details you are ignoring when reasoning about code. While abstracting details is a great way to gain a higher level understanding of code, some forms of thinking about code might abstract relevant details.

**EXERCISE 6.4** List three examples of notional machines and the levels at which they operate. Fill out the following table by listing notional machines and selecting their level of abstraction.

| Notional machine | Programming language | Compiler/ interpreter | Virtual machine/ bytecode | Operating system |
| --- | --- | --- | --- | --- |
| | | | | |

## 6.4    *Notional machines and language*

We often use notional machines not only to reason about how machines work but also to talk about code. We say, for example, that a variable "holds" a value, even though of course there is not a physical object that has a numeric value stored in it. This language indicates a mental model of a variable that is like a box containing a value.

There are many examples of language about programming that hint at underlying notional machines and lead to certain mental models. For example, we say that a file is "open" or "closed," where we technically mean we are allowed to read the file or forbidden to do so. We use the word "pointer" and commonly say that a pointer "points" to a certain value, and we say that a function "returns" a value when it places the value on the stack so the caller (also a mental model) can use it.

Notional machines that are commonly used to explain how things work find their way into the language we use to talk about code, and even into programming languages themselves. For example, the concept of a pointer is present in many programming languages, and many IDEs allow you to see where a certain function is "called."

> **EXERCISE 6.5**  List three more examples of language we use about programming that indicate the use of a certain notional machine and lead to a certain mental model.

### 6.4.1    *Expanding sets of notional machines*

Earlier I used the term "notional machine" as if there is just one notional machine at play at any given moment. In reality, programming languages do not necessarily have just one all-encompassing notional machine but rather a set of overlapping ones. For example, when learning about simple types, you might have been told that a variable is like a box holding a value. Later in your programming career, you learned about compound types, which can be thought of as stacks of boxes each holding a simple value. These two notional machines are built on each other, as shown in figure 6.5.

There are numerous other examples of expanding sets of abstractions we use to understand programming language concepts. For example, consider the notional machine used to think of parameter passing in a language that supports functions. Initially, you can think of a function without parameters as a package for several lines of code. When input parameters are added and we move from a procedure to a function, the function can be seen as a traveler that packs a set of values in its backpack and brings the values to the call location in the code. When output parameters are also considered, the traveler also brings back a value in its backpack, as illustrated in figure 6.6.

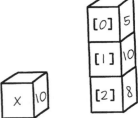

**Figure 6.5**  **Two notional machines that are composable. On the left is a visualization of a variable as a box, and on the right an array is shown as a stack of boxes.**

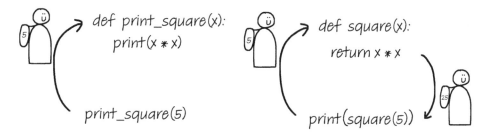

**Figure 6.6  Two notional machines for functions. On the left is a machine that only supports input parameters, and on the right is an extended model that also incorporates output parameters.**

### 6.4.2  *Different notional machines can create conflicting mental models*

In the previous section you saw that some notional machines can be composed, like the notional machine of a variable as a box, which composes with the notional machine of an array as a stack of boxes. However, notional machines can also create mental models that conflict with each other.

For example, the notional machine describing a variable as a box differs from the one where a variable is imagined as a name tag. The two notional machines cannot be combined into one consistent mental model; we either think of a variable as one or the other. Each of these notional machines has upsides and downsides. For example, the variable as a box representation implies that a variable might hold multiple values, like a box can hold multiple coins or candies. This (flawed) way of thinking is less likely if you think of a variable as a name tag or a sticker. A sticker can only be placed on one thing, so a variable then can only be used to describe one value. In 2017 my research group ran a study at the NEMO Science Museum in Amsterdam where we explored this concept.[2] The 496 participants, who did not have any programming experience before the study, all received an introductory programming lesson in Scratch. Scratch is a block-based programming language developed by MIT to be welcoming and accessible to children who are learning to program. Although it's meant for beginners taking their first steps in programming, it does support more advanced features, including defining and using variables. Creating a variable is done by pressing a button and entering the name of the variable, while setting a variable is done with the programming block depicted in figure 6.7.

In our study, we introduced all the participants to the concept of a variable but not in the same way. Half of the participants, the "label" group, received an introductory programming lesson in which we explained a variable as being

**Figure 6.7  Setting the variable `points` to 0 in Scratch**

---

[2] "Thinking Out of the Box: Comparing Variables in Programming Education," 2018, https://dl.acm.org/doi/10.1145/3265757.3265765.

a label, like a temperature or the age of a person. The other half, the "box" group, received a lesson in which we explained variables as being boxes, like a piggy bank or a shoebox. We consistently used the same metaphor in both lessons; for example, we used the phrase "x contains 5?" for the box group and "x is 5?" for the label group.

After this introductory lesson, the participants were tested on their understanding of programming. This included simple questions about variables with one variable, but we also included questions where one variable was set twice to investigate whether the participants had understood that a variable can only hold one value.

Our results clearly showed that both metaphors for variables have their benefits and downsides. For simple questions relating to variables with one assignment, the box group did better. We assume that thinking of a box is an easy thing to do, because people put stuff in boxes all the time. Therefore, visualizing the concept of a box for storage of a variable might help them grasp the idea. However, when we analyzed how many participants thought that a variable could hold two values, we found that people in the box group were likely to suffer from this misconception.

The important takeaway of our study is that you should be careful about describing programming concepts and the corresponding workings of the computer in terms of objects and operations in the real world. While these metaphors can be valuable, they might also create confusion, especially since old mental models can remain in the LTM and occasionally pop up in the working memory too.

> **EXERCISE 6.6**  Think of a notional machine you commonly use when reasoning about code or when explaining code. What are some of the downsides or limitations of the mental models this notional machine creates?

## 6.5    *Notional machines and schemata*

While there can be downsides to using notional machines, in general they work well as a means of thinking about programming. The reason for this is related to a few topics we covered earlier in this book. Notional machines that work well relate programming concepts to everyday concepts that people have already formed strong schemata for.

### 6.5.1    *Why schemata matters*

Schemata are ways in which the LTM stores information. For example, the idea of a box is very likely a concept people have strong associations with. Placing something in a box, retrieving it later, and opening it just to see what's inside are likely operations people are familiar with. As such, thinking of a variable as a box causes no extra cognitive load. If we were to say instead "A variable is like a monocycle," that would be a lot less helpful, precisely because most people have no strong mental model of all the operations a monocycle supports.

What you can assume people will know is not fixed in time and place, of course. When explaining a concept, it is therefore important to choose a comparison that the person you are explaining it to will be familiar with. For example, when explaining a computer's functionality to children in rural India, some educators have used elephants as computers and their trainers as the programmers since that is a principle familiar to the children.

### 6.5.2 *Are notional machines semantics?*

The way I've defined notional machines might remind you of the definition of the *semantics* of a computer program. Semantics is the subfield of computer science concerned with the study of the *meaning* of programs rather than their appearance, which is called *syntax*. You might wonder whether the notional machine of a programming language simply indicates its semantics. However, semantics aim to formalize the working of a computer in mathematical equations and with mathematical precision. They do not aim to abstract details, but rather to specify the details precisely and completely. In other words, notional machines are not simply semantics.

## Summary

- How you represent a problem can heavily influence the way you think about it. For example, thinking of customers as a list versus as a collection can influence how you store and analyze customer objects.
- Mental models are mental representations we form while thinking of problems. People can hold multiple mental models that can compete with each other.
- Notional machines are abstract versions of how a real computer functions that are used when explaining programming concepts and reasoning about programming.
- Notional machines help us understand programming because they enable us to apply existing schemata to programming.
- Different notional machines sometimes nicely complement each other but may also create conflicting mental models.

# Misconceptions: Bugs in thinking

**7**

**This chapter covers**
- How knowing one programming language can help you learn a new one
- Avoiding problems when learning a second programming language
- Understanding how the brain can hold misconceptions and how misconceptions lead to bugs
- How to avoid misconceptions in thinking and prevent bugs

In the last few chapters, we covered techniques for thinking about code, such as creating visualizations, using frameworks to support the working memory, and using mental models to help solve code problems. No matter how helpful the techniques are that we use to support our brains, we will sometimes make mistakes in thinking about code.

The focus of this chapter is bugs. Sometimes bugs are the result of sloppiness, for example, when you forget to close a file or make a typo in a filename. More often, though, bugs are the result of a mistake in thinking. You might not know that a file needs to be closed after use, or you might assume that the programming language closes the file for you automatically.

In this chapter, we will first explore the topic of learning multiple programming languages. There are many possible sources of erroneous assumptions when you learn a new language, one being that different programming languages have different conventions for various concepts. Python, for example, will close a file after a block starting with `open()` without requiring an explicit `file.close()` statement, but in C you always have to use `fclose()`. In the first part of this chapter, I'll show you how to best use your existing knowledge to learn new programming languages, as well as how to avoid frustrations and errors resulting from differences between languages.

The second part of the chapter teaches you about erroneous assumptions about code. We'll cover various programming-specific misconceptions, and we will dive into the origins of misconceptions. Being aware of what misconceptions you may hold about code will help you catch errors earlier and even prevent some.

## 7.1    Why learning a second programming language is easier than learning the first one

In the previous chapters, you learned that keywords and mental models stored in your LTM can help you comprehend code. Sometimes when you've learned something, that knowledge is also useful in another domain. This is called *transfer*. Transfer happens when information you already know helps you do new things. For example, if you already know how to play checkers, it will be easier to learn chess because some of the rules are similar. Likewise, if you already know Java, learning Python is easier because you already know the basic programming concepts, such as variables, loops, classes, and methods. Also, some of the skills you picked up while programming, such as using a debugger or a profiler, might come in handy when you're learning the second programming language.

There are two ways programming knowledge stored in your LTM can support learning new programming concepts. First, if you already know a lot about programming (or any other subject), learning more about it is easier. Information stored in your LTM helps you learn new things; this is known as *transfer during learning*.

You learned in chapter 2 that when you encounter new information, it travels from the sensory memory to the STM, and it enters the working memory when it is being processed. This process is illustrated in figure 7.1. When you activate your working memory by thinking about a new programming concept, the LTM is also activated and starts a search for relevant information.

As shown in figure 7.1, when your LTM is searched, information related to the newly learned information might be found. If information exists that is related to the new information, it's relayed to the working memory. This information might include procedural memories, schemas, plans, or episodic memories.

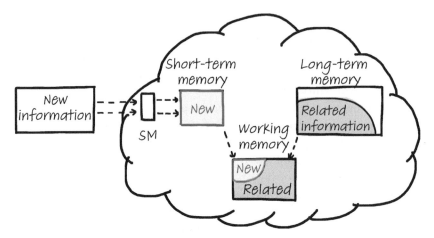

**Figure 7.1  When you learn new information, it is processed first by the sensory memory (SM) and then by the STM. The new information is subsequently sent to the working memory, where you can think about it. At the same time, the LTM is searched for related information. If related information is found, it too is sent to the working memory to support thinking about the new information.**

For example, when you already know Java and are learning about methods in Python, you might be reminded of methods in Java. That will help you to learn the Python methods more quickly even though they work a bit differently than methods in Java.

In chapter 3, we talked about the use of elaboration when learning a new concept. Elaboration is the practice of explicitly relating new information to things you already know. The reason elaboration works well is that explicitly searching your LTM for related information increases the chances of relevant information being found that can help you perform the task at hand. Therefore, elaboration can help increase transfer during learning.

> **EXERCISE 7.1**  Think of a new programming concept or library you learned recently. What concepts that you already knew helped you learn the new concept?

The second way knowledge stored in your LTM can support learning is called *transfer of learning*. Transfer of learning happens when you can apply things you already know in entirely unfamiliar situations. When people are talking about cognitive science and use the term "transfer," they almost always mean transfer of learning.

Sometimes transfer of learning happens without you thinking about it at all. For example, when you buy a new pair of pants, you don't have to think about how to close its button. You just know how to do it, even though these particular pants and its button are unfamiliar to you. Similarly, when you buy a new laptop, you know how its keyboard works without thinking about it, even if you have never operated this specific type of laptop before. Transfer of learning can also happen consciously, like when you learn a new programming language. If you are learning JavaScript and already know Python, you might explicitly think, "I know I need to indent the body of a loop in Python; would that be true for JavaScript too?"

Transfer of learning is similar to transfer during learning because in both situations the brain searches the LTM looking for relevant strategies to apply.

### 7.1.1 How to increase the chances of benefiting from existing programming knowledge

As a professional programmer, I am sure you have been in situations where knowledge could have transferred but didn't. Maybe you were confused about how some function in a certain library worked, and it later turned out to be exactly the same as in a library you already knew. Sadly, not all knowledge that is useful will automatically transfer to new situations.

The amount of learning you can transfer from one task to another can vary widely and is influenced by many factors. Factors that can influence how much transfer takes place include the following:

- *Mastery*—How well you've mastered the task for which knowledge is already stored in your LTM. The better you know a task, the more likely it is you'll be able to apply it in another domain. For example, an expert Java programmer will likely benefit more from their prior knowledge when learning Python than a novice Java programmer. As we've seen in previous chapters, an expert programmer has a larger arsenal of strategies, chunks, and mental models that can be applied to problems in any different programming language.

- *Similarity*—Commonalities between the two tasks. For example, if you are implementing an algorithm you already know in an unfamiliar programming language, that will be easier than implementing a new algorithm in a new programming language.

- *Context*—How similar the environments are. It's not only the similarity between the tasks that matters, but also the context in which you are executing them. For example, transfer between two programming languages is more likely if you program those different languages in the same IDE, which is a strong argument for using one IDE for multiple languages. Context extends beyond the computer, though; it can also matter whether you are sitting in the same office with the same people. The more similarities there are, the more likely it is that knowledge will transfer.

- *Critical attributes*—How clear it is to you what knowledge may be beneficial. If someone points out that knowing JavaScript might be beneficial in learning Python, you will be more likely to actively look for similarities. It can therefore be important to actively search for commonalities and to reflect on them before learning a new programming language or framework. What existing knowledge could help with the new task?

- *Association*—How strongly you feel that the tasks are similar. For example, Java and JavaScript sound similar, even though conceptually the languages are not all that alike. Therefore, a stronger association might exist in your LTM between Java and JavaScript than between Python and Scala. Your episodic memory, which stores memories of things you have experienced, can also play a role. For example, if you learned Java and C# in the same lecture hall, you might connect them more strongly than if you'd learned them in different settings.

- *Emotions*—How you feel about the task. Your emotions can also play a role in the likeliness of transfer. For example, if you find working with binary trees pleasurable and a new task reminds you of it, you might try to apply similar strategies to the new task more actively.

## 7.1.2  Different forms of transfer

There are several different ways we can look at transfer. If you have a vocabulary for the different forms of transfer, you can set more realistic expectations of transfer between programming languages. Programmers sometimes assume that the syntax of programming languages is irrelevant and that if you know one language, you can pick up a second one with ease, and a third one with no effort at all. Certainly, knowing one language can make learning a new one easier, but it doesn't always help. Understanding different forms of transfer will prepare you to learn a new language or framework more effectively.

### HIGH- AND LOW-ROAD TRANSFER

Transfer of automatized skills is different from transfer of skills you mastered consciously. Transfer of automatized skills is called *low-road transfer*. In programming, low-road transfer might occur if you use Ctrl-C and Ctrl-V in a new editor without thinking about it. Transfer of more complex tasks is called *high-road transfer*. When high-road transfer occurs, you are often aware that it is happening. For example, you might assume that you need to declare a variable in a new programming language because you know that is the case in most languages.

### NEAR AND FAR TRANSFER

Earlier, you learned that if two domains are more similar, that impacts the amount of transfer. Looking at the distance between the domains is another way we can divide different forms of transfer. *Near transfer* happens when knowledge transfers from domains that are seen as close to each other, like calculus and algebra or C# and Java. We speak of *far transfer* when skills transfer between very different domains, like Latin and logic, or Java and Prolog. Because similarity is a factor that influences transfer, far transfer is far less likely to happen than near transfer.

> **EXERCISE 7.2**  Think of a few situations in which you experienced transfer. What form of transfer occurred? Fill in the following table to guide your thinking.

| Situation | High-road | Low-road | Near | Far |
|---|---|---|---|---|
|  |  |  |  |  |

### 7.1.3   *Already knowing something: Curse or blessing?*

In addition to high- and low-road and near and far transfer, there are two more main categories of transfer. The type of transfer we've been looking at so far, where knowing something supports learning a new thing or performing a new task, is called *positive transfer*.

When positive transfer occurs, you don't have to create a fresh, new mental model from scratch; instead, your brain gets help in constructing a mental model of a new situation by basing it on mental models the LTM already holds for other domains. For example, when you know Java, you already have a mental model of a loop and know that a loop has a counter variable, a body, and a stop condition. In almost any new programming language you encounter, loops will also have these aspects, so you know what to look for. This helps you create a new mental model. However, as you might have experienced, transfer is not always positive. When existing knowledge prevents you from learning something new, we call this *negative transfer*. Edsger W. Dijkstra, Dutch computer science professor and creator of Dijkstra's algorithm, famously said that teaching BASIC should be forbidden because "it cripples the mind."

While I do not believe at all that brains can be ruined forever by learning a certain programming language, there is some truth in this saying because mistakes can be caused by wrong assumptions about code. Wrong assumptions can in turn be caused by negative transfer. For example, in Java, variables cannot be used without initialization. An experienced Java programmer might assume that in Python too, all variables must be initialized and that the compiler will warn them if they forget. This can cause confusion and lead to bugs.

Even in very similar languages, like Java and C#, there are risks of negative transfer because the mental models of both languages are similar but not identical. For example, Java has a concept called *checked exceptions*, which are exceptions checked at compile time. If you don't wrap these exceptions in a `try-catch` block, the code will fail to compile. Checked exceptions are a Java-specific language feature, so people coming from C# might not realize they are different from what they are used to. Not only do they have the wrong mental model, but they think they have the right one!

Forgetting to initialize a variable or mishandling an exception are relatively small errors that can be easily fixed. But there are examples of negative transfer that run deeper. For example, many people have a hard time learning a functional language like F# when they are already familiar with object-oriented languages because functions exist in both paradigms but work differently.

**EXERCISE 7.3**   Think of a situation where you made an incorrect assumption about a language concept in a programming language. Could that be attributed to negative transfer from one language to another?

### 7.1.4   *The difficulties of transfer*

In the previous section you saw that transfer of knowledge can be both negative and positive and that positive transfer is not a given. Situations need to be similar enough to each other to make transfer more likely. Far transfer, in which knowledge from one domain "hops over" to a domain that is not very similar to the original domain, is unlikely to happen spontaneously.

Sadly, research shows that transfer indeed is hard and does not come automatically to most people. Chess is often named as a candidate source for transfer—many people believe that chess knowledge will improve general intelligence as well as logical reasoning skills and memory. However, scientific studies have not been able to support these assumptions. In chapter 2 we discussed the work of Adriaan de Groot, whose experiments showed that the memory of experienced chess players was no better than that of novices when the setups were random. Other studies have confirmed this and shown that proficient chess players are not necessarily any better at remembering numbers or visual shapes. Chess skills don't appear to transfer to other logical games either, like the Tower of London (a puzzle similar to Towers of Hanoi).

What is true for chess seems to be true for programming too. Many programmers argue that by learning to program you will gain skills in logical reasoning, or even increase your general intelligence. However, the small number of studies that have researched the cognitive effects of programming show a pattern similar to that found with chess. An overview study done in 1987 by Gavriel Salomon of the University of Tel Aviv revealed that most studies of the impact of programming education show little effect. Many of the studies examined by Salomon do show that children are successful in acquiring certain programming skills, but those skills do not appear to transfer to other cognitive domains.

The takeaway here is that the fact that you've already mastered one programming language will not always help you learn a new one. This might be frustrating because you already see yourself as an expert, and the slow pace of a beginner and corresponding learning activities, like using flashcards to learn syntax, might feel unnecessary. A related piece of advice to consider is that if you set out to learn a new language to expand your way of thinking, it's important to pick a language that is fundamentally different from the ones you've already mastered—that is, you should avoid a false broadening of your tastes from "country music" to "Western music."

However, this section has shown that far transfer, say, from something like SQL to JavaScript, is not all that likely, and that you will probably need to learn a lot of new syntax as well as new strategies to regain your expert level in a new programming language. Practices might differ too; for example, much of what you know about reuse and abstraction in JavaScript has to be considered rather differently in SQL.

Paying deliberate attention to similarities and differences will ease the task of learning a new language.

**EXERCISE 7.4** Consider a programming language you are learning or one you want to learn. Compare it to language(s) you already know. What is similar and what is different?

Filling out the following table can help streamline your thinking and show where you can expect transfer and where you will need to pay specific attention while learning.

| | Similarities | Differences | Remarks |
|---|---|---|---|
| Syntax | | | |
| Type system | | | |
| Programming concepts | | | |
| Runtime | | | |
| Programming environment/ IDE | | | |
| Testing environment/ practices | | | |

## 7.2 Misconceptions: Bugs in thinking

In the first part of this chapter, we focused on how knowledge transfers from one situation to another. When stored information interferes with us performing a new task, we call this negative transfer. In this section, we'll explore the consequences of negative transfer.

Think about a situation in which you created a bug, for example by forgetting to initialize an instance in the right way, by calling the wrong function, or with an off-by-one error in a list. Situations where bugs occur can be caused by a simple slip of the mind where you accidentally forgot some code, selected the wrong method, or made a mistake in calculating a boundary value.

However, bugs can also have a deeper underlying reason, where you made a faulty assumption about the code at hand. Maybe you counted on the fact that the instance would be initialized elsewhere in the code, or maybe you were sure this was the right method or assumed that data structure would prevent you from accessing elements out of its bounds. When you are sure your code will work, but it still fails, chances are that you are suffering from a *misconception.*

In regular conversation, the word "misconception" is often used as a synonym for a mistake or for being confused, but the formal definition is slightly different. For a belief to be a misconception, it must

- be faulty,
- be held consistently, across different situations, and
- be held with confidence.

There are many common misconceptions. For example, many people think that the seeds of chili peppers are the spiciest part. The seeds of chilies are not spicy at all! This is an example of a misconception because

1  It is faulty
2  If people believe the seeds of one kind of chili are spicy, they will believe the seeds of all kinds of chilies are spicy, and
3  They believe it to be true and act on it, for example by removing the seeds of chili peppers before cooking them.

The "seeds of chilies are spicy" misconception is the result of an urban legend people have simply repeated to each other, but negative transfer often plays a role in the creation of misconceptions. For example, many people believe that searing meat will "seal in the juices" because the outer surfaces of other forms of food, like eggs, solidify when heated. These people assume that heat always creates a solid "shield," which will be impenetrable by the moisture trapped inside. Knowledge from one type of food is incorrectly transferred to another type of food, leading to a misconception—in fact, searing meat leads to a greater net loss of moisture.

Misconceptions commonly occur in programming too. New programmers sometimes assume that a variable, like `temperature`, can only hold one value that cannot be changed. While that assumption might sound absurd to an experienced programmer, there are reasons why assuming that a variable can only hold one value is sensible. For example, this assumption might be transferred from prior knowledge of mathematics, where variables indeed do not change within the scope of a mathematical proof or exercise.

Another source of this misconception lies within the realm of programming itself. I have seen students with prior exposure to files and filesystems incorrectly transfer beliefs about files to variables. Because operating systems typically allow you to only create one file with a certain name (in a folder), students might incorrectly assume that the variable `temperature` is already in use and cannot hold a second value, just like a file name can only be used for one file.

### 7.2.1  *Debugging misconceptions with conceptual change*

Misconceptions are faulty ways of thinking held with great confidence. Because misconceptions are held with such high confidence, it can be hard to change someone's mind about them. Often, it is not enough to point out the flaw in their thinking. Instead, to change a misconception, the faulty way of thinking needs to be replaced with a new way of thinking. That is, it's not enough to tell a novice programmer that a variable can be changed; they need to get a new understanding of the variable as a concept.

The process of replacing a misconception based on a programming language you already know with the right mental model for the new language you are learning is called *conceptual change*. In this paradigm, an existing conception is fundamentally changed, replaced, or assimilated by the new knowledge. It is this change in knowledge, rather than the addition of new knowledge to an already existing schema, that distinguishes conceptual change from other types of learning.

The fact that knowledge you have already learned needs to be changed in your LTM makes conceptual change learning harder than regular learning. That is why misconceptions can linger for a very long time; simply being presented with information on why your thinking is wrong often does not help or does not help enough.

Therefore, you will have to spend a lot of energy when you learn a new programming language "unlearning" existing knowledge about prior programming languages. For example, if you're learning Python when you already know Java, you will have to unlearn some syntax, like that you must always define the types of variables. You'll also have to unlearn some practices, like relying on the types of variables to make decisions in code. Even though it is not hard to remember the simple fact that Python is dynamically typed, learning to think about types while you are programming might take longer because it requires conceptual change.

### 7.2.2 *Suppressing misconceptions*

Remember when we considered dressing a snowman in a sweater and I asked you to decide if the snowman would melt faster or slower than when he is "naked?" Your first thought likely was that he would melt quicker—after all, putting on a sweater makes one warmer, right? Well, not for a snowman. When wearing a sweater, the snowman is insulated, trapping in the cold and slowing the melting process.

What likely happened is that your brain instantly activated an existing conception: sweaters make you warmer. This conception, which is correct in (warm-blooded) people, was then wrongly transferred to the situation of the snowman. This is not because you are not a smart person!

It was long assumed that when people learn how things work, old, incorrect notions are deleted from their memories for good and replaced by better, more correct notions. Knowing what we know about the brain, that is unlikely. Memories are now assumed not to be forgotten or replaced; rather, our retrieval of them lessens over time. However, the old memories of wrong ways of thinking are still there, and paths to them might be triggered, even if we would prefer that they weren't.

Research has shown that people often fall back on old notions, even if they can also successfully work with the correct ones. The work of Igal Galili and Varda Bar of the Hebrew University of Jerusalem showed that students could work well with mechanics in familiar exercises but regressed to more basic but wrong reasoning for more complicated questions.[1] This illustrates that multiple notions can be present in the memory at the same time, like in the snowman example: we can have the idea that a sweater means warmth in our brains, as well as the notion that a sweater insulates and thus keeps in the cold. These ideas compete with each other when we have to decide whether a sweater makes a snowman warm, so we have to actively suppress the older idea that sweater equals warmth to come to the right conclusion. That likely happened when you thought about the puzzle and you experienced a "wait a minute" moment when you reasoned rather than reacted intuitively.

We do not know exactly how the brain decides which of the stored concepts to use, but we know that *inhibition* plays a role. We typically associate inhibition with a feeling of self-consciousness, holding back, or feeling shy. However, recent research has started to indicate that when inhibitory control mechanisms are active, an incorrect conception can lose the competition with a correct conception.

**EXERCISE 7.5**  Think of a situation where you were you held a misconception about a concept in a particular programming language. For example, I assumed for an embarrassingly long time that all functional languages used lazy evaluation and that all lazy languages must be functional because I only knew one language that was lazy and functional: Haskell. What misconception did you hold for a long time, and what was its origin?

### 7.2.3  *Misconceptions about programming languages*

Extensive research has been done into misconceptions in the domain of programming, especially the misconceptions that novice programmers hold. Juha Sorva, now a senior university lecturer at Aalto University in Finland, wrote a PhD dissertation in 2012 that contains a list of 162 different misconceptions novices can hold.[2] All these misconceptions are rooted in research. While the full list is very interesting, and I recommend reading it, some of the misconceptions in Sorva's thesis are especially worth noting:

- *Misconception 15: Primitive assignment stores equations or unresolved expressions.* This misconception indicates that sometimes people assume variable assignments store relationships. A person who suffers from this misconception assumes that if we write total = maximum + 12 it somehow links the value of total with the value of maximum.

   That leads to the belief that were maximum to be changed later in the code, total would change along with it. The interesting thing about this misconception is that it is very sensible. You can imagine a programming language in

---

[1] See "Motion Implies Force: Where to Expect Vestiges of the Misconception?" by Igal Gaili and Varda Bar, 1992, https://www.tandfonline.com/doi/abs/10.1080/0950069920140107.
[2] See table A-1 (pp. 3593–68) of "Visual Program Simulation in Introductory Programming Education," http://lib.tkk.fi/Diss/2012/isbn9789526046266/isbn9789526046266.pdf.

which the relationships between variables could be expressed like a system of equations. There are even programming languages that work this way to a certain extent, such as Prolog.

This misconception often occurs in people with prior mathematical knowledge. A related misconception we covered earlier in the chapter is the idea that a variable can only hold one value. This is true in mathematics too.

- *Misconception 33: While loops terminate as soon as condition changes to false.* This misconception expresses confusion about when the stop condition of a while loop is evaluated. When suffering from this misconception, people assume the loop condition is checked at each line and that it stops immediately when the condition is false and does not finish executing. This misconception is likely to have a relationship with the meaning assigned to the keyword *while*. When we hear someone say, "I will sit here and read my book while it is raining," we assume the speaker of this sentence regularly monitors the weather, leaves when it stops raining, and does not first finish the whole book. Here, too, the misconception is not a sign of a person being utterly confused and having no concept of how programming works. It's quite a reasonable assumption to think that code so similar to English would behave similarly.

  This misconception is an example of where the meaning of English (key)words interfere with programming understanding. Also, you could again imagine a programming language in which the stop condition of a while loop is evaluated continuously and the loop halts immediately when the condition becomes false.

  A related misconception is assuming that the name of the variable influences what value it can hold—for example, thinking that a variable called `minimum` can never hold a large value (this is misconception 17 on Sorva's list).

- *Misconception 46: Parameter passing requires different variable names in call and signature.* People with this misconception tend to assume that a variable name can only be used once, including inside functions. When you are learning to program, you learn that variable names can only be used once. If a new variable is needed, you need to define a new name too. The limitation on one use of variables, however, is no longer true when we talk about methods or functions and their invocations. Suddenly, it is allowed to use the same name both inside a function and outside of it. In fact, it's more than allowed; using the same names for different variables in and outside of functions is common practice. This is often shown in introductory examples of functions. For example, code like this is quite common when teaching functions:

```
def square(number):
return number * number

number = 12
print(square(number))
```

Such code also occurs in real life. For example, when you use the extract method functionality in an IDE, most IDEs will replicate the variable name both in defining and calling the function. Hence, real code is filled with this pattern too, which might be why educators use it. This misconception is an interesting example of a misconception that transfers within a programming language rather than being influenced by prior knowledge of math or English. Sometimes when we understand a specific concept of a programming language, the knowledge we acquire about that part does not transfer even to other concepts within the same language.

### 7.2.4   *Preventing misconceptions while learning a new programming language*

There's not a lot we can do about misconceptions. When learning a new programming language or system, inevitably you will be confronted with negative transfer. However, there are some strategies that can be helpful.

First, it is important to be aware that even if you're sure you've gotten something right, you could still be wrong. Keeping an open mind is key.

Second, you can deliberately study common misconceptions to prevent yourself from falling prey to them. It can be hard to know when you are making erroneous assumptions and what assumptions are valid. Therefore, it can be helpful to use a checklist of common misconceptions. Exercise 7.5 can help you get a first sense of potential areas where you might hold misconceptions, and Sorva's list can be used when learning a new programming language as a guideline for determining what misconceptions you should watch out for. Use the list to identify misconceptions that could apply to the programming language you are learning.

A final tip is to ask the advice of programmers who also learned the same programming languages in the same order. Every pair of programming languages has its own interactions that can create misconceptions, so there are too many to list here. Asking for advice from people who might have encountered the same traps can be tremendously helpful.

### 7.2.5   *Diagnosing misconceptions in a new codebase*

In this section, we have talked mainly about misconceptions in programming languages in general, which can be caused by prior knowledge that negatively transfers to a new programming language.

Similarly, you can have misconceptions about the codebase you are working on. Whenever you make assumptions about code based on prior experience with a programming language, framework, or library, or about the domain of the code, the meanings of variable or other names, or the intentions of other programmers, there is a risk of misconception.

One way to detect misconceptions is to program in pairs or in a larger group. If you expose yourself to the ideas and assumptions of others, it will soon be clear that there are conflicts and that one person has a misconception.

Especially for expert programmers (or experts in anything), it can be hard to realize that the error is yours, so always verify assumptions you make about code by running it or making use of a test suite. If you are sure a certain value can never be below zero, why not add a test to verify it? That test can not only help you detect whether your assumption is wrong, but also serves as documentation of the fact that the value indeed will always be positive. The test can communicate this information to you in the future, which is important because, as we've seen, misconceptions rarely go away and can always resurface, even when we have learned the correct model.

As this suggests, documentation is a third way of battling misconceptions about a certain method, function, or data structure within a codebase. If you've discovered a misconception, in addition to adding a test, you might also want to add documentation in relevant places to prevent yourself and other people from falling into the same trap.

## Summary

- Knowledge you already have stored in your LTM can be transferred to new situations. Sometimes existing knowledge helps you learn faster or perform new tasks better. This is called positive transfer.
- Transfer of knowledge from one domain to another can also be negative, which happens when existing knowledge interferes with learning new things or executing new tasks.
- You can use positive transfer to learn new things more effectively by actively searching for related information in your LTM (for example, by elaboration, as covered earlier in the book).
- You may hold misconceptions, which occur when you are sure you are right but are actually wrong.
- Misconceptions are not always addressed by simply realizing or being told you are wrong. For misconceptions to be fixed, you need a new mental model to replace the old, wrong model.
- Even if you have learned a correct model, there is always the risk you will fall back to using the misconception.
- Use tests and documentation within a codebase to help prevent misconceptions.

# Part 3

# On writing better code

In parts 1 and 2, we examined the roles of the short-term memory, the long-term memory, and the working memory when reading and thinking about code.

In part 3, we move our attention to writing better code: how to write code that is understandable and avoid vague names and code smells. We will also discuss how to improve your skills in writing code for complex problems.

# How to get better
# at naming things

## This chapter covers

- Comparing different perspectives on good naming practices
- Understanding the relationship between names and cognitive processes
- Exploring the effect of different naming styles
- Investigating the effect of bad names on bugs and errors
- Learning how to structure a variable name to maximize understanding

Part 1 covered the different cognitive processes involved in reading code, including storing information in the LTM and retrieving it when needed, storing information in the STM, and processing code in the working memory. In part 2, we looked at how we think about code, what mental models are formed about code, and how we talk about code. In Part 3, we will zoom into the process of writing code rather than reading or thinking about it.

This chapter aims to study how to best name things in code, like variables, classes, and methods. Since we now know quite a bit about how the brain processes code, we can more deeply understand why naming is so important for code comprehension. Good names help activate your LTM to find relevant information you already know about the domain of the code. Bad names, on the other hand, can cause you to make assumptions about the code, leading to misconceptions.

Even though naming is important, it is also very hard. Names are often created while modeling a solution or solving a problem. During such an activity, it is likely you are experiencing a high cognitive load: your working memory is at full capacity to create a mental model and use the mental model to reason. In such a situation, thinking about a good variable name might simply cause too much cognitive load, which your brain wants to prevent. As such, it makes sense from a cognitive perspective to pick an easy name or a placeholder name so as not to exceed the capacity of the working memory.

This chapter covers the importance but also the difficulty of naming in depth. Once we have covered the basics of naming and cognitive processing, we will zoom into the effect of names on two different aspects of programming. We will first study what types of names make code easier to comprehend. Secondly, we will look at the effect of bad names on the occurrence of bugs. We close the chapter with concrete guidelines for coming up with great names.

## 8.1   Why naming matters

Choosing a good variable name is hard. Phil Karlton, a programmer at Netscape, famously said that there are only two hard problems in computer science: cache invalidation and naming things. And indeed, many programmers struggle with naming things.

Representing everything a class or data structure does in one unambiguous word is not an easy task. Dror Feitelson, Berthold Badler professor of computer science at the Hebrew University of Jerusalem, recently ran an experiment to understand exactly how hard it is to come up with an unambiguous name. Feitelson performed an experiment in which almost 350 subjects were asked to choose names in different programming scenarios. The subjects in the study were both students and programming professionals with an average of six years' work experience. Participants were asked to choose names for variables, constants, and data structures, and also for functions and their parameters. Feitelson's experiment confirmed that naming is hard, or at least that it is hard to choose names that others also choose. In the experiment, the probability that two developers selected the same name was low. Overall, for the 47 objects that had to be named (i.e., variables, constants, data structures, functions, and parameters combined) the median probability of two people choosing the same name was only 7%.

Even though naming is hard, choosing the right names for objects we reason about in code is important. Before we dive into the connection between naming and cognitive processes in the brain, let's look at why naming is important.

### 8.1.1 *Why naming matters*

With identifier names, we mean all the things in a code base named by the programmer. Identifier names include names we assign to a type (class, interface, struct, delegate, or enum), variable, method, function, module, library, or namespace. There are four main reasons that identifier names matter.

#### NAMES MAKE UP A LARGE PART OF CODEBASES

The first reason variable names matter is that in most codebases a large part of what you will read will be names. For example, in the source code of Eclipse, which consists of about two million lines of code, 33% of tokens and 72% of characters are devoted to identifiers.[1]

#### NAMES PLAY A ROLE IN CODE REVIEWS

In addition to their frequent occurrence in code, programmers talk about names a lot. Miltiadis Allamanis, now a researcher at Microsoft Research in Cambridge, has investigated how often identifier names are mentioned in code reviews. To that end, Allamanis analyzed over 170 reviews with over 1,000 remarks in them. He found that one in four code reviews contained remarks related to naming and that remarks about identifier names occurred in 9%.

#### NAMES ARE THE MOST ACCESSIBLE FORM OF DOCUMENTATION

While formal documentation of code might contain a lot more background information, names serve as an important type of documentation because they are available right inside the codebase. As we saw in earlier chapters, piecing information together from different places can increase cognitive load. As such, having to navigate outside your codebase to read documentation is an act programmers try to avoid. Hence the "documentation" read most will be comments in the code and names.

#### NAMES CAN SERVE AS BEACONS

In previous chapters we discussed beacons, parts of code that help an unfamiliar reader unlock the meaning of the code. Variable names are important beacons that help readers make sense of code in addition to comments.

### 8.1.2 *Different perspectives on naming*

Choosing a good name is important. Many different researchers have tried to define what makes a variable name good or bad, and they all have different perspectives on this question. But before we look at those different perspectives, let's activate your LTM and look at your take on variable names with an exercise.

> **EXERCISE 8.1** What defines a good identifier name in your opinion? Can you think of an example of a good name?
>
> What defines a bad name? Is that simply the opposite of a good name, or can you think of properties that characterize bad names you've seen? Do you know of an example of a bad name from your practice?

---

[1] Florian Deißenbock and Markus Pizka, "Concise and Consistent Naming," https://www.cqse.eu/fileadmin/content/news/publications/2005-concise-and-consistent-naming.pdf.

Now that you have thought about what makes a name a good name, let's look at three different perspectives on good naming practices by researchers who study naming.

### A GOOD NAME CAN BE DEFINED SYNTACTICALLY

Some people believe there are several rules based on the syntax of names that should hold. For example, Simon Butler, associate senior lecturer at the Open University in the UK, created a list of issues with variable names, as shown in table 8.1.

Table 8.1   Butler's list of naming conventions

| Name | Description | Example of a bad name |
|---|---|---|
| Capitalization anomaly | Identifiers should use proper capitalization. | `page counter` |
| Consecutive underscores | Identifiers should not contain multiple consecutive underscores. | `page__counter` |
| Dictionary words | Identifiers should consist of words and only use abbreviations when they are more commonly used than the full words. | `pag_countr` |
| Number of words | Identifiers should be composed of between two and four words. | `page_counter_ converted_and_ normalized_value` |
| Excessive words | Identifiers should not be composed of more than four words. | `page_counter_ converted_and_ normalized_value` |
| Short identifier name | Identifiers should not consist of fewer than eight characters, except for c, d, e, g, i, in, inOut, j, k, m, n, o, out, t, x, y, z. | `P, page` |
| Enumeration identifier declaration order | Unless there are clear reasons not to do so, enumeration types should be declared in alphabetical order. | `CardValue = {ACE, EIGHT, FIVE, FOUR, JACK, KING...}` |
| External underscores | Identifiers should not begin or end in an underscore. | `__page_counter_` |
| Identifier encoding | Type information should not be encoded in identifier names using Hungarian notation or similar. | `int_page_counter` |
| Long identifier name | Long identifier names should be avoided where possible. | `page_counter_ converted_and_ normalized_value` |
| Naming convention anomaly | Identifiers should not combine uppercase and lowercase characters in nonstandard ways. | `Page_counter` |
| Numeric identifier name | Identifiers should not be composed entirely of numeric words or numbers. | `FIFTY` |

While Butler's list contains different types of rules, most are syntactic. For example, the rule "External underscores" states that names should not start with or end in an underscore. Butler's rules also imply a ban on the systems Hungarian notation, which would prescribe variable names like `strName` for a variable representing a name stored as a string.

While rules about the precise formation of variable names might sound a bit petty, in previous chapters we saw that unnecessary information in code can cause extraneous cognitive load and distract from understanding the code, so it is sensible to also have syntactic rules such as the ones in table 8.1.

Many programming languages, of course, have conventions about how to format variable names, such as PEP8 in Python, which prescribes snake case for variable names, and the Java naming convention, which states variable names should be camel case.

#### NAMES SHOULD BE CONSISTENT WITHIN A CODEBASE

Another perspective on good naming is consistency. Allamanis, whose work on code reviews and naming we covered earlier in the chapter, has also thought about good names. He states that the most important aspect of a good naming scheme is similar execution across a codebase.

Objecting against inconsistent naming practices fits with what we know about cognitive science. If the same word is used for similar objects across a codebase, it will be easier for the brain to find relevant related information stored in the LTM. Simon partly agrees with Allamanis's view; his list contains a rule saying that names should not use capital letters inconsistently.

> **EXERCISE 8.2** Select a piece of code you have worked on recently. Make a list of all the variable names that occur in that piece of code. Now reflect on the quality of these names, given the three perspectives outlined. Are the names syntactically clear? Do they consist of words? Are they used consistently across your codebase?

| Name | Syntactic issues | Consistent in the codebase |
|---|---|---|
|  |  |  |
|  |  |  |
|  |  |  |

### 8.1.3 Initial naming practices have a lasting impact

Dawn Lawrie, a senior research scientist at Johns Hopkins University who has studied naming extensively, has also investigated trends in naming.[2] Are naming practices different than they were a decade ago? And how do names change within a codebase over longer periods?

To answer these questions, Lawrie analyzed a total of 186 versions of 78 code bases written in C++, C, Fortran, and Java. Together these versions had over 48 million lines of code and spanned three decades. The set Lawrie analyzed contained both proprietary code and open source projects, including well-known codebases such as Apache, Eclipse, mysql and gcc, and samba.

To analyze the quality of identifier names, Lawrie investigates two aspects of naming practices. First, she looked at whether names split words within names, for example by using underscores between words or using capitals. Lawrie argues that names that split words are easier to understand. Second, she looked at whether the words that occur within variable names occur in the dictionary, following Butler's rule that names should consist of words.

Because Lawrie studied different versions of the same codebase over time, she could analyze how naming practices change over time. She looked at how naming quality has changed over time across all 78 code bases combined and found that modern code uses identifiers consisting of dictionary words in names more than older code, both using more dictionary words and more commonly splitting the words within variable names. Lawrie attributes these improved naming practices to programming maturing as a discipline. The size of the code base showed no correlation with quality, so bigger codebases do not do better (or worse) when it comes to the quality of identifier names.

Lawrie did not only compare older codebases to younger ones; she also looked at previous versions of the same code base to see if naming practices changed over time within a codebase. She found that within a single code base, naming does not improve as the code gets older. Lawrie draws an important and actionable conclusion here, saying that "identifier quality takes hold early in a program's development." So, when you start a new project, you might want to take extra care in choosing good names, because the way you create names in the early stages of a project is likely going to be the way the names will be created forever.

Research on test usage in GitHub found a similar phenomenon: new contributors to a repository often look at existing tests and modify them rather than reading the project's guidelines.[3] When a repository has tests in place, new contributors feel obligated to also add tests, and as such comply with how the project is organized.

### FINDINGS ON NAMING PRACTICES OVER TIME

- Modern code follows naming guidelines better
- But within one code base, naming practices remain constant
- There is no difference between smaller and larger codebases in terms of naming practices

---

[2] Dawn Lawrie, Henry Field, and David Binkley, "Quantifying Identifier Quality: AN. Analysis of Trends," http://www.cs.loyola.edu/~lawrie/papers/lawrieJese07.pdf.

[3] Raphael Pham et al., "Creating a Shared Understanding of Testing Culture on a Social Coding Site," 2013, http://etc.leif.me/papers/Pham2013.pdf.

So far in this chapter, we have seen two different perspectives on naming, as shown in table 8.2.

**Table 8.2   Different perspectives on naming**

| Researcher | Perspective |
|---|---|
| Butler | Syntactically similar names |
| Allamanis | Names should be consistent across a codebase |

Butler's perspective is that we can follow several mainly syntactic guidelines to choose the right names. Allamanis, on the other hand, prescribes no fixed rules or guidelines on the quality of names but takes the stance that the codebase should be leading and that consistent and bad is better than good but inconsistent. It would be great if there was one clear way to name identifiers in code, but the fact that even researchers have varying opinions underlines that what is a good name is in the eye of the beholder.

## 8.2   Cognitive aspects of naming

Now that we have covered why naming matters and what different perspectives on naming are, let's dive into naming from the perspective of what we know about cognition.

### 8.2.1   Formatting names supports your STM

Given what we know about the cognitive processing of code in the brain, we can see that both perspectives make sense from a cognitive perspective, as outlined in table 8.3. Having clear rules for how to format variable names is likely going to help your STM make sense of the names you are reading.

**Table 8.3   Different perspectives on naming and their connection to cognition**

| Researcher | Perspective | Fits cognition because |
|---|---|---|
| Allamanis | Names should be consistent across a codebase. | Supports chunking |
| Butler | Syntactically similar names | Lower cognitive load while processing names |

Allamanis's approach, for example, prescribes using consistent naming practices across a codebase. That is sensible since it is likely to support chunking. If all names were formatted in different ways, you would have to spend effort on every name to find its meaning.

Butler's perspective also fits with what we know about cognitive processing. He promotes the use of names that are syntactically similar, for example by disallowing leading underscores and using consistent capitalization. Similar names are also likely to lower your cognitive load while reading the names because the relevant information is presented in the same way every time. Butler's limit of four words in one identifier name, while seemingly a bit random, fits with the limit of the working memory, which is now estimated to be between two and six chunks.

**IMPROVE CONSISTENCY OF NAMES IN YOUR CODEBASE**  To improve the consistency of names in code bases, Allamanis implemented his approach to detect inconsistent names into a tool called Naturalize (http://groups.inf.ed.ac.uk/naturalize/), which uses machine learning to learn good (consistent) names from a codebase and can then suggest new names for locals, arguments, fields, method calls, and types. In a first study, the authors of Naturalize used it to generate 18 pull requests on existing codebases with suggestions to improve names. Of these, 14 were accepted, which gives some credibility to its success. Sadly, in its current form, Naturalize only works for Java.

In their paper on Naturalize, the authors share a lovely story of a time they used Naturalize to generate a pull request for Junit. This pull request was not accepted, because according to the developers, the proposed change was not consistent with the codebase. Naturalize could then point them to all the other places where this convention was violated, causing the suggestion. Their own convention was broken so often that, to Naturalize, it seemed the wrong version was more natural!

### 8.2.2  *Clear names help your LTM*

The two perspectives on naming that we have seen so far are different from each other but share some similarities. Both methods are syntactic or statistical, and a computer program can be used to measure the quality of names according to both models. As we have seen, Allamadis's model is also implemented into the software.

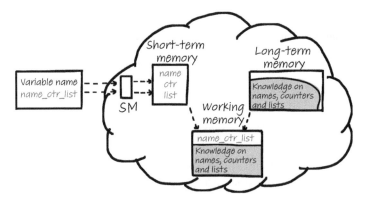

**Figure 8.1  When you read a name, the name will first be broken up into separate chunks and then sent to the working memory. At the same time, the LTM is searched for information related to the different parts of the variable name. Related information from the LTM is also sent to the working memory.**

But naming, of course, is more than selecting the right syntax for a variable name. The words we choose also matter, especially from a cognitive perspective. We saw earlier in the book that when thinking about code, the working memory processes two types of information. This is illustrated in figure 8.1. First, the variable name is processed by sensory memory and then is sent to the STM. We know that the STM is limited in size and therefore tries to make the variable names separate words. The more systematic names are formatted, the more likely it is that the STM can identify individual parts. For example, in a name like nmcntravg, it can take considerable effort to find and understand the components. Alternatively, in a name like name_counter_average it is a lot easier to see what the name concerns. Despite being roughly twice as many characters, it requires a fraction of the mental effort when you read it.

When processing variable names, it is not only the STM that provides information to the working memory. The working memory also receives information from your LTM after it has been searched for related facts. For this second cognitive process, the choice of words in the identifier name is important. Using the right domain concept for a variable name or class can help the reader of code find relevant information in their LTM.

### 8.2.3 Variable names can contain different types of information to help you understand them

As outlined in figure 8.2, three types of knowledge can exist in identifier names and can help you quickly understand an unfamiliar name:

1. Names can support your thinking about the domain of the code. A domain word like "customer" will have all sorts of associations in your LTM. A customer is probably buying a product, needs a name and an address, and so on.
2. Name can support your thinking about programming. A programming concept like a tree will also unlock information from the LTM. A tree has a root, can be traversed and flattened, and so on.
3. In some cases, the choice of a variable name also contains information about conventions your LTM is aware of. For example, a variable named j will remind you of a nested loop in which j is the counter of the inside-most loop.

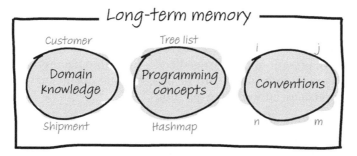

**Figure 8.2** Three types of knowledge stored in your LTM can occur in variable names and can help you to understand the names: domain knowledge (like customer or shipment), programming concepts (like list, tree, or hashmap), and conventions (for example, i and j will likely be loop counters and n and m will be dimensions).

Considering how a variable name will support both the STM and the LTM of a future reader can be a great help in choosing names.

**EXERCISE 8.3** Select a piece of not-too-familiar source code. It should not be entirely unfamiliar, for example, it could be some code you worked on a while ago, or a piece of code written by someone else within a codebase you also work on.

Go through the code and write down a list of all the identifier names in the code: variable names, method names, and class names. For each of the names, reflect on how the name supports your cognitive processing:

- Does the formatting of the name support your STM? Can the name be improved to make the individual parts clearer?
- Does the name support your LTM in understanding the domain? Can the name be improved to be clearer?
- Does the name support your LTM in understanding the programming concepts used? Can the name be improved to be clearer?
- Does the name support your LTM in understanding because its use is based on a programming convention?

### 8.2.4 *When to evaluate the quality of names*

We have seen that naming is hard because of the cognitive processes related to coding. When you are engaged in solving a problem, you are likely experiencing a high cognitive load. Maybe your load was so high while solving the problem that you had nothing left to come up with a good variable name. I think we have all written complex code in which we named a variable foo because we did not want to think about naming in addition to solving the problem at hand. Additionally, maybe the meaning of the thing you were naming didn't become clear until later in the programming process.

Therefore, coding is not a great moment to think about names and to improve their quality. It is better to reflect on naming quality outside of the coding process. Code reviews can be a good moment to reflect on the code quality of your identifier names. Exercise 8.4 can serve as a checklist for names to use, which you can use in code reviews to specifically direct attention to names in code.

**EXERCISE 8.4** Before starting the code review, mechanically list all identifier names that are present in the changed code. List those names outside of the code, for example on a whiteboard or in a separate document. For each of the identifier names, answer these questions:

- Without knowing anything about the code, is it clear what the name means? For example, do you know the meaning of the words this name consists of?
- Are any of the names ambiguous or unclear?
- Do the names use abbreviations that could be confusing?
- What names are similar? Do these similar names also refer to similar objects in the code?

## 8.3 What types of names are easier to understand?

So far, we have investigated why good names are important, and we have explored the impact of names on cognitive processes. We will now zoom into more detailed choices about how to format identifier names.

### 8.3.1 To abbreviate or not to abbreviate?

Thus far, we have seen the opinion that names should be created by combining dictionary words. While using full words seems a reasonable choice, it is good to dive into the evidence we have that identifiers consisting of full words are indeed easier to understand.

Johannes Hofmeister, a researcher at the University of Passau in Germany, conducted an experiment with 72 professional C# developers in which the developers had to find bugs in C# code snippets. Hofmeister was interested in whether the meaning or the form of identifier names is more important for successful bug finding. He presented the developers with three different types of programs: one program where identifiers were letters, a second program in which the identifiers were abbreviations, and finally a program in which the identifiers were words. Hofmeister asked participants to find both syntax and semantic errors. He then measured the time it took for the participants to find bugs in the given programs.

Participants on average found 19% more defects per minute when reading programs in which the identifiers were words compared to letters and abbreviations. There was no significant difference in speed between letters and abbreviations.

While other studies confirm that variables consisting of words aid comprehension, there might also be downsides to using longer variable names.[4] Lawrie, whose work we covered earlier in the chapter, ran a study in which 120 professional developers with an average of 7.5 years of professional experience were asked to comprehend and remember source code with the same three different types of identifiers: words, abbreviations, or single letters.

Participants in the study were shown a method using one of the three identifiers' styles. The code was then removed from view, after which participants were asked to explain the code in words and then recall the variable names that occurred in the program. Contrary to Hofmeister, Lawrie measured how well the summaries of the code corresponded with the actual functionality of the code by rating the answers participants gave on a scale from 1 to 5.

Lawrie found results like Hofmeister's: identifiers consisting of words are easier to understand than both other categories. Summaries of code using word identifiers were rated almost one point higher by the researchers than summaries of code using single-letter identifiers.

---

[4] Dawn Lawrie et al., "Effective Identifier Names for Comprehension and Memory," 2007, https://www.researchgate.net/publication/220245890_Effective_identifier_names_for_comprehension_and_memory.

The study also revealed a downside of using word identifiers. When investigating the results of the recall assignment, Lawrie found that longer variables names are harder to remember, and it takes more time to remember them. It is not the length per se that makes variable names harder to remember, but the number of syllables the names contain. This of course is understandable from a cognitive perspective: longer names might use more chunks in the STM, and syllables are a likely method for chunking words. Thus, choosing a good variable name is a careful balance between clarity of words, which will improve the reader's capability of understanding the code and finding bugs, and the brevity of abbreviations, which might improve recall of names.

Based on her study, Lawrie advises being careful with the use of naming conventions that involve prefixing or suffixing an identifier. These practices should be carefully evaluated to ensure that the added information outweighs the added cost of the names being hard to remember.

**BEWARE OF PREFIXES AND SUFFIXES**   Lawrie advises being careful with the use of naming conventions that involve prefixing or suffixing an identifier.

### SINGLE LETTERS ARE COMMONLY USED AS VARIABLES

Thus far, we have seen that words are better identifiers than abbreviations or letters, both in terms of more quickly finding bugs and in terms of better comprehension. Single letters, however, are commonly used in practice. Gal Beniamini, a researcher at the Hebrew University of Jerusalem, studied how often single letters are used in C, Java, JavaScript, PHP, and Perl. For each of these five programming languages, Beniamini downloaded the 200 most popular projects from GitHub, together with over 16 GB of source code.

Beniamini's results showed that different programming languages have quite different conventions for the use of single-letter variable names. For example, for Perl, the three most-used single-letter names are, in order, v, i, and j, while for JavaScript the most common single-letter names are i, e, and d. Figure 8.3 shows the use of all 26 letters in the five different programming languages Beniamini analyzed.

Beniamini did not only look at the occurrence of single-letter variable names; he was also interested in the associations programmers have for letters. For a letter like i, most programmers will think of a loop iterator, and x and y will likely be coordinates on a plane, but what about other letters, such as b, f, s, or t? Are these letters associated with a common meaning by many programmers? Knowing about the assumptions people make about variable names might help you prevent misconceptions, and also help you understand the ways others are confused about code.

To gain an understanding of the types that programmers associate with variable names, Beniamini ran a survey with 96 experienced programmers, where he asked them to list one or more types that they would associate single-letter variables with. As you can see in figure 8.4, there is little consensus on the types of most letters. Notable exceptions are s, which is overwhelmingly voted to be a string, c, which is overwhelmingly a character, and i, j, k, and n, which are integers. But for all other letters, almost anything goes.

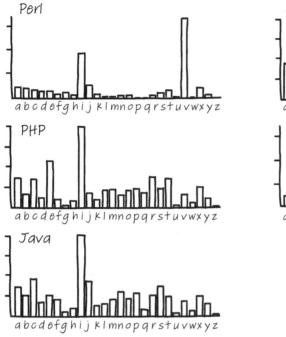

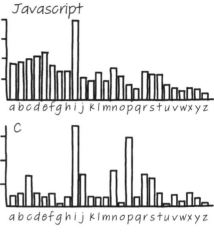

**Figure 8.3** Single-letter variables used in five different programming languages that Beniamini analyzed

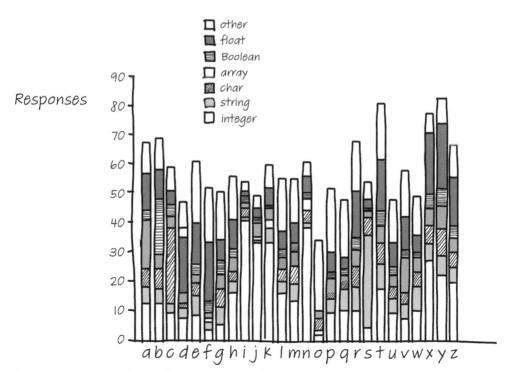

**Figure 8.4** Types associated with single-letter variables

Somewhat surprisingly, d, e, f, r, and t tend to be associated with floating-point numbers, and variables x, y, and z are as strongly associated with integers as they are with floating-point numbers, which could mean that when used as coordinates, they are used both in places where the coordinates are integers and in places where they are floating-point numbers.

Beniamini's results on type associations for one-letter variable names mostly remind us that we cannot take assumptions of others for granted. We might think that a certain letter will surely convey the idea of a certain type, helping the reader make sense of the code, but that is unlikely, apart from a few specific cases. Therefore, choosing words as names or agreeing on conventions is a better bet for future code comprehension.

**EXERCISE 8.5**  Write down the types you would expect for all 26 single-letter variable names in the following table. Then compare notes with your team members. Are there letters where your assumptions differ? Can you find places in your codebase where these letters are used as variables?

| Letter | Type | Letter | Type | Letter | Type |
|--------|------|--------|------|--------|------|
| a |  | j |  | s |  |
| b |  | k |  | t |  |
| c |  | l |  | u |  |
| d |  | m |  | v |  |
| e |  | n |  | w |  |
| f |  | o |  | x |  |
| g |  | p |  | y |  |
| h |  | q |  | z |  |
| i |  | r |  |  |  |

### 8.3.2   Snake case or camel case?

While most programming languages have a style guide that also describes what variable names should look like, not all style guides agree. Famously, C-family languages, including C, C++, C#, and Java, all use camel case where the first letter of any variable is lowercase, and each new word within the name starts with an uppercase letter, for example, `customerPrice` or `nameLength`. Python, on the other hand, uses a convention called snake case, which separates words in identifier names with underscores, for example, `customer_price` or `name_length`.

Dave Binkley, a professor of computer science at the Loyola University in Maryland, performed a study investigating the differences in comprehension between variables written in camel case and those written in snake case.[5] Binkley wanted to know if

---

[5] Dave Binkley, "To Camel Case or Under_Score," 2009, https://ieeexplore.ieee.org/abstract/document/5090039.

the two identifier styles impact the speed and accuracy with which people can adapt programs. In Binkley's study, 135 people participated, both programmers and non-programmers. Participants in the study were first shown a sentence describing the variable, for example, "Extends a list to a table." After studying the sentence, participants were given four multiple-choice options to choose from, of which one represented the sentence. Examples of options participants could pick from are `extendListAsTable`, `expandAliasTable`, `expandAliasTitle`, or `expandAliasTable`.

The results of Binkley's study show that the use of camel case leads to higher accuracy among both programmers and non-programmers. The model finds that there is a 51.5% higher chance of selecting the right option for identifiers written in the camel case style. But there is a cost to this higher accuracy: speed. It took participants half a second more to find identifiers written in camel case.

In addition to comparing the two different identifier styles and looking at the results of both programmers and non-programmers, Binkley also looked at the effect of programming education on the subject's performance, comparing people with no training to people with more years of training. The participants in Binkley's study who had received training had been mostly trained using camel case.

When comparing people with varying levels of experience, Binkley found that programmers with more training in camel case were quicker at finding the right identifiers written in the camel case style. Training in one identifier style seems to negatively impact a person's performance in using other styles. Binkley's results demonstrated that subjects with more training in camel case were slower on identifiers written in snake case than subjects without any training at all.

Knowing what we know about cognitive processing, these results are a bit less surprising than they might seem. If people practice using names in camel case a lot, they get better at chunking names and finding meaning in them.

Of course, if you are working in an existing code base that uses snake case, it would be unwise to change all variable names according to this study. Consistency is an important aspect also. However, should you find yourself in the position to decide on a naming convention, you might want to opt for camel case.

## 8.4 The influence of names on bugs

In this chapter so far, we have looked at why naming matters and what types of names are easier to understand. However, bad naming practices can also directly have an impact on the occurrence of bugs.

### 8.4.1 Code with bad names has more bugs

Simon Butler, whose work on naming guidelines we covered earlier in the chapter, also analyzed the relationship between bad names and bugs. Butler performed a study in 2009[6] that investigated the relationship between bad naming and bad code by investigating open source repositories written in Java, including Tomcat and Hibernate.

---

[6] Simon Butler, "Relating Identifier Naming Flaws and Code Quality: An Empirical Study," 2009, http://oro.open.ac.uk/17007/1/butler09wcreshort_latest.pdf.

Butler created a tool to extract variable names from Java code and also detect violations of naming guidelines. Using his tool, Butler located places in the eight case bases where bad naming styles occurred. As explained in section 8.1, Butler looked both at structural naming issues, such as two consecutive underscores, as well as the components of the names, such as whether they occur in a dictionary.

Butler then compared the locations in the code with a bad naming style to the locations of bugs, as found with FindBugs, a tool that locates potential bug locations using static analysis. Intriguingly, Butler's study found statistically significant associations between naming issues and code quality. Butler's findings suggest that a bad naming style might point to code that is likely to be wrong as opposed to code that is merely hard to read, understand, and maintain.

Of course, the correlation between bug locations and the locations of bad names does not necessarily imply causation. It could be that both bugs and bad names are the result of code written by a novice or sloppy programmer. It could also be the case that the location where the bugs occur is where complex issues are being solved. Those complex issues might relate to the naming errors in other ways. As we have discussed before, maybe the cognitive load of the programmer was very high when creating the code because they were solving a hard problem. It might also be the case that the domain of the code is complex, and therefore coming up with a good name is hard, and the complexity of catching the right name led to confusion and thus a bug.

So, while addressing naming issues is not necessarily going to solve or prevent bugs, inspecting your codebase to find locations where bad naming practices occur might help you find places where code could be improved and bugs could be prevented. That is an extra reason to go on the hunt for bad names in code: improving names might indirectly result in fewer bugs, or at least shorter fix times because better names will make code easier to comprehend.

## 8.5    How to choose better names

We have seen that the effects of bad naming are severe, might lead to lower chances of comprehending code, and might even increase the chance of bugs. Feitelson, whose work on choosing names we covered earlier, also studied how developers can select better names.[7]

### 8.5.1    Name molds

In his survey where developers were asked to select variable names, Feitelson saw that even though developers rarely selected the same name for variables, they would be able to understand names chosen by other developers. When a specific name was chosen in Feitelson's experiment, it was typically understood by most developers. A reason for this seeming contradiction is that developers used what Feitelson calls *name molds*.

Name molds are patterns in which elements in a variable name are typically combined. For example, when a name was needed for the maximal benefits someone can

---

[7] Dror G. Fietelson, "How Developers Choose Names," https://www.cs.huji.ac.il/~feit/papers/Names20TSE.pdf.

receive per month, the names in table 8.4 were all chosen. The names are also normalized, so "max" could be "max" or "maximum" and "benefit" could be "benefits." The table lists the names in order of most to least chosen.

**Table 8.4  Most to least chosen forms of variable names**

```
max_benefit

max_benefit_per_month

max_benefit_num

max_monthly_benefit

benefits

benefits_per_month

max_num_of_benefit

max_month_benefit

benefit_max_num

max_number_of_benefit

max_benefit_amount

max_acc_benefit

max_allowed_benefit

monthly_benefit_limit
```

Looking at these molds helps us understand why the chance of two developers choosing the same variable name in Feitenson's study was so low. The plethora of different names in the experiment was mostly from developers using different name molds.

While all these names conceptually represent the same value, there are a lot of differences in style. The developers in Fcitclson's study did not all work in the same code base, but even within the same code base it is likely that these different molds occur. Knowing what we know now about both cognitive load and LTM, using different molds within a codebase is not a good idea.

First, in terms of cognitive load, looking for the relevant concept in the variable name (in this case, benefit) and in different locations within the variable name adds unnecessary, extraneous cognitive load. The mental energy you will spend on looking for the right concept cannot be spent on understanding the names. Earlier in the chapter, we saw that people can be trained to recognize variables in a certain style, such as camel case or snake case. While no studies have been done on name molds, people will likely get better at recognizing variables written in a certain mold when they use them often.

Second, if variable names are similar, using the same mold is likely going to make it easier for your LTM to find related information. For example, max_benefit_amount might remind you of code you wrote before to calculate the maximum interest amount if that variable was named max_interest_amount. Your LTM will have a harder time remembering similar code when the variable involved was called interest_maximum, even if the calculation was similar.

Because similar molds support your working memory and your LTM best, it is advisable to agree on a limited number of different molds to use in each codebase. When you start a project, agreeing on the molds can be a good step in this direction. In an existing code base, you can start by creating or extracting a list of existing variables names for the code base, see what molds are already in use, and decide on these molds going forward.

**EXERCISE 8.6**    Create a list of variable and function/method names in part of your codebase. This can be one class, all code in one file, or all code related to a certain feature. For each of the names, check which mold they follow using the following table. In the names in the table, X represents a quantity or value like interest of VAT, and Y represents a certain filter on the quantity, such as per month, for a given customer.

Discuss the results with your team. What mold(s) are commonly used? Can some variables be written using a different mold to reach more consistency in your codebase?

| Mold | Variable | Function/method |
|------|----------|-----------------|
| max_X | | |
| max_X_per_Y | | |
| max_X_num | | |
| X | | |
| X_per_Y | | |
| max_num_of_X | | |
| max_Y_X | | |
| X_max_num | | |
| max_number_of_X | | |
| max_X_amount | | |
| max_acc_X | | |
| max_allowed_X | | |
| Y_X_limit | | |
| max_X | | |
| Other | | |

### 8.5.2    *Feitelson's three-step model for better variable names*

We have seen that programmers often use many different name molds for the same objects, while using similar molds can help comprehension. Based on these findings, Feitelson designed a three-step model to help developers choose better names:

1   Select the concepts to include in the name.
2   Choose the words to represent each concept.
3   Construct a name using these words.

#### THE THREE-STEP MODEL IN DETAIL

Let's explore these three steps in more detail. The first step, selecting the concepts to include in the name, is very domain-specific, and the decision on which dimensions to include might be the most important decision in naming. The main thing to take into consideration when choosing which parts to include in the name is, according to Feitelson, the intent of the name, which should represent what information the object holds and what it is used for. When you feel the need to write a comment to explain the name, or when you encounter a comment close to a name in code you use, wording from the comment should probably be included in the variable name. In some cases, it can be important to also include an indication of what kind of information this is, for example, that a length is in the horizontal or vertical dimension, that a weight in stored in kilos, or that a buffer contains user input and should therefore be considered unsafe. Sometimes we might even use a new name when data is converted. For example, after the input is validated, it could be stored in another variable with a name indicating that it is safe.

The second step of Feitelson's model is choosing the words to represent each concept. Often choosing the right words is straightforward, with one specific word being the obvious choice because it is used in the domain of the code or has been used across the codebase. However, in his experiments Feitelson observed that there were also many cases in which for at least one of the words many different contending options were suggested by participants. Such diversity can cause problems when developers become confused about whether synonyms mean the same thing or represent nuanced differences. A *project lexicon*, in which all important definitions are noted and alternatives for synonyms are registered, can help programmers select names consistently.

Feitelson notes that the steps of his model do not necessarily need to be executed in order. Sometimes you might think of words to use in a variable name without considering the concepts they represent. In such cases, it is important to still consider the concepts.

The third step of Feitelson's model is constructing a name using the chosen words, which comes down to selecting one of the naming molds. As we have explained, when choosing a mold, alignment with your codebase can be important. Consistent names will make it easier for others to locate the important elements within the name and to relate the name to other names. A second consideration Feitelson advises is to use molds so they fit with the natural language the variables are defined in. For example, in an English sentence you would say, "the maximum number of points" rather than "the point maximum." Therefore, you might prefer `max_points` over `points_max`. Another way to make variable names sound more natural is to add a preposition, such as in `indexOf` or `elementAt`.

### THE SUCCESS OF FEITELSON'S THREE-STEP MODEL

After defining the three-step model, Feitelson ran a second experiment with 100 new participants.

The researchers explained the model to new participants, who were given an example. After the explanation, participants were given the same names as the participants in Feitelson's original study. Two external judges were then asked to compare pairs of two names: one from the first study, where participants were not aware of the model, and one stemming from the second experiment, in which participants were trained in using the model. The judges did not know which name came from which study.

The judges' choices showed that names selected by subjects using the model were seen as superior to names chosen in the original experiment by a ratio of two to one. Thus, using these three steps leads to better names.

## Summary

- There are different perspectives on what makes a good name, ranging from syntactic rules, such as using camel case, to emphasis on consistency within a codebase.
- Without other differences, camel case variables are easier to remember than variables written in snake case, but people are quicker to identify variables when using snake case.
- Locations in code where bad naming occur are also more likely to contain bugs, but that does not necessarily mean there is a causation.
- There are many different name molds used to shape variable names, but limiting yourself to a smaller number of molds will likely help comprehension.
- Applying Feitelson's three-step model (what concepts to use in a name, what words to use for those concepts, and how to combine them) leads to higher quality names.

# Avoiding bad code and cognitive load: Two frameworks

**This chapter covers**

- Explaining the connection between code smells and cognitive processes, especially cognitive load
- Surveying the connection between bad names and cognitive load

As a professional programmer, I am sure you have seen code that was easy to read, as well as code you had to spend a lot of effort to understand. The reason code can be hard to understand is something we covered in earlier chapters when discussing STM, LTM, and working memory: you are experiencing too much cognitive load. Cognitive load happens when your working memory becomes too full and your brain cannot properly process anymore. In earlier chapters, we focused on how to read code. We have seen that sometimes you need to gain more knowledge of syntax, concepts, or domain knowledge to read code with greater ease.

In this chapter, we will explore what is known about writing code from a cognitive perspective. We will look at what type of code causes a high cognitive load and how to improve code so it is easier to process. In particular, we will dive into two different reasons code can cause cognitive load. First, code can be hard to understand because it is structurally confusing, and second, it can be confusing because its contents are confusing. By examining what makes code hard to read, you can learn to write code that is easier to understand and easier to maintain, which means your team members (including future you) will need less effort to read and adopt the code and the risk of bugs will be lower.

## 9.1 Why code with code smells creates a lot of cognitive load

In this chapter, we examine how to write code that is not confusing for others; in other words, code that does not pose too much cognitive load for the reader. The first framework we use to study why code can be confusing is the idea of *code smells*: parts of code that are not structured ideally. (Code smells were coined by Martin Fowler in his 1999 book *Refactoring: Improving the Design of Existing Code* [Addison-Wesley Professional].) Examples of code smells are very long methods or overly complex switch statements.

You might already be familiar with code smells. If you are not, the next subsection provides a brief overview. After the brief recap of code smells, we dive into code smells and their connection to cognitive processes, especially cognitive load. Simply saying "That class is too big" is helpful, but sometimes it is not helpful enough because we want to understand precisely how big is "too big" and on what factors that depends.

### 9.1.1 A brief intro to code smells

Fowler describes a catalog of different code smells, paired with strategies to relieve code smells, which he called *refactorings*. Examples of code smells are very long methods, classes that try to do too much at the same time, and overly complex switch statements. As we have seen earlier in this book, the term "refactoring" has become somewhat separate from code smells in that a refactoring can now also indicate an improvement to code in a more generic sense, apart from relieving a code smell. For example, changing a loop into a list comprehension is seen by most people as a refactoring, even though a loop does not necessarily contain a code smell.

Fowler's book describes a catalog of 22 code smells, which we summarize in table 9.1. While Fowler does not make this distinction in his book, the 22 code smells can be divided into different levels, also indicated in table 9.1 Some code smells concern a single method, like the long method, while others pertain to an entire codebase, like comments. The next subsection dives into the code smell at each of the levels.

Table 9.1　Overview of Fowler's smells and the levels they pertain to

| Code smell | Explanation | Level |
|---|---|---|
| **Long method** | A method should not consist of many lines of code performing different calculations. | Method level |
| **Long parameter list** | A method should not have many parameters. | Method level |
| **Switch statements** | Code should not contain large switch statements; polymorphism could be used to ease the code. | Method level |
| **Alternative classes with different interfaces** | There should not be two different classes that seem different at first glance but have similar fields and methods. | Class level |
| **Primitive obsession** | Avoid the overuse of primitive types in a class. | Class level |
| **Incomplete library class** | Methods should not be added to random classes instead of to a library class. | Class level |
| **Large class** | A class should not have too many methods and fields, making it unclear what abstraction the class provides. | Class level |
| **Lazy class** | A class should not be doing too little to justify its existence. | Class level |
| **Data class** | Classes should not contain only data; they should contain methods as well. | Class level |
| **Temporary field** | Classes should not contain unnecessary temporary fields. | Class level |
| **Data clumps** | Data often used in combination belongs together and should be stored together in a class or structure. | Class level |
| **Divergent change** | Generally, code changes should be local, preferably to one class. If you have to make many different changes in different places, that indicates a poor structure in the code. | Codebase level |
| **Feature envy** | When many methods in class A are referenced from class B, they belong in B and should be moved there. | Codebase level |
| **Inappropriate intimacy** | Classes should not be connected to other classes extensively. | Codebase level |
| **Duplicated code or code clones** | The same or very similar code should not occur in multiple different places in a codebase. | Codebase level |
| **Comments** | Comments should describe why the code is there, not what it does. | Codebase level |
| **Message chains** | Avoid message chains that are long chains of message calls, where methods call methods call methods, and so on. | Codebase level |
| **Middle man** | If a class is delegating too much responsibility, should it exist? | Codebase level |
| **Parallel inheritance** | When you make a subclass of one class, you need to make a subclass of another. This indicates that the functionality of both classes might belong in one class. | Codebase level |

**Table 9.1  Overview of Fowler's smells and the levels they pertain to (continued)**

| Code smell | Explanation | Level |
|---|---|---|
| **Refused bequest** | When classes inherit behavior they do not use, the inheritance might not be necessary. | Codebase level |
| **Shotgun surgery** | Generally, code changes should be local to one class. If you have to make many different changes in different places, that indicates a poor structure in the code. | Codebase level |
| **Speculative generality** | Do not add code to a codebase "just in case"; only add features that are needed. | Codebase level |

#### METHOD-LEVEL CODE SMELLS

An example of a code smell that pertains to an individual method is a method that consists of many lines of code and has a lot of functionality. Such a method is said to suffer from the long method or God method smell. Another code smell occurs when a method has a large number of many parameters. According to Fowler, such a method suffers from the many parameters smell.

For readers unfamiliar with the concept, reading Fowler's book is advised. Table 9.1 provides an overview of Fowler's 22 code smells, including the level they occur.

#### CLASS-LEVEL CODE SMELLS

In addition to code smells that exist at the method level, there are code smells at the class level. An example is a large class, sometimes also called a *God class*. A large class is a class that has so much functionality that it is no longer a meaningful abstraction. God classes are typically not created at once, but occur over time. First you might create a class to handle displaying a customer's account, which might contain methods relating to nicely marking up customer information, such as `print_name_and_title()` or `show_date_of_birth()`. Slowly, the class's functionality is expanded with some method that also performs some simple calculations like `determine_age()`. Over time, methods are added that do not consider one individual customer but can also list all clients of a certain representative, and so on. At some point in time, the class no longer represents the logic related to one customer but contains logic for all sorts of processes within the application and thus becomes a God class.

Similarly, a class can have too few methods and fields to be a meaningful abstraction, which Fowler calls the lazy class. A lazy class can also be created over time, when functionality is moved to other classes, or the lazy class might have been created as a stub, meant to be extended, which then never happened.

#### CODEBASE-LEVEL CODE SMELLS

Code smells do not only occur at the level of individual methods or classes; a codebase as a whole can also have smells. For example, when a codebase contains very similar code in different places, the codebase has the duplicated code smell, also called code clones. An example of cloned code in shown in figure 9.1. Another example of a code smell in a codebase is when it contains several methods that continuously pass each other information. That phenomenon is called message chain.

```
int foo(int j) {
    if (j < 0)
        return j;
    else
        return j++;
}
```
Product A

```
int goo(int j) {
    if ( j < 0 )
        return j;
    else
        return j+2;
}
```
Product B

Figure 9.1  An example of code clones; functions foo and goo are very similar but not the same.

### IMPACT OF CODE SMELLS

The presence of a code smell does not necessarily imply the code has an error. However, it is known that code with smells is more likely to contain errors. Foutse Khomh, professor of software engineering at Polytechnique Montréal in Canada, studied the codebase of Eclipse, a well-known IDE for Java and other languages. Khomh inspected different versions of the Eclipse codebase and looked at how code smells impacted errors. He found that God classes were a significant contributor to error proneness in all versions of Eclipse analyzed, and God methods were significant contributors to errors in Eclipse 2.1.[1, 2]

Khomh looked not only at the impact of code smells on errors, but also at change proneness. He found that code containing smells is also more likely to change in the future than non-smelly code. The large class and long method smells were shown to have a significantly negative impact on change proneness: classes suffering from these smells are more likely to change than classes without in more than 75% of Eclipse releases.[3]

**EXERCISE 9.1**  Think of code you recently edited or fixed that was very hard to understand. Was that related to a code smell? At what level did those code smells occur?

## 9.1.2  *How code smells harm cognition*

Now that we have covered the code smells in detail, let's look at the deeper cognitive issues connected to them. If you want to avoid writing code that contains code smells, it is important to understand why they are harmful to understanding. We will therefore explore the connection of code smells to cognitive processes in the brain and especially to cognitive load.

---

[1] Wei Le and Raed Shatnawi, "An Empirical Study of the Bad Smells and Class Error Probability in the Post-Release Object-Oriented System Evolution, *Journal of Systems and Software*, vol. 80, no. 11, 2007, pp. 1120–1128, http://dx.doi.org/10.1016/j.jss.2006.10.018.

[2] Aloisio S. Cairo et al., "The Impact of Code Smells on Software Bugs: A Systematic Literature Review," 2018, https://www.mdpi.com/2078-2489/9/11/273.

[3] Foutse Khomh et al., "An Exploratory Study of the Impact of Antipatterns on Software Changeability," http://www.ptidej.net/publications/documents/Research+report+Antipatterns+Changeability+April09.doc.pdf.

Fowler's code smells are based on prior work and his personal experience in writing code. While Fowler does not make the connection, a lot of the code smells could be related to cognitive functions of the brain. Based on what we know about working memory and LTM, we can interpret the effect of code that contains code smells.

In previous chapters, we have seen different forms of confusion related to different cognitive processes. Similarly, different code smells have an origin in different forms of cognitive processes, which we will outline.

### LONG PARAMETER LIST, COMPLEX SWITCH STATEMENTS: OVERLOADING THE CAPACITY OF THE WORKING MEMORY

Knowing what we know about the working memory, we can understand why long parameter lists and complex switch statements are hard to read: both smells are related to an overloaded working memory. In part 1 of this book, we explained that the capacity of the working memory is as low as 6, so it makes sense that a parameter list of more than about six parameters will be too much for people to remember. While reading code, it will be impossible to hold all the parameters in working memory. As such, the method will be harder to understand.

There are, of course, some nuances here. Not all individual parameters will be necessarily treated as separate chunks when you read them. For example, consider a method with a signature like the one in the next listing.

---

Listing 9.1   **Java method signature takes two x- and two y-coordinates as parameters**

```
public void line(int xOrigin, int yOrigin, int xDestination, yDestination) {}
```

Your brain will likely treat this as two rather than four chunks: one chunk origin with an x- and y- coordinate and one chunk destination with its coordinates. The limited number of parameters is thus context-dependent and depends on the prior knowledge you have about elements in the code. However, long lists of parameters are more likely to overload the working memory. The same is true for complex switch statements.

### GOD CLASS, LONG METHOD: NO POSSIBILITY FOR EFFICIENT CHUNKING

When working with code, we create abstractions continuously. Rather than placing all functionality in one `main()` function, we now prefer to divide functionality into separate small functions with meaningful names. Groups of coherent attributes and functions are be combined into classes. A benefit of dividing functionality over separate functions, classes, and methods is that their names serve as documentation.

If a programmer calls `square(5)`, they immediately have a sense of what might be returned. But another benefit of function and class names is that they help chunk the code. For example, if you see a block of code that contains a function called `multiples()` and one called `minimum()`, you might conclude that this function calculates the least common denominator without even inspecting the code in detail. This is why code smells related to large blocks of code, including God classes and long methods, are harmful: there are not enough defining characteristics to quickly comprehend the code, and we have to fall back on reading code line by line.

### CODE CLONES: CHUNKING GONE WRONG

*Code clones*, or the duplication smell, occur when a codebase has a lot of code with small differences.

With what we now know about the working memory, we might understand why clones are considered a code smell. Consider the previous two methods, shown again in figure 9.2. When you see a function call very similar to `foo()`, like `goo()`, your working memory might collect information on `foo()` from long-term storage. It is like your working memory is telling you "This might come in handy." Next, you might inspect the implementation of `goo()` itself. Just glancing over it, and strengthened by your prior knowledge of `foo()`, it is likely you will think "Ah, that is a `foo()`."

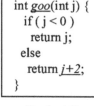

```
int foo(int j) {
    if (j < 0)
        return j;
    else
        return j++;
}
```
Product A

```
int goo(int j) {
    if ( j < 0 )
        return j;
    else
        return j+2;
}
```
Product B

**Figure 9.2  Two functions with similar names and similar, but not exactly the same, functionality. Because the names and implementation of the two functions are so similar, our brains are likely going to confuse both methods.**

Thus, your brain will group the method `goo()`, with its small differences from `foo()`, into one category with `foo()`, much like a few different variants of the Sicilian opening are all grouped under "Sicilian" in the mind of a chess player. As such, the misconception that `goo()` is a `foo()` might be born, even though it returns a different value. We have saw earlier in this book that such misconceptions can linger in your mind for a long time. You might need several exposures to the fact that `goo()` is not the same as `foo()` to really realize your mistake.

> **EXERCISE 9.2**  Revisit the smelly code you examined in exercise 9.1. What cognitive processes were involved in misunderstanding the code?

## 9.2  The influence of bad names on cognitive load

In this chapter, we are focusing on creating code that is easy to understand. So far we have looked at the framework of Fowler's code smells, like long methods and code clones, and their effect on cognitive load.

Code smells are parts of code that suffer from *structural antipatterns*: the code is correct but not structured in a way that is easy to process. However, code can also have *conceptual antipatterns*: the code might be structured in the right way, in neat classes with short methods, but these have confusing names. Such issues with code are described in the second framework, *linguistic antipatterns*. Because both frameworks cover different aspects of code, they complement each other well.

### 9.2.1 Linguistic antipatterns

Linguistic antipatterns were originally defined by Venera Arnaoudova, now a professor at Washington State. Arnaoudova describes linguistic antipatterns as inconsistencies between linguistic elements in code and their roles. Linguistic elements of code are defined as natural language parts of code, including method signatures, documentation, attribute names, types, or comments. Antipatterns occur when the linguistic elements do not correspond with their role. A simple example would be a variable that is called `initial_element`, which doesn't contain an element but an index of an element, or a variable that suggests it is a Boolean, like `isValid`, which turns out to contain an integer.

Linguistic antipatterns commonly occur in method or function names, too, when its name describes something the method or function does not do. An example of this occurs when the name of a function sounds like it will return a collection but returns a single object, such as a method `getCustomers` that returns a Boolean. While this can be somewhat sensible behavior in a case where the method is checking whether there are customers, it can also be confusing.

Arnaoudova describes six categories of linguistic antipatterns, summarized in table 9.2.

**Table 9.2   Arnaoudova's six linguistic antipatterns**

| |
|---|
| Methods that do more than they say |
| Methods that say more than they do |
| Methods that do the opposite of what they say |
| Identifiers whose names say that they contain more than what the entity contains |
| Identifiers whose names say that they contain less than what the entity contains |
| Identifiers whose names say the opposite of what the entity contains |

After defining the linguistic antipatterns, Arnaoudova studied their occurrence in seven open source projects. She found that these antipatterns are relatively common; for example, 11% of setters also return a value in addition to setting a field. In 2.5% of methods, the method name and the corresponding comment gave opposite descriptions of the working of the method, and a whopping 64% of identifiers starting with "is" turned out not to be Boolean.

> **CHECK THE LINGUISTIC ANTIPATTERNS IN YOUR CODEBASE** Are you curious about whether your codebase suffers from linguistic antipatterns? Based on her research, Arnaoudova created Linguistic Anti-Pattern Detector (LAPD), which can detect antipatterns in Java code. LAPD is available as an extension of Eclipse Checkstyle plugin.[4]

---

[4] http://www.veneraarnaoudova.ca/linguistic-anti-pattern-detector-lapd/.

While we can all intuitively guess that linguistic antipatterns are confusing, and thus might cause a higher cognitive load, science also confirms this as fact. But before we can dive into the effects of linguistic antipatterns on cognitive load, we must first understand how cognitive load can be measured.

### 9.2.2   *Measuring cognitive load*

In earlier chapters, we introduced cognitive load, the overloading of the working memory. We also showed some examples of tasks that induce high cognitive load, for example reading code when relevant information is located in different methods or files, or reading code that contains a lot of unfamiliar keywords or programming concepts. We have, however, not covered how we measure cognitive load.

#### THE PAAS SCALE FOR COGNITIVE LOAD

When measuring cognitive load, scientists often use the *Paas Scale*, designed by Dutch psychologist Fred Paas, who is now a professor at the Erasmus University in Rotterdam, shown in table 9.3.

The Paas Scale has received some criticism over the past years because it is a relatively small questionnaire, consisting of just one question. It is also unclear whether participants can reliably distinguish between, for example, having a very high load and a very, very high load.

Despite its shortcomings, the Paas Scale is commonly used. In previous chapters, we covered strategies for reading code and exercises to practice. When engaging in the task of reading unfamiliar code, the Paas Scale can be used to help you reflect on code and your relationship with the code.

**Table 9.3   In the Paas Scale, participants are asked to self-rate the cognitive load on this 9-point scale.**

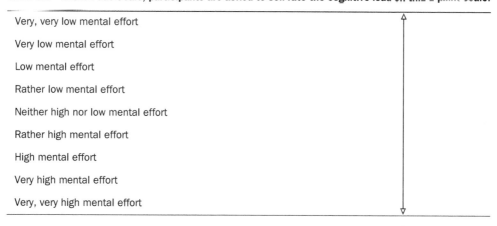

EXERCISE 9.3   Choose an unfamiliar piece of code and use the Paas Scale to rate the cognitive effort you had to exert to understand this code. Then, also reflect on why this code caused you a certain amount of cognitive load. This exercise can help you to understand what types of code are hard for you to read.

| | Level of cognitive load | Reason |
|---|---|---|
| Very, very low mental effort | | |
| Very low mental effort | | |
| Low mental effort | | |
| Rather low mental effort | | |
| Neither high nor low mental effort | | |
| Rather high mental effort | | |
| High mental effort | | |
| Very high mental effort | | |
| Very, very high mental effort | | |

### EYE-BASED MEASUREMENTS

In addition to metrics based on the perception of participants, newer research also makes increasing use of biometrics. By measuring the body's reaction to a certain task, it is possible to estimate the cognitive load being caused by whatever the person is doing at that moment.

An example of a biometric measurement is eye tracking. With an eye tracker we can determine how concentrated people are. This can be done, for example, by examining a person's blink rate, which is a measure of how often you blink. Several studies have shown that blinking behavior is not stable but can differ based on what you are doing at the moment. Several studies have also found that cognitive load affects blinking; the harder a task is, the less you will blink. A second eye-related metric that can predict cognitive load is the pupil. Studies have shown that more difficult tasks induce more cognitive load as measured by pupil size.[5]

The current hypothesis for why blinking correlates with cognitive load is that it can indicate how hard your brain tries to maximize your exposure to the difficult task and thus tries to get as many visual stimuli as possible. For similar reasons, larger pupils occur when performing complicated tasks, because with a larger pupil, the eye can absorb more information, which is what the brain searches for when engaged in a difficult task.

### SKIN-BASED MEASUREMENTS

In addition to measurements based on the eyes, the skin can also tell us the cognitive load of a person. Skin temperature and the presence of sweat are indicators of cognitive load too.

While these biometric methods of measuring cognitive load might sound cool, research has shown they often correlate with the Paas Sscale, so even though you might consider using your fitness tracker to decide on the readability of your code, simply using exercise 9.3 will probably do.

---

[5] Shamsi T. Iqbal et. al., "Task-Evolved Pupillary Response to Mental Workload in Human-Computer Interaction," 2004, https://interruptions.net/literature/Iqbal-CHI04-p1477-iqbal.pdf.

## BRAIN-BASED MEASUREMENTS

In chapter 5, we discussed the fMRI scanner as a method to measure what type of activities the brain is performing. fMRI machines are precise in their measurement but also have big limitations. Since participants have to lie still, they are not able to write code while in the machine. Even reading code is a bit artificial since it can only be shown on a small screen. The fact that people are not able to move in the machine also greatly limits their possible interactions with the code; for example, they would not be able to scroll through the code, to click on identifiers to navigate to their definitions in the code, or to search for keywords or identifiers using ctrl-f. Because of these fMRI limitations, alternative brain measurements are also used.

## ELECTROENCEPHALOGRAM

One alternative measure of brain activity is the *electroencephalogram* (EEG). EEG devices measure variance in the activity of neurons in the brain caused by measuring the variance in voltage that brain activity causes. A second alternative is the use of functional near infrared spectroscopy (fNIRS). fNIRS can also be measured with a headband, and as such allows for more realistic experiments than fMRI.

As we will discuss in the next subsection, fNIRS has been used to gain a deeper understanding of the relationship between linguistic and cognitive load.

An fNIRS device uses infrared light and corresponding light sensors. Because hemoglobin in the blood absorbs the light, this device can be used to detect oxygenation the brain. The infrared light moves through in the brain, but some of it reaches the light detectors on the headband. By determining the amount of light sensed by the detector, the amount of oxygenated and deoxygenated hemoglobin in the area can be calculated. If blood is more oxygenated, there is an increase in cognitive load.

fNIRS devices are highly sensitive to motion artifacts and light, so users should remain relatively still and not touch the device during recording. While this is still a lot less intrusive than fMRI, it is a bit more inconvenient than wearing an EEG headband.

## FUNCTIONAL FNIRS AND PROGRAMMING

In 2014, Takao Nakagawa, a researcher at the Nara Institute of Science and Technology in Japan, measured brain activity during program comprehension using a wearable fNIRS device.[6] Participants in Nakagawa's study were asked to read two versions of an algorithm written in C. One version was a regular implementation, and the second was deliberately made complicated. For example, loop counters and other values were changed such that the variables were updated frequently and irregularly. These modifications did not change the functionality of a program.

While wearing the fNIRS headband, participants were presented with the original and the deliberately complicated versions of the program. To rule out the possibility that participants would learn from the easy version and transfer that learning to the

---

[6] Takao Nakagawa et al., "Quantifying Programmers' Mental Workload during Program Comprehension Based on Cerebral Blood Flow Measurement: A Controlled Experiment," https://posl.ait.kyushu-u.ac.jp/~kamei/publications/Nakagawa_ICSENier2014.pdf.

more complicated program, the setup was randomized. That meant some participants first saw the original version while others first saw the modified program.

The results of Nakagawa's study showed that for 8 out of the 10 participants, the oxygenated blood flow while studying the complicated program was larger than when reading the original programs. This result suggests that cognitive load during programming could be quantified using cerebral blood flow measurement with an fNIRS device.

### 9.2.3   *Linguistic antipatterns and cognitive load*

Using fNIRS, researchers have been able to measure the effects of linguistic antipatterns on cognitive load. Sarah Fakhoury, currently a graduate student supervised by Arnaoudova, studied the relationships between linguistic antipatterns and cognitive load in 2018. Fifteen participants each read code snippets gathered from open source projects. The researchers deliberately added bugs to the snippets and asked the participants to find the bugs. The bug detection task in itself was not so important; what mattered was that finding the bug would make the participants able to comprehend the code.

The researchers make some more adaptions to the code such that they had four variants of the code snippets:

1  Snippets that were altered to contain either linguistic antipatterns
2  Snippets that were altered to contain structural inconsistencies
3  Both issues
4  No issues

The participants were divided into four groups, and each of the groups read the snippets in a different order to rule out any learning effects.

The researchers used an eye tracker to detect where in the code people were reading, and the participants also wore an fNIRS machine to detect cognitive load. The results of the study showed first that the parts of the code where linguistic antipatterns occurred were inspected a lot more than the rest of the code, as indicated by the eye tracker results.

Furthermore, the results from the fNIRS device indicate that the presence of linguistic antipatterns in the source code significantly increases the average oxygenated blood flow that a participant experiences (i.e., the cognitive load that is induced by the snippet is higher).

What was also interesting in this particular study was that some of the snippets contained structural antipatterns that the researchers added to the code. The code was formatted in a way that is contrary to conventional Java formatting standards; for example, opening and closing brackets were not on their lines and were not indented properly. They also increased the code's complexity, for example by adding extra loops.

This allowed the researchers to compare the effect of bad structure with the effect of linguistic antipatterns. Participants disliked the structurally inconsistent snippets, with one participant commenting that "terrible formatting severely increases readers' burden." However, the researchers found no statistical evidence that structural inconsistencies increased the average cognitive load that participants experienced compared to the control snippets that were unaltered.

### 9.2.4 *Why linguistic antipatterns cause confusion*

We know that code with more linguistic antipatterns induces greater cognitive load. More studies using brain measurements are needed to confirm these connections, but we can speculate on the effect of linguistic antipatterns based on what we know about the working memory and the LTM.

There are two likely cognitive issues in play when reading code containing linguistic antipatterns. In part 1 of this book, we covered transfer while learning: when you are reading something unfamiliar, such as code that you did not write yourself, your LTM searches for related facts and experiences. When reading a conflicting name, the wrong information will be presented to you. For example, reading a function name `retrieveElements()` might cause you to think of information on functions returning a list of things. That gives you the idea that you could sort, filter, or slice the returning element, which is not true for a single element.

A second reason linguistic antipatterns can confuse is that they might lead to "mischunking," just like code clones. When you are reading a variable name such as `isValid`, you can simply assume the variable is a Boolean. That means there is no need for your brain to dig deeper to see that in fact it is used as a list of possible return values. By trying to save energy, your brain made a wrong assumption. As we have seen earlier, such assumptions may linger for long periods of time.

## *Summary*

- Code smells, such as long methods, indicate structural issues with code. There are different cognitive reasons why code smells cause a higher cognitive load. Duplicated code, for example, makes it harder to chunk code properly, while long parameter lists are heavy on your working memory.
- There are different ways to measure cognitive load, including biometric sensors like measuring blinking rate or skin temperature. If you want to measure your own cognitive load, the Paas Scale typically is a reliable instrument.
- Linguistic antipatterns indicate places in a codebase where code does something different than names involved suggest, leading to a higher cognitive load. This is likely caused by the fact that your LTM finds wrong facts while trying to support your thinking. Linguistic antipatterns can also lead to wrong chunking because your brain assumes a meaning of code that is not actually implemented.

# Getting better at
# solving complex problems

## This chapter covers

- Comparing the role that different memory systems play in problem solving
- Investigating how automatization of small skills can help you solve larger and harder problems
- Understanding how to strengthen your LTM to solve problems with greater ease

In the last few chapters, we mainly looked at what you should *not* do while coding and why. We investigated the effect of bad names in chapter 8 and the impact of code smells on your ability to understand code in chapter 9.

Earlier in the book, in chapter 6, we discussed different strategies to support your working memory when solving programming problems. This chapter again covers techniques to help you in problem solving, but focuses on strengthening your LTM.

We will first investigate what it means to solve a problem. After exploring problem solving in depth, we dive into how to get better at it. By the end of this chapter, you will know two techniques to improve your programming and problem-solving skills. The first technique that we will cover is *automatization* (i.e., being able to do small tasks without thinking about them). This is useful because the less time you spend on figuring out small things, the easier it is to solve hard problems. Then we will explore problem solving from others' written code as a means to improve your own problem-solving skills.

## 10.1 What is problem solving?

The goal of this chapter is to teach you strategies that will help you improve your problem-solving skills by examining the LTM's role in problem solving. But before we can tell you how to better solve problems, we will first dive into what it means to engage in problem solving.

### 10.1.1 Elements of problem solving

Problem solving has three important elements:

- The goal state, which is what we want to achieve. When we reach the goal state, the problem is considered solved.
- The start state from where the problem has to be solved
- The rules that dictate how we can reach the goal state from the start state

For example, consider playing tic-tac-toe. In that situation, the start state is an empty field, your desired state is three crosses in a row, and the rules are that you can place a cross in any empty field on the board. When you are adding a search box to an existing website, your start state is the existing code base and your desired state might be passing unit tests or a satisfied user. The rules of the problem in programming often come in the form of constraints, such as implementing the feature in JavaScript or not breaking additional tests while implementing this new feature.

### 10.1.2 State space

All steps that we could consider while solving a program are called the problem's *state space*. When playing tic-tac-toe, all possible fields are the state space. For small problems like tic-tac-toe, the whole state space can be visualized. Figure 10.1 shows a small part of the state space of a tic-tac-toe game.

For example, when adding a button to a website, all possible JavaScript programs are the state space. It is up to the problem solver to make the right moves or add the right lines of code to reach the start goal. In other words, problem solving means traversing the state space in the optimal way, reaching the goal state in as few steps as possible.

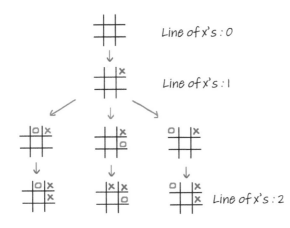

**Figure 10.1   A part of the state space of a tic-tac-toe game, where link arrows indicate moves for o's and blue arrows are moves for x's. The goal state for x is to get three x's in a row.**

**EXERCISE 10.1**   Examine something you created with code within the last few days. What were the aspects of this problem?

- What was the goal state you wanted to achieve?
- How was the goal state checked: manually by you, by someone else, or with unit tests or acceptance tests?
- What was the start state?
- Which rules and constraints applied?

## 10.2   *What is the role of the LTM when you solve programming problems?*

Now that we have defined what it means to solve a problem, we can dive into what happens in your brain when you do. Chapter 6 covered what happens in your working memory when you solve programming problems. If you experience too much cognitive load, your brain cannot properly process and programming gets harder. However, the LTM also plays a role in problem solving, as we will explore in this chapter.

### 10.2.1   *Is problem solving a cognitive process on its own?*

Some people think that problem solving is a generic skill and thus also a specific process in your brain. Hungarian mathematician George Pólya is a famous thinker on problem solving. In 1945, Pólya wrote a short and famous book called *How to Solve It.* His book proposes a "system of thinking" to solve any problem involving three steps:

1   Understanding the problem
2   Devising a plan
3   Carrying out the plan

However, despite the popularity of generic approaches, research has consistently shown that problem solving is neither a generic skill nor a cognitive process. There are two reasons why generic problem-solving methods do not work so well, and both have to do with the role of the LTM.

## YOU USE LTM WHEN SOLVING PROBLEMS

First, when you solve a problem, you take into account knowledge about the desired goal state and the rules by which we have to play. The problem itself will influence the solutions we can design. Let's consider the influence of prior knowledge on solutions with a programming example. Suppose you have to implement code to detect whether a given input string s is a palindrome. We ask you to write code for this problem in Java, APL, and BASIC. Let's investigate Polya's steps and see how they would pan out when programming.

- Understand the problem.

    We assume that for you, being a programmer, understanding the problem is not a problem. You are likely able to formulate a few solid test cases to check your code too.

- Devise a plan (translate).

    The second step of Polya's method is harder to do. Your plan depends heavily on the capabilities of the programming language in which you are going to implement the solution.

    Does the language at hand, for example, have a reverse-like method or function? In that case, you can simply check whether the string s is equal to reverse(s). You might know that that in Java you can use StringBuilder, which has a reverse() function, but is such a method available for BASIC and APL? Not having access to the information, to the building blocks of the solution, makes it hard to create a plan.

- Carry out the plan (solve).

    The third step of Polya's method is also influenced by your understanding of the programming language at hand. I can tell you that APL indeed has a reverse() function (BASIC does not), but you have seen a bit of APL now, and you know it is not going to be called reverse(), because all APL keywords are operators, so carrying out the plan is still challenging.

## IT IS EASIER FOR YOUR BRAIN TO SOLVE FAMILIAR PROBLEMS

There is a second reason generic problem-solving methods often fall short that also relates to the workings of the LTM. In chapter 3, we explained that memories in the LTM are stored as a network in relation to each other. Earlier in this chapter, we also covered the fact that while thinking about a problem, the brain retrieves information from the LTM, which could be relevant to the problem at hand.

Using a generic problem-solving technique like Polya's "devise a plan" creates a cognitive problem. You might have a lot of useful strategies stored in your LTM, which the brain tries to retrieve when solving the problem. When we try to solve the problem in a generic way, however, the relevant strategies might not be found. As we outlined in chapter 3, the LTM needs clues to retrieve the right memories. The more specific the clue, the more likely we are to find the right memory. For example, when you have to perform tail division, thinking of a plan is unlikely to give your LTM enough clues to find the approach stored in memory. Thinking of things like tail division or sub-tracting multiples of the divisor are more likely to result in the right plan.

Like we covered in chapter 7, transfer of knowledge from one domain, like chess, to another domain, like mathematics, is unlikely to happen. Similarly, transfer from the very generic domain of problem solving back to other domains is not very likely.

### 10.2.2  *How to teach your LTM to solve problems*

We have seen that problem solving is not a cognitive process. This brings us to this question: How should we train for problem solving instead? To explore that in more depth, we need to dive even deeper into how the brain thinks. Earlier in the book we explained that thoughts are formed in the working memory. We also saw that your working memory does not form thoughts alone but operates in strong collaboration which both the LTM and the STM.

When you think about a certain problem, let's say implementing a sorting button on a web application, your working memory will make the decisions on what you implement. However, before your working memory you can make such a decision, it needs to do two things. First is to get information from the STM about the context of the problem, such as the requirements for the button or the existing code you just read.

At the same time, the LTM is searched for relevant background knowledge. Relevant memories that you might have, such as how to implement sorting or information about the code base, are also sent to the working memory. To understand problem solving better, we need to explore this second process of searching the LTM.

### 10.2.3  *Two types of memories that play a role in problem solving*

Later in this chapter we will explore two techniques to strengthen your problem-solving skills. Before that, however, we need to explore different types of memories people have and what role they play when solving problems. Understanding the different forms of memories matters because different types are created in different ways,

The LTM can store different types of memory, which are outlined in figure 10.2. First there is *procedural* (sometimes called *implicit*) memory, which is the memory for motor skills or skills you are not consciously aware of. Implicit memories are, for example, knowing how to tie shoelaces or ride a bike.

The second type of memory that plays a role when solving a problem is *declarative* (sometimes called *explicit*) memory. There are facts you can remember, and you also know you know them, such as the fact that Barack Obama was the 44th president of the United States, or that the way to write a for-loop in Java is for (i = 0; i < n; i++).

As shown in figure 10.2, declarative memories can be subdivided into two catego-ries: episodic memory and semantic memory. Episodic memories are what we often mean when we colloquially use the word "memory." Those are memories of experi-ences, like going to summer camp when you were 14, meeting your spouse for the first time, or spending three hours chasing a bug only to find out there was an error in a unit test.

The other part of declarative memory is called *semantic* memory. Semantic memory is memory for meanings, concepts, or facts, such as that frog in French is "grenouille," or 5 times 7 equals 35, or a class in Java is used to combine data and functionality.

Semantic memories are the memories we trained in chapter 3 with flashcards. Episodic memories are created without you spending additional effort, although, similar to semantic memories, retrieval strength will be higher for memories you have thought about often.

### WHAT TYPES OF MEMORIES PLAY A ROLE WHEN YOU SOLVE PROBLEMS?

All these forms of memory play a role when programming, as outlined in figure 10.2 When considering the memories you use for programming, explicit memory might be the first that comes to mind. While programming, a programmer must remember how to construct a loop in Java. However, other forms of memory also play a role, as illustrated by figure 10.2

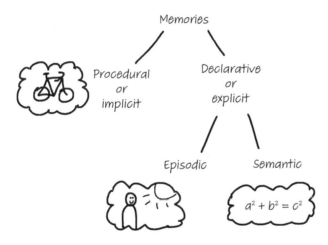

**Figure 10.2  There are different types of memories. Procedural (or implicit) memory showcases how to do something. Declarative (explicit) memory consists of memories we are explicitly aware of. Declarative memory is further divided into things you have experienced and that are stored in episodic memory and facts you know that are stored in semantic memory.**

Episodic memory is used when you remember how you solved a problem in the past. When you have to solve a problem involving hierarchy, for example, you might remember that you used a tree in the past. Research shows that experts especially rely heavily on episodic memory when solving problems. In a sense, experts recreate, rather than solve, familiar problems. That means that instead of finding a new solution, they rely on solutions that have previously worked for similar problems. In chapter 10, we will dive deeper into how we can strengthen episodic memories to become better problem solvers.

In addition to both forms of explicit memory, programming activities also rely on implicit memory, as illustrated in figure 10.3. For example, many programmers can touch type, which is procedural memory. In addition to the alphabet, there are numerous keystrokes you can use without explicit attention, such as hitting ctrl-z when you make a mistake or automatically adding a closing bracket to an opening bracket. In problem-solving activities, implicit memory can also play a role, for example, when you automatically place a break point on a line where you suspect a bug might be present. Sometimes what we call intuition, in fact, happens when you solve a problem similar to one you have solved before; you just know what to do without really knowing how to do it.

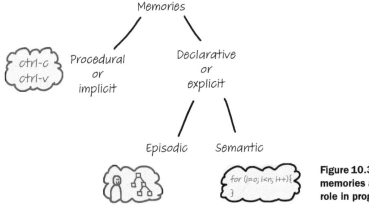

**Figure 10.3    Different types of memories and how they play a role in programming**

### UNLEARNING

While we have seen that implicit memory can help you quickly execute known tasks, having implicit memories can also be harmful. In chapter 7, we discussed the idea of negative transfer: knowing something harms learning something else. Having a lot of implicit memory can harm your flexibility as well. For example, once you have learned how to touch type on a Qwerty keyboard, learning to use a Dvorak keyboard will be harder than if you had never learned Qwerty. This is partly due to the fact that you have a large set of implicit memories of how to do things.

You might have experienced the difficulty of unlearning implicit memory, as well, if you have ever learned a second programming language with a syntax quite different from the first language you learned. For example, when moving from C# or Java to Python, it is likely you will unconsciously type curly brackets around blocks or functions for a while. I personally moved from C# to Python years ago, and I still very often type `foreach` instead of `for` when iterating over a list, which is due to implicit memory I built when programming C# and that is still strongly present.

**EXERCISE 10.2**    The next time you write code, try to actively monitor the memories you use.

Use the following table to reflect on what type of programs or problems activate which type of memories. It can be interesting to do this exercise a few times for different programs. If you do the exercise a few times and follow your progress for a while, it is likely you will see that for more unfamiliar programming languages or projects, you rely more on semantic memory, whereas for more familiar situations, you use more procedural and episodic memories.

| Program or problem | Procedural | Episodic | Semantic |
|---|---|---|---|
|  |  |  |  |

## 10.3 *Automatization: Creating implicit memories*

Now that we have understood why problem solving is hard, and how different types of memories play a role when solving problems, let's explore how you can improve your problem-solving skills in two ways. The first technique is *automatization*. Once you have practiced a skill so many times that you can do it without thinking about it, like walking, reading, or tying your shoelaces, we say that you have automatized this skill.

Many people have automatized day-to-day skills like driving or biking, but also domain-specific skills like math. For example, you might have learned to factor out equations like $x^2 + y^2 + 2xy$. If you are one of the people who has automatized the distributive law, you can immediately translate this formula to $(x + y)^2$, with no more effort than reading this line. The important thing here is that being able to factor out equations without effort allows you to perform more complex calculations. I often think of automatization as a process that unlocks new skills in a game. Once you can double jump in a game, it allows you to reach areas of a level you could not reach before.

For example, once you can factor out equations with great ease, you can look at an equation like the one that follows and immediately see that the answer is $(x + y)$. If you have not automatized factoring out, this problem will be a lot harder to do, if not impossible.

$$\frac{x2 + y2 + 2xy}{(x + y)}$$

So, automatization of programming skills is key to being able to solve larger and more complex problems. But how do you reach the point of having automatized skills?

To know how to automatize skills, we first need to explore how to strengthen your implicit programming memories. Earlier in the chapter, we discussed the fact that sometimes implicit memories can get in the way when moving to a new programming language, for example, when you keep inserting curly brackets into a Python problem. While you might think that is a small mistake, it does cause some cognitive load. As covered in chapter 9, cognitive load indicates how busy or full your brain is. When you experience too much cognitive load, thinking can become really hard. The interesting thing about implicit memories is that when you have trained implicit memories well enough, it takes your brain hardly any energy to use them. For example, when you know how to bike, or how to touch type, you can do it without any effort. Because these tasks create hardly any cognitive load, you can bike and also eat an ice cream or drive a car while talking.

### 10.3.1  *Implicit memories over time*

The more implicit memories you have for programming, the easier it will be to solve larger problems because you will have more cognitive load to spare. How do you create more implicit memories? To understand that, we have to dive into how they are created in the brain.

In chapter 4 we covered how to create memories, for example, by using a deck of flashcards on which you write facts you want to remember and revisiting those cards often. However, these types of techniques are mainly useful for declarative knowledge. Facts stored in your explicit memory need your explicit attention to be stored. For example, it probably took you some time to memorize that a for-loop in Java is written for (i = 0; i < n; i++){}, and you knew that you really wanted to learn it. This is why we also call it explicit memory; it needs your explicit attention to be stored.

Implicit memories, on the other hand, are created in a different way: by repetition. When you were a kid, you tried to eat soup with a spoon many times, and after a while you knew how to do it. The memory of how to do it was created though practice rather than thinking. That is why we call this implicit memory. Implicit memories are formed in three different phases, as illustrated in figure 10.4.

#### COGNITIVE PHASE

First, someone who is learning something new is in the cognitive phase. In this phase, a new piece of information needs to be split into smaller parts and you have to explicitly think about the task at hand.

For example, when you learned to index a list that is zero-based, you probably needed to spend energy to keep track of that index, as shown in the left-most part of figure 10.4. In the cognitive phase, schemata are formed or updated. For example, when you learned to index a list starting at zero, you already had a schema saved in your brain for counting outside of programming. That schema dictated that counting starts at one and needed to be adapted to also include the possibility of starting at zero.

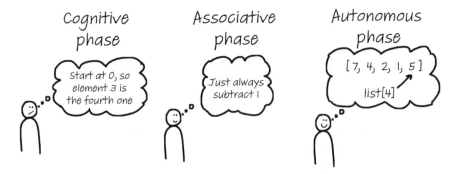

Figure 10.4  The three phases of storing information: cognitive phase, associative phase, and autonomous phase

## ASSOCIATIVE PHASE

The associative phase is next. In this phase you need to actively repeat the new information until patterns of response emerge. You see an opening bracket and get nervous if you do not see the closing one. You might also realize that typing both brackets is a great strategy to not forget the closing one. In other words, effective actions are remembered and ineffective actions are discarded.

The harder a task is, the longer it takes to complete the associative phase. Easier facts or tasks are more quickly remembered. In the example of counting at zero, after a while you might realize that you can simply think of the element you want to retrieve and subtract 1 from it to get to the right index.

## AUTONOMOUS PHASE

Finally, you reach the autonomous phase (also called the procedural phase), where the skill is perfected. For example, you have reached the autonomous phase when you index into a list and you always do it correctly, no matter the context, the data type, or the operations on the list. When you see a list and a list operation, you can now tell its number immediately, without relying on counting or thinking explicitly.

Once you reach the autonomous phase, we say that you have automatized the skill. You can perform the task without any effort, and performing the skill will not add to the cognitive load a problem poses.

To experience the power of automatizing, look at exercise 10.3. If you are an experienced Java programmer, you can probably fill in the blanks in the code without thinking about it. The pattern of a for-loop is so well known you can complete it without thinking about the bounds, even in a slightly more uncommon situation like a reverse loop.

**EXERCISE 10.3** Finish these Java programs by completing the missing pieces on __ as quickly possible:

```
for (int i = ;  __ <= 10; i = i + 1) {
  System.out.println(i);
}

public class FizzBuzz {
    public static void main(String[] args) {
        for (int number = 1; number <= 100; __++) {
            if (number % 15 == 0) {
                System.out.println("FizzBuzz");
            } else if (number % 3 == 0) {
                System.out.println("Fizz");
            } else if (number % 5 == 0) {
                System.out.println("Buzz");
            } else {
                System.out.println(number);
            }
        }
    }
}
```

```
public printReverseWords(String[] args) {
    for (String line : lines) {
        String[] words = line.split("\\s");
        for (int i = words.length - 1; i >= 0; i__)
            System.out.printf("%s ", words[i]);
        System.out.println();
    }
}
```

### 10.3.2  Why automatization will make you program quicker

By creating a large repository of techniques (skeptics might call them tricks), we can create an ever-growing toolbox of new techniques. Gordon Logan, an American psychologist, argues that automatization is done by retrieving memories from the episodic part of the LTM, in which regular memories about daily life are also stored. Executing a task like factoring out an equation or reading a letter creates a new memory, which is an instance of a memory about the task. Because each memory is seen as an instance of an abstract class, like the class "memories about factoring," the theory is called the *instance theory*.

When you are confronted with a similar task, rather than reasoning about the task—as someone might do who lacks enough instance memories—you can remember how you did it before and apply the same method. According to Logan, automatization is complete when you fully rely on episodic memory and do not use any reasoning at all. This automatic performance of tasks is quick and effortless because retrieval from memory is faster than actively thinking of the task at hand and can be done with little or no conscious attention. If you have fully automatized a task, you will also feel no need to go back and check your work, which you might be tempted to do when completing a task by reasoning.

For many of the skills you need for programming and problem solving, you have likely reached the autonomous phase by now. Writing a for-loop, indexing into a list, or creating a class are skills that you have likely automatized. As such, these tasks do not add to your cognitive load while programming.

Depending on your experience and skills, however, there are likely tasks you are still struggling with. As I mentioned before, I personally struggled with the for-loop when I started to learn Python. It was not that I could not remember the for syntax; I had even used flashcards to practice the syntax! However, often when I tried to type the words, for each came out of my fingers rather than for. My implicit memories needed to be rewired. Before we dive into techniques to rewire your memories, it would be a great idea to diagnose your own skills so that you know where to improve.

**EXERCISE 10.4**  Start a new programming session while thinking about the tasks or skills you are using while programming. For each skill, examine at what level you have automatized the skill or task and write the results in the following table. These questions can help you decide the level of your skills:

- Do you need to spend explicit attention to the task at hand in isolation? That means you are still in the cognitive phase.
- Can you do the task but are relying on tricks? You are likely in the associative phase.
- Can you perform the task with ease while also thinking about other problems? You have reached the autonomous phase.

| Task or skill | Cognitive | Associative | Autonomous |
|---|---|---|---|
|  |  |  |  |

### 10.3.3 *Improving implicit memories*

Now that we understand the three different levels at which you can master a skill, let's look at how you can use deliberate practice to improve skills that have not yet reached the autonomous stage. As we covered in chapter 2, the idea of deliberate practice is to use very small tasks and execute them repeatedly until you have reached perfection. For example, in sports interval training, a deliberate way to increase your speed is running, and in music, tone ladders are deliberate practice to train finger placement.

In programming, deliberate practice is not commonly used. When you are struggling with creating for-loops without errors, deliberately typing 100 for-loops is not something commonly done in programming culture. However, building these small skills will help you solve larger problems with greater ease because it frees up cognitive load for those larger problems.

Executing deliberate practice can be done in different ways. First, you can write a lot of similar but different programs for which you need the skill you want to practice. If you are practicing for-loops, for example, write many different forms of for-loops: forward, backward, using a stepper variable with different steps, and so on.

When you are struggling with a more complex programming concept, you can also consider adapting programs rather than writing them from scratch. Adapting programs helps you focus on how new concepts differ from those you already know. For example, if you are struggling with list comprehensions, you can first write many different programs that use loops instead. You subsequently take the programs and adapt the code until they use list comprehensions. It can also work well to revert the changes in the code manually to reflect on the difference from a different perspective. By comparing the different forms of code actively, the equivalence of the programming concepts is strengthened in your memory, as we saw in chapter 3 with the use of flashcards.

Just like with flashcards, spaced repetition is key to learning. Set some time aside every day to practice and continue until you can consistently perform the tasks without any effort. I want to stress again how uncommon this technique is in programming, so it might feel weird, but keep trying. It is really like weight lifting; each repetition makes you a little bit stronger.

## 10.4   *Learning from code and its explanation*

In this chapter we have seen that there is no such thing as generic problem-solving skills and that simply doing a lot programming is unlikely to make you a better problem solver. We have also seen that you can use deliberate practice to improve small programming skills. While mastering small skills at the autonomous level is needed, it is not sufficient to solve larger problems.

A second technique you can use to improve your problem-solving skills is to deliberately study how others have solved problems. Solutions of how other people have solved problems are often called *worked examples*.

Australian professor John Sweller, who also introduced the idea of cognitive load, covered in chapter 4, has extensively researched the importance of domain-specific strategies for problem-solving abilities.

Sweller taught children mathematics by having them solve algebra equations, but soon he grew frustrated by how little they were learning from only working on traditional algebra problems. At that point, Sweller got interested in experimenting with the way problem solving is taught. To gain more insight, Sweller performed a series of experiments in the 1980s. In these experiments, Sweller studied 20 ninth graders (children aged 14–15) in an Australian high school. He divided the students into two groups, who were both asked to solve typical algebra equations, such as "a = 7 – 4a; solve for a."

However, there was a difference between the groups, as illustrated in figure 10.5. Both groups solved the same algebra equations, but group 2 simply solved the equations

**Figure 10.5   Both groups of children solved the same algebra problems, but the left group received recipes, called worked examples, which tell the students how to solve the problem step by step.**

without further help, much like you probably also solved algebra equations in high school. Group 1 received the algebra equations but also received *worked examples* of the equations, which explain how to solve the problems in detail. You can think of worked examples as recipes that describe in detail the steps needed to solve the equations.

After both groups of children finished the equations, Sweller and Cooper compared how the students performed. It probably does not come as a surprise that the first group did better; after all, they got recipes to solve the problems. Group 1 did spectacularly better; they solved the equations five times faster than group 2.

Sweller and Cooper also tested the performance of both groups on different problems because that is what makes some people reluctant to teach with these recipes; the idea that children will only be able to blindly follow the recipes and don't really learn anything. And here is the kicker: the children in group 1 also performed better on different problems, for which calculation rules could be used (which were present in the recipe), like subtracting the same value from both sides of an equation or dividing both sides of the equation by the same.

The worked example effect has been replicated in many studies for different age groups and subjects, including mathematics, music, chess, sports, and programming.

### 10.4.1 A new type of cognitive load: Germane load

To many professional programmers, Sweller's results might have been surprising. We often assume that if we want children to be good problem solvers, we should let them solve problems; if we want to be good programmers, we should program a lot. However, Sweller's results seem to show that is not the case, and we will now dive into the details of why that is true. Why did the group who received the recipes do better than the group who had to solve the problems by themselves? The explanation Sweller offers relates to cognitive load of the working memory.

We have learned these things: the working memory is the STM applied to a given problem. Thus, while the STM can only hold two to six items, as explained in chapter 2, the working memory can only process about two to six slots available to store information.

We have also seen that when the working memory is full, it cannot properly think. There is a second thing the brain cannot do when the working memory is too full: store information back to the LTM. This is illustrated in figure 10.6.

We've reviewed two types of cognitive load: intrinsic load caused by the problem itself and extraneous load caused by the phrasing of the problem. But there is a third type of cognitive load we have not covered: germane cognitive load.

Germane load, which means something like relevant load, is the effort it takes your brain to store information back to the LTM. When all the cognitive load you have room for is filled with intrinsic and extraneous load, there is no room left for germane load; in other words, you cannot remember the problems you have solved and their solutions.

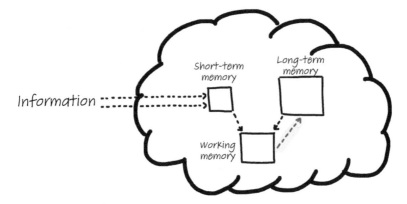

**Figure 10.6   Germane load is needed to enable the highlighted arrow and form the working memory into the LTM. If the working memory is working too hard (that is, experiencing too much load) no information can be stored.**

This is why sometimes after a heavy coding session you are unable to remember what you did. Your brain was so engaged that it could not store the solutions.

Now that you are familiar with the three types of cognitive load, including germane load, we can reconsider the Australian experiment with the ninth graders. We now understand why the group who used the recipes did better at new equations: because their cognitive load was not that high, they could reflect on and remember these recipes. They learned that when solving an algebra problem, it might be a good idea to move part of the equation to the other side of the equal sign, which requires turning a plus into a minus, or that they can always divide both sides by the same values.

The type of skills students learned from the recipes are exactly the type of approaches that come in handy in almost all algebra problems, and thus the first group could also apply them to the new equations. The second group, while engaged in deep thinking, was more focused on the problem at hand rather than on generic rules.

The people who worry about teaching recipes have it backward. I agree, it sounds so sensible: if we want children to be problem solvers, they should solve problems. This same line of thinking is present in the programming community: if you want to be a better programmer, program a lot! Have side projects and just try out things and you will learn. But that seems to not be true.

Although Sweller's experiments focused on math teaching, similar experiments have been done for programming. Those studies showed similar results: kids learn more from reading programs, plus an accompanying explanation, than from programming.[1] As Dutch psychologist Paul Kirschner says, "You don't become an expert by doing expert things."

---

[1] Marcia C. Linn and Michael J. Clancy, "The case for case studies of programming problems," Communications of the ACM, vol. 35, no. 3, 1992, https://dl.acm.org/doi/10.1145/131295.131301.

### 10.4.2 *Using worked examples in your working life*

We have seen that explicitly studying code, and studying the process of how it was created, can help you strengthen your programming skills. There are a number of sources you can use when you study code.

#### COLLABORATE WITH A COLLEAGUE

First, you don't have to study code alone; it is more useful to do it with someone. You could start a code reading club at work with other colleagues who are interested in studying code. If you do it together, it will be easier to keep up the habit of reading code regularly (https://code-reading.org/). If you are in a club, you can exchange code and its explanation and learn from each other.

In chapter 5, we covered techniques to understand code, including making summaries of code. Those summaries can serve as the explanation to use when reading code. You can study your own code and summaries, but it is even more powerful if you use a two-step process where you first write a summary for code you wrote, and then exchange it to learn from the code of a colleague.

#### EXPLORE GITHUB

If you are exploring the practice of code reading alone, luckily there is a plethora of source code and documentation online. GitHub, for example, is an excellent place to start reading code. Just go to the code of a repository you know somewhat, for example a library you use, and read the code. It is best if you choose a repository in which the domain is at least a bit familiar to you, so there are not too many unfamiliar words and concepts causing additional extraneous load, and you can focus on the programming itself.

#### READ BOOKS OR BLOG POSTS ABOUT SOURCE CODE

There are many blog posts that describe how people solved a certain programming problem, and these too can serve as study tools. And although there are not many, there are a few books that also describe code and its explanation; for example, the two volumes of *The Architecture of Open Source Systems* by Amy Brown and Greg Wilson, or *500 Lines or Less* by Amy Brown and Michael DiBernardo.

## Summary

- While many people in programming argue that problem solving is a generic skill, it is not. Your prior knowledge of programming, coupled with the current problem you are solving, influence how quickly you can solve programming problems.
- Your LTM stores different types of memories, which all play a different role when solving problems. The two overarching categories of memories are implicit and explicit memories. Implicit memories are "muscle memories," tasks you can execute without thinking about them, like touch typing. Explicit memories are memories you are aware of that you need to actively recall, such as the syntax of a for-loop.

- To strengthen your implicit memories related to programming, it is best to automatize related skills, such as touch typing and memorizing relevant keyboard shortcuts.
- To strengthen your explicit memories related to programming, study existing code, preferably with an explanation about how the code was designed.

# *Part 4*

# *On collaborating on code*

So far in this book, we've focused on the individual developer. But in reality, software is developed by teams. In the final part of this book we will discuss how to get into the flow state, where you can code without being interrupted by your colleagues. We will also discuss how to create larger systems other people can easily start working in, as well as the process of onboarding.

# The act of writing code

**This chapter covers**

- Comparing different activities people perform while interacting with code
- Examining how to support your brain in performing different activities more effectively
- Exploring how interruptions impact your work as a developer
- Understanding how to use your memory to best recover from an interruption

So far in this book, we have examined what cognitive processes play a role when reading and writing code. In the previous chapters, we looked at how to write code that is easier to read and how to solve problems better.

In this chapter, we direct our attention away from the code itself and instead look at what cognitive processes play a role when you are executing the act of programming. We will first examine what we mean when we say that someone is programming. We will dive into different activities that make up the act of programming and explore how to best support these different activities.

179

Second, we will look at the cognitive implications of a much-dreaded occurrence in the life of programmers: interruptions. We will investigate why interruptions while programming are so annoying and examine what can you do to make them less disruptive. By the end of this chapter you will be better able to support activities of programming and better equipped to deal with interruptions.

## 11.1 Different activities while programming

When you program, there are a lot of different types of things you might be doing. These different activities were first described by British researchers Thomas Green, Alan Blackwell, and Marian Petre (whose work we will cover in more depth in chapter 12) in their cognitive dimensions of notation (CDN) framework, which evaluates the cognitive impact of a programming language or code base and describes five activities: searching, comprehension, transcription, exploration, and incrementation.

Figure 11.1 provides an overview of the five programming activities, what programming tasks you likely do in these activities, and what makes each activity hard.

| Activity | Task | | | | | Hard on |
|---|---|---|---|---|---|---|
| | Executing | Coding | Testing | Reading | Refactoring | |
| Searching | ✓ | | | ✓ | | Short-term memory |
| Comprehension | ✓ | | ✓ | ✓ | ✓ | Working memory |
| Transcribing | | ✓ | | | | Long-term memory |
| Incrementation | ✓ | ✓ | ✓ | ✓ | ✓ | All three |
| Exploration | ✓ | ✓ | ✓ | ✓ | ✓ | All three |

Figure 11.1   An overview of programming activities and the memory systems they use most

### 11.1.1 Searching

Searching in code is the activity where you are looking through a code base, searching for a specific piece of information. This can be the precise location of a bug you need to address, all calls of a certain method, or the location in which a variable should be initialized.

While searching, you will mainly be reading and executing code, potentially using breakpoints and a debugger, or replying on print statements while executing the code. The activity of searching is hard on your STM. You have to remember what you were searching for, what paths in the code you have already explored and why, and what you still need to explore in more depth. Therefore, this activity is best supported by making notes to offload some of the memories to paper or to a separate document on your code. Write down what information you are looking for, where you will search next, and what you have already found.

As discussed earlier, it can sometimes be beneficial to make temporary changes to code to ease a certain task. When searching within code, it can help if you leave little breadcrumbs for yourself in comments indicating why you visited the code. For example, a comment like "I read this method because I thought it might be involved in the initialization of the page class" can help you when you visit the code later on in the same search. This especially matters when you suspect you might not be able to finish the search in one go because a meeting or the end of the workday is approaching. Writing down the steps of the search will help you finish it later.

### 11.1.2 Comprehension

When you are performing the activity of comprehension, you are reading and executing code to gain an understanding of its functionality. It is similar to searching, but with comprehending, you lack a good understanding of what the code does in detail, possibly because it is code you wrote a long time ago or because someone else wrote the code.

As we saw in chapter 5, developers on average spend as much as 58% of their time comprehending existing source code, so this activity is pretty common in your day-to-day life.

In addition to reading and executing code, comprehension can also include running test code to gain a better understanding of the way the code is intended to work. And as we covered in chapter 4, comprehension can also include executing refactorings to make the code easier for you to understand.

Refactoring code helps because comprehension is an activity that is heavy on your working memory. You have to reason about code you do not yet fully understand. As such, supporting the working memory is the best strategy you have when it comes to comprehension. Try to draw a model of the code and update it each time you learn new information. This way, instead of retrieving information from your brain, you can retrieve it from an external source, which is easier. And having a model at hand can also help to detect misconceptions you might hold about the code. Also, should you have to finish the task of comprehension at a later time, all your notes and drawings can help you to get back into the task with more ease.

### 11.1.3 Transcription

Transcription is the activity where you are "just coding." You have a concrete plan of what you want to add or change to the code base, and you are going to do just that. In its most pure form, in transcribing you are just coding and nothing else.

Transcription is mainly hard on the LTM because you will have to be able to recall syntactic constructions for implementation.

### 11.1.4 Incrementation

Incrementation is a mix of searching, comprehension, and transcription. When you are incrementing a code base, you are adding a new feature, which is likely to include both searching for the location(s) to add code and comprehending the existing code to understand where to add code and how to do that, followed by the actual transcribing of the idea into syntax.

Because incrementation is a mix of activities, it can also be hard on all three memory systems. As such, incrementation tasks, which are the most common in a professional programmer's life, have the greatest need of support for the memory systems in the form of notes and refactoring for comprehension.

Your personal experience with the programming language and code base at hand affects which system is most heavily impacted. If you know the programming language well, your LTM might not be working very hard to remember syntax. On the other hand, if you know the code base well, your working memory and STM might not be impacted by searching and comprehending the code.

But if either the code base or the language (or both) is less familiar, incrementation can be a hard task. Where possible, try to split the task of incrementation into separate smaller tasks. Being deliberate about what subtask you are doing can help you support the right memory system. Tell yourself that you will start by searching for the relevant information, then comprehending it, followed by adding the needed code.

### 11.1.5  *Exploration*

The final activity Green, Blackwell, and Petre discuss is exploring code. When you are performing the activity of exploration, you are in essence sketching with code. You might have a vague idea of where you want to go, but by programming you gain clarity about the domain of the problem and about the programming constructs you will need to use.

As in incrementation, when exploring you are probably performing a number of different programming-related tasks in quick succession: writing code, executing the code, running tests to see if you are going in the right direction, reading existing code, and potentially refactoring code to make it more in line with your newly found plans for it.

While exploring, it is likely you heavily rely on tools in the IDE—for example, running tests to see if small changes have impacted any tests, using automated refactoring tools, or relying on "find dependents" to quickly navigate code.

Because exploration also relies on different activities, it is hard on all three memory systems, but especially on the working memory because you are making plans and designs on the fly while programming. While you might feel that documenting your plans will disrupt your flow and slow you down, it can be very helpful to make some rough notes of your design direction or design decisions so you can free up mental space to think about the problem in more depth.

### 11.1.6  *What about debugging?*

When discussing this framework with developers, they often wonder why the activity of debugging is missing. The answer is that when you are debugging, you are often engaging in all five activities. Debugging entails fixing a bug, but it often also includes finding the location of the bug before you can fix it.

Therefore, debugging is often a sequence of exploration, searching, and comprehension, followed by writing code, and can often be described as a mix of the five activities.

**EXERCISE 11.1**  During your next coding session, reflect on the five activities of the CDN framework. What activity are you performing most of the time? What barriers did you encounter while searching, comprehending, transcribing, incrementing, and exploring?

| Activity | Task | Time spent |
| --- | --- | --- |
| Exploration | | |
| Searching | | |
| Comprehension | | |
| Transcription | | |
| Incrementation | | |

## 11.2  Programmer interrupted

Many programmers nowadays work in open plan offices, where distractions are common. What sort of results do these interruptions have on our brains and our productivity? Rini van Solingen, now professor at Delft University of Technology in the Netherlands, studied programmer interruptions as early as the mid-90s.

Van Solingen studied two different organizations and found surprisingly similar results in both organizations. He found that interruptions are common and take 15–20 minutes each. About 20% of a developer's time is spent on interruptions. With the increasing use of Slack and other messaging apps, it is likely that nowadays interruptions are more common.[1]

There is more recent work on interruptions too. Chris Parnin, whose work we briefly covered in chapter 3, also studied interruptions by recording 10,000 programming sessions of 86 programmers. With this study, Parnin confirmed van Solingen's results, finding that interruptions are common. According to Parnin's study,[2] the average programmer will have just one uninterrupted two-hour session in a day. Developers also agree that interruptions are an issue. A study at Microsoft revealed that 62% of developers regard recovering from interruptions as a serious problem.[3]

### 11.2.1  Programming tasks require a warm-up

In chapter 9, we discussed fNIRS devices as a technique to measure cognitive load. With the help of fNIRS, we have gained not only an understanding of what type of code causes cognitive load, but also how cognitive load is distributed over tasks.

---

[1] Rini van Solingen et al., "Interrupts: Just a Minute Never Is," *IEEE Software*, vol. 15, no. 5, https://ieeexplore .ieee.org/document/714843.

[2] Chris Parnin and Spencer Rugaber, "Resumption Strategies for Interrupted Programming Tasks," https:// ieeexplore.ieee.org/document/5090030.

[3] Thomas D. LaToza et al., "Maintaining Mental Models: A Study of Developer Work Habits," https://dl.acm .org/doi/10.1145/1134285.1134355.

In 2014, Takao Nakagawa, a researcher at the NARA Institute of Science and Technology in Japan, measured brain activity with an fNIRS device.[4] Participants in the study were asked to read two versions of an algorithm written in C. One version was a regular implementation, while the second was deliberately made complicated by the researchers. For example, they changed loop counters and other values such that the variables were updated frequently and irregularly. These modifications did not change the functionality of a program.

Nakagawa found two interesting results. First, for 9 out of the 10 participants, there was a large variation in the cognitive load during the task. Programming was not hard all the time; some things were hard, while other things were relatively easy. Second, the researchers also looked at the time in the task where the largest increase in blood flow, and thus in cognitive load, occurred. Their results showed that cognitive load in the middle of the task was highest.

Nakagawa's results might suggest there is a sort of warm-up and cooling down phase in program comprehension tasks, between which the hardest work is performed. Professional programmers will likely recognize this warm-up time that is needed to get "in the zone" to build a mental model of the code and to get ready to start the activity of transcribing. As discussed earlier in the chapter, it can help to actively delineate subactivities in a larger programming task.

### 11.2.2  What happens after an interruption?

Parnin also looked at what happens after an interruption and determined they are, unsurprisingly, quite disruptive to productivity. It takes about a quarter of an hour to start editing code after an interruption. When interrupted during an edit of a method, programmers could resume their work in less than a minute only 10% of the time.

What do people do to get back to the code? From Parnin's results, we can see that the working memory lost vital information about the code programmers were working on. Programmers in his study needed to put in deliberate effort to rebuild the context. They would often navigate to several locations to rebuild context before continuing the programming work. The participants in the study also left breadcrumbs for themselves, for example, by inserting some random characters, causing a compile error, and thus forcing what Parnin called a *roadblock reminder*: a way to ensure that the code would be finished rather than remain in a half-completed state. Some participants also used a source diff between their current version and master as a last-resort way to recover state, but it can be cumbersome to find the actual differences.

---

[4] Takao Nakagawa et al., "Quantifying Programmers' Mental Workload during Program Comprehension Based on Cerebral Blood Flow Measurement: A Controlled Experiment," https://posl.ait.kyushu-u.ac.jp/~kamei/publications/Nakagawa_ ICSENier2014.pdf.

### 11.2.3 *How to better prepare for interruptions*

Now that we know that interruptions are common and hard to recover from, let's examine what happens in your brain when you are interrupted in more depth so that we can better prepare for interruptions. This chapter suggests three techniques to help deal with interruptions.

**STORE YOUR MENTAL MODEL**

Earlier in the book we discussed various techniques that can be used to support the working memory and STM, such as making notes, drawing models, and refactoring code to be easier on

**Figure 11.2   Three techniques to help recover after an interruption**

the brain. These techniques can also be useful for recovering from an interruption.

Nakagawa's results showed a warm-up period in comprehension activities, which is most likely spent on building a mental model of the code at hand. If parts of the model are stored apart from the code, that can help you to quickly regain your mental model. Leaving notes about your mental model in comments is also helpful.

The use of extensive comments has gotten a bad reputation among some developers because code should be "self-documenting," making comments unnecessary. However, code very seldom explains the thought processes of the programmer and thus most often does not adequately represent the mental model of the creator. We are not used to writing down in the code, for example, why a certain approach was chosen, what the goals of the code are, or what alternatives were considered for an implementation. When these kinds of decisions are not written down anywhere, they can at best be implicitly rediscovered, which obviously is a time-consuming process. John Ousterhout nicely describes this in his book *The Philosophy of Software Design* (Yaknyam Press, 2018): "The overall idea behind comments is to capture information that was in the mind of the designer but couldn't be represented in the code."

In addition to being very useful for others reading the code, documenting decisions can also be helpful in storing your own mental model temporarily, making it easier to continue programming at a later time. In his book the *Mythical Man-Month* (Addison-Wesley, 1995), Fred Brooks says that comments are most important in the program comprehension process because they are always present. While notes on paper or in documents are useful, finding relevant documents when you start again can cause extra mental notes.

When you are interrupted and have the option to hold off the interruption for a little while—for example, when it is a Slack message or a colleague at your desk who can wait for a little while, rather than a ringing phone—it can be very useful to just "brain dump" your latest mental model of the code into a comment. It will not always help, but in some cases it might.

## HELP YOUR PROSPECTIVE MEMORY

For the second technique, we have to dive a bit deeper into different types of memories. In chapter 10, we looked at two types of memories: implicit and explicit, or declarative and procedural.

There is one additional type of memory that concerns the future rather than the past, called *prospective memory*, the memory of remembering to do something in the future. This type of memory is closely related to planning and problem solving. When you tell yourself that on the way home you have to remember to pick up some milk at the store, or when you remind yourself to refactor a certain piece of ugly code later, you are using your prospective memory.

How developers support their prospective memory has been the topic of a few studies. Various studies have described how developers have tried to cope with prospective memory failures. For example, developers often add "to-do" comments in the part of the code they are working on to remind them to complete or improve part of the code.[5] Of course, as most programmers have experienced, these to-do comments can linger for a long time and often remain unresolved. Figure 11.3 shows a recent search on GitHub resulting in 136 million code results containing the word "to-do."

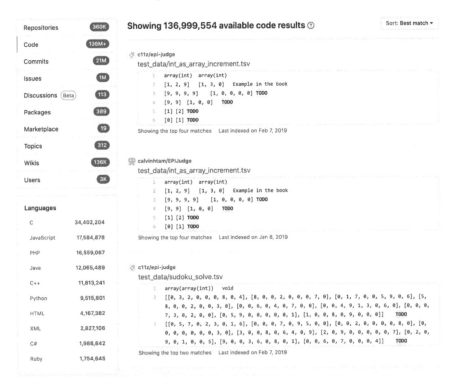

**Figure 11.3    To-do comments can remain in code bases without being resolved.**

---

[5] Margaret Ann Storey et al., "TODO or to Bug: Exploring How Task Annotations Play a Role in the Work Practices of Software Developers," https://dx.doi.org/doi:10.1145/1368088.1368123.

In addition to to-do comments and intentional compile errors, programmers also use techniques that other office workers use: leaving sticky notes on their desk and sending emails to themselves. Paper notes and emails, of course, have the downside of being disconnected from the code base, but can still be helpful.

Parnin also developed a Visual Studio plugin that allows you to support your prospective memory when you have to stop programming.[6] For example, it allows you to add to-do items to your code and give them an expiration date so you do not forget to work on tasks.

### LABEL SUBGOALS

A third practice that can help protect against interruptions is called subgoal labeling, in which you explicitly write down into what small steps a problem can be divided. For example, when parsing and restructuring text, these steps could be

1 Parse text and receive parse tree.
2 Filter the parse tree.
3 Flatten tree back into text format.

While these steps in themselves are not hard to imagine or to remember, when you are interrupted in between them, it can be cumbersome to return to the code and remember what you were planning to do. If I program a larger task, I try to start with writing the steps in my code as comments, like this:

```
# parse text
# receive parse tree
# filter the parse tree and
# flatten tree back into text format
```

This way, I can fill out small parts of the code, and I always have a plan to fall back on. A study on programmers by Lauren Margulieux, professor of learning technologies in the Department of Learning Sciences at Georgia State University, showed that when you provide subgoals, programmers use them in mentally organizing the solution.[7]

Subgoals are useful for organizing your own thinking after an interruption, but are also useful in other situations. For example, some of the subgoals placed in the code can remain as comments and serve as documentation later on. They can also be used in collaboration where a senior programmer designs the subgoals and other programmers implement parts of a larger solution.

## 11.2.4 *When to interrupt a programmer*

In chapter 9, we covered various ways to detect cognitive load that people experience, including questionnaires and brain-based metrics. But there are other ways to access the cognitive load a certain task creates.

---

[6] https://marketplace.visualstudio.com/items?itemName=chrisparnin.attachables.
[7] Lauren E. Margulieux et al., "Subgoal-Labeled Instructional Material Improves Performance and Transfer in Learning to Develop Mobile Applications," https://doi.org/10.1145/2361276.2361291.

One example is to use a *dual-task measure*. A dual task is a second task a participant performs while working on the original task. For example, when solving a mathematical equation, at random times a letter A will appear on the screen. Whenever the A appears, the participant needs to click the A as soon as possible. How quickly and accurately a participant can perform the second task is a good measure of how much cognitive load is experienced. Researchers have shown that a dual-task measurement can be a good way to estimate cognitive load. There are downsides to using a dual task, too, as you might imagine; the second task itself can also add cognitive load, interfering with the original task.

Using a dual-task measurement, research has explored the connection between cognitive load and interruptions. Brian P. Bailey, a professor of computer science at the University of Illinois, has devoted a large part of his career to understanding the cause and effect of interruptions.

In a study from 2001,[8] 50 participants were asked to perform a primary task while being interrupted. The experiment used different types of tasks, from counting the occurrence of words in a grid to reading some text and answering questions about the text. While executing these primary tasks, participants were interrupted by irrelevant information such as breaking news headlines and stock market updates. This study was run as a controlled experiment, with two groups. One group received the interruptions during a primary task, while the other group received them after completing a task.

While Bailey's results were not surprising, they do offer a deeper insight into disruptions. Bailey found that it takes longer to complete an interrupted task than a non-interrupted task (without counting the time of the actual interruption), and that people perceive interrupted tasks to be more difficult to complete than a noninterrupted task.

Bailey did not only measure the time and difficulty of tasks; he also investigated the emotional state of participants. Participants answered questions on their annoyance and anxiety levels each time an interrupting task would appear. The results of these questions showed that the level of annoyance experienced is influenced when the interrupting task is displayed. Participants in the group where the interruptions appeared during the primary task were more annoyed than in the group that saw the interruptions after a task. The same was true for anxiety. Participants whose primary task was disrupted experienced more anxiety. A follow-up study from 2006 that used a very similar setup revealed interrupted people also make twice as many mistakes.[9]

Based on these results, we could conclude that it could help for programmers, who will unavoidably be interrupted now and then, to be interrupted at more convenient

---

[8] Brian P. Bailey et al., "The Effects of Interruptions on Task Performance, Annoyance, and Anxiety in the User Interface," http://mng.bz/G6KJ.

[9] Brian P. Bailey, "On the Need for Attention-Aware Systems: Measuring Effects of Interruptions on Task Performance, Error Rate, and Affective State," Computers in Human Behavior, vo. 22, no. 4, pp. 685–708, 2006, http://mng.bz/zGAA.

times (for example, after having completed a task). Based on this idea, Manuela Züger, then a PhD student at the university of Zurich, developed an interactive light called the FlowLight.

The FlowLight (https://emea.embrava.com/pages/flow) is a physical light a developer can place on their desk or on top of their screen. Based on computer interactions, like typing speeds and mouse clicks, FlowLight detects whether the programmer is deeply engaged in a task and experiencing high cognitive load. Colloquially this state is sometimes also called being "in the flow" or "in the zone." When the programmer is very much in the zone and should not be interrupted, the FlowLight will blink red. With a little bit less activity, FlowLight will glow continuously red. If a developer seems available, the light turns green.

Züger tried out the FlowLight in a large-scale field study with over 400 participants from 12 countries and found that the FlowLight can reduce interruptions by 46%. Many participants in the study kept using the FlowLight after the experiment ended, and the FlowLight is now available as a commercial product.[10]

### 11.2.5 Some thoughts on multitasking

While reading about interruptions, you might have pondered the concept of multitasking. Are disruptions really that bad? Can't our brains do multiple things at the same time, like a multicore processor?

#### MULTITASKING AND AUTOMATIZING

Sadly, there is overwhelming evidence that people cannot multitask while doing deep cognitive tasks. This might not be all that convincing, because you might be reading this book while listening to music, or listening to this book while running or knitting, so how can I say that a person cannot do two things at the same time?

Remember the three phases of storing information: cognitive, associative, and autonomous. Let's phrase it differently: you cannot do two or more tasks at the same time when you have not reached the autonomous phase for them. Reading English is probably not something you still need to learn, so you can do it while engaging in other tasks you have also automatized, like knitting. Sometimes, though, when you are reading a passage that is especially hard because it contains many new ideas, you feel the need to turn down the music to be able to focus better. This is your brain telling itself you cannot multitask, and this is why people also feel compelled to turn down the radio when they park their car.

If you do not believe your own brain, there is some science that shows multitasking does not work as well as you might think.

---

[10]Manuela Züger, "Reducing Interruptions at Work: A Large-Scale Field Study of FlowLight," https://www.zora.uzh.ch/id/eprint/136997/1/FlowLight.pdf.

### RESEARCH ON MULTITASKING

In 2009, Annie Beth Fox, now professor of quantitative methods at the Massachusetts General Hospital's Institute of Health Professions,[11] compared students who were reading a text while also using an instant messenger to students who were fully focused on the text. While both groups understood the text equally well, the group that was interrupted by messages needed about 50% more time for both reading the text and answering questions about it afterward.

Dutch psychologist Paul Kirschner performed a study in 2010 with about 200 students in which he asked them about their Facebook habits. Heavy Facebook users studied just as long as nonusers, but heavy users had a significantly lower grade average. This was especially true for students who reported replying to messages immediately after they came in. The interesting thing is that people who multitask often feel very productive.[12]

In a controlled experiment where students were performing a task while also communicating with a partner using online messaging, students themselves found their performance satisfactory, but their partners gave them a much lower rating. This is likely to mean that programming while also chatting on Slack might not be the best way to get work done.[13]

## Summary

- When you are programming, you perform a combination of different programming activities: searching, comprehending, transcription, incrementation, and exploration. Each activity puts pressure on different memory systems. Therefore, each activity should be supported by different techniques.
- Interruptions while you are programming are not only annoying; they are detrimental to productivity because it takes time to rebuild your mental model of the code.
- To better deal with interruptions, offload mental models into notes, documentation, or comments.
- Deliberately support your prospective memory if you cannot complete a task by documenting your plans.
- Try to limit interruptions to moments you experience low cognitive load, for example, through automation using a FlowLight or manually by setting your status in Slack.

---

[11]Annie Beth Fox et al., "Distractions, Distractions: Does Instant Messaging Affect College Students' Performance on a Concurrent Reading Comprehension Task? *Cyberpsychology and Behavior*, vol. 12, pp. 51–53, 2009. https://doi.org/10.1089/cpb.2008.0107.

[12]Paul A. Kirschner and Aryn C. Karpinski, "Facebook® and Academic Performance," *Computers in Human Behavior*, vol. 26, no. 6, pp. 1237–1245, 2010, http://mng.bz/jBze.

[13]LingBei Xu, "Impact of Simultaneous Collaborative Multitasking on Communication Performance and Experience, 2008, http://mng.bz/EVNR.

# Designing and
# improving larger systems

## 12

## This chapter covers

- Examining what effect different design decisions have on the understandability of codebases
- Exploring trade-offs between different design decisions
- Improving the design of existing codebases for better cognitive processing

So far in this book, we have discussed how to best read and write code. To do so, we have examined how cognitive processes play a role when reading and writing code. For larger codebases, however, it is not just small parts of code that influence how easy it is for people to comprehend it. The way in which you organize code also greatly influences how easily other people can interact with the code. This is especially true for code in libraries, frameworks, and modules that other programmers use rather than change.

Often when we talk about libraries, frameworks, and modules, we talk about their technical aspects, like the language they are created in. However, codebases

191

can also be viewed through a cognitive lens. In this chapter we will discuss CDN, which is a technique to examine codebases from a cognitive perspective. CDN helps you answer questions about existing large codebases, such as "Will this code be easy for people to change?" or "Will this codebase be easy for people to find information in?" Examining codebases from a cognitive rather than technical perspective can help you gain a better perspective on how people interact with your code.

Once we have discussed CDN and studied how it can support our understanding of codebases, we will dive into how to use it to improve the design of existing codebases using an adapted framework called *cognitive dimensions of codebases* (CDCB).

In the previous chapter we described five different programming activities. This chapter will also examine how properties of a codebase influence the different programming activities in different ways.

## 12.1  *Examining the properties of codebases*

Often when we talk about libraries, frameworks, and modules, we talk about their technical aspects. We commonly say things like "This library is written in Python," "This framework uses node.js," or "This module is precompiled."

When we discuss programming languages, we also often look at the technical domain, for example their paradigm (object-oriented, functional, or a mix of both), perhaps the existence of a type system, or whether the language is compiled to byte code or interpreted by a program in another language. You can also look at where the language, framework, or library can run; for example, does this program run in the browser or on a virtual machine? All these aspects concern the technical domain (that is, what the language can do).

However, when we discuss different libraries, frameworks, modules, or programming languages, we can also discuss what they do to your brain rather than your computer.

> **EXERCISE 12.1**  Think of a codebase you recently used that you did not write yourself. This can be a library you use, of which you had to read the code to understand how to call a function, or a framework in which you fixed a bug.

Now consider these questions:

- What made performing your task easier (for example, the presence of documentation, good variables names, comments)?
- What made performing your task harder (for example, complex code or lack of documentation)?

### 12.1.1  *Cognitive dimensions*

CDN can be used to assess the usability of existing large codebases. It was originally created by British researchers Thomas Green, Alan Blackwell, and Marian Petre and consists of a number of different dimensions, each of which represents a different way to examine the codebase at hand. The dimensions were originally created to examine visualizations such as flowcharts, and were later applied to programming languages, also, hence the name. Programming languages, like flowcharts, can be seen as notations, a way to express thoughts and ideas.

The dimensions as Green, Blackwell, and Petre describe them apply only to notations, but in this book we generalize the use of CDN to codebases rather than programming languages. We call this version cognitive dimensions of code bases (CDCB) and use it to examine a codebase to understand how it can be understood and improved. CDCB is especially useful for code written in libraries and frameworks, which other programmers often call rather than adapt.

We will first discuss each of the dimensions in isolation and then dive into how the different dimensions interact with each other and how we can use them to improve existing codebases.

## ERROR PRONENESS

The first dimension to discuss is called *error proneness*. In some programming languages it is easier to make a mistake than in other languages. JavaScript is currently one of the most popular languages, but it is known to have a few eccentric corner cases.

In JavaScript and other dynamically typed languages, variables are not initialized with a type when they are created. Because it is unclear what the type of an object is at runtime, programmers can become confused about the types of variables that are leading to errors. Also, unexpected coercion of a variable of one type into another type can cause errors. Languages that have strong type systems, such as Haskell, are thought of as being less error-prone because the type system will provide guidance when coding.

Codebases, rather than programming languages, can also be error-prone, for example because of inconsistent conventions, a lack of documentation, or vague names.

Sometimes, codebases inherit dimensions from the programming language that they were created in. For example, a module written in Python could be more error-prone than a very similar library written in C because Python does not have a type system as strong as C's to catch errors.

> **TYPE SYSTEMS DO PREVENT ERRORS** You might wonder whether it is true that type systems prevent errors. In an extensive set of experiments comparing Java to Groovy, German researcher Stefan Hanenberg demonstrated that type systems can indeed help programmers locate and fix errors more quickly. In many cases in Hanenberg's experiments, the place in the code where the compiler pointed out an error was the same as where the code would crash at runtime. Running code, of course, takes more time, and as such relying on errors at runtime is generally slower.
>
> Hanenberg tried various methods to improve dynamically typed code to make it less error-prone, including better IDE support and documentation, but even in those situations, static-type systems outperformed dynamic ones in terms of time and accuracy of programmers finding bugs.

## CONSISTENCY

Another way to examine how people will interact with a programming language or codebase is *consistency*: How similar are similar things? Are names always structured in the same way, for example, using the same name molds we discussed in chapter 8? Is the layout of code files similar for different classes?

An example of a situation where many programming languages show consistency is in the definition of functions. Maybe you never thought of this, but built-in functions typically have the same user interface as user-defined functions. When you are looking at a function call like `print()` or `print_customer()`, you cannot see from the call who created the function, the creator of the programming language, or the code creator.

A framework or language that is inconsistent in its use of names and conventions might lead to greater cognitive load because it will take your brain more energy to understand what is what, and it might take you more time to find relevant information.

Consistency is related to error-proneness, as we saw in chapter 9. Code in which linguistic antipatterns occur (for example, names do not match the implementation of the code) are more error-prone and cause greater cognitive load.

## DIFFUSENESS

In an earlier chapter we covered code smells, which can make code harder to read. A well-known code smell is a long method, in which a method of a function consists of a lot of code lines, making it harder to understand.

A long method can be the programmer's fault if they added unnecessary complexity to a method or tried to fit too much functionality into one method. However, some programming languages also need more space than others for the same functionality. The dimension diffuseness covers this. Diffuseness refers to how much room or space a programming construct takes.

For example, a for-loop in Python looks like this:

```
for i in range(10):
    print(i)
```

In C++, the same code would be

```
for (i=0; i<10; i++){
    cout << i;
}
```

Simply counting the lines of code, C++ has three lines, while Python has two. However, diffuseness does not only concern the number of lines of code; you could also consider how many chunks the code consists of. If you count the individual elements, which you might chunk if you are a novice, then the Python code has seven elements, while the C++ code contains nine, as illustrated in figure 12.1.

**Figure 12.1   Different chunks in a simple for loop Python (top) and C++(bottom)**

This difference between the number of chunks lies in the fact that there are elements in the C++ code that are not present in the Python version (for example, i++).

We too might have more and less diffuse versions of the same code within the same programming language. We covered the example of list comprehensions in Python in earlier chapters; here again are two Python code snippets that do the same thing:

```
california_branches = []
for branch in branches:
  if branch.zipcode[0] == '9'
    california_branches.append(branch)
```

```
california_branches = [b for b in branches if b.zipcode[0] == '9']
```

The second version of the code is less diffuse, which might impact readability and understandability.

### HIDDEN DEPENDENCIES

The *hidden dependencies* dimension indicates to what extent dependencies are visible to the user. An example of a system with high hidden dependencies is an HTML page with a button controlled by JavaScript, which is stored in a different file. It can be hard to see from the JavaScript file what HTML pages call the function in such a situation. Another example is requirements for files separate from code files. From the codebase it might be hard to see all libraries and frameworks that need to be installed for the code to properly run.

In general, in code the functions that are being called within another function or class are more visible than the other way around: which functions or classes call a given function. In the first case, we can always read a function text and see what functions are being called in the body.

While modern IDEs can reveal hidden dependencies, as shown in figure 12.2, finding the dependencies still requires the use of mouse clicks or shortcuts.

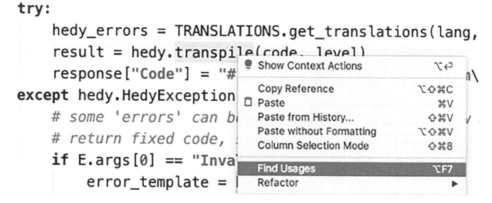

**Figure 12.2**  Option in PyCharm to find all call locations of a given function

Creators of code can compensate for hidden dependencies with more extensive documentation. Teams might consider having a policy for discussing and adopting new dependencies as well as documenting them when the adoption occurs.

### PROVISIONALITY

The dimension of *provisionality* describes how easy it is to think while using the tool. As we covered in chapter 11, sometimes you are programming in an exploratory way when you are not yet sure what exactly you are creating. When you are exploring, you might use pen and paper or whiteboards. These are tools that have ultimate provisionality because you can sketch freely, write down all sorts of annotations, and write incomplete or wrong code without any issues.

When we start coding in a codebase, however, we lose some freedom. If we write code that has syntax errors, it cannot by type checked, and if it does not type check, the code cannot be run. While it is useful to have these types of checks in place, they can hamper our ability to try things and use code as a means of thought rather than an execution model.

If a codebase or programming language is very strict (for example, using types, assertions, and post conditions), it can be hard to use code to express a thought. We then say this tool has low provisionality.

Provisionality is an essential factor in learnability because expressing vague ideas and incomplete code might be needed if you are a beginner in a certain system. Thinking of a plan for your code while also thinking about types and syntax can cause too much cognitive load in beginners.

### VISCOSITY

Related to provisionality is *viscosity*: how hard it is to make changes in a certain system. Typically, codebases written in dynamically typed languages are a bit easier to change. You can simply change code and do not have to change all corresponding type definitions. Code that is not very modular and contains large blocks of code can also be easier to change because it can be changed directly, and you do not have to make changes in multiple places to multiple functions or classes.

Whether a system is easy to change depends not only on the programming language and the codebase itself; factors surrounding the codebase also impact viscosity. For example, if it takes a long time for a codebase to compile or run tests, that adds to each change's viscosity.

### PROGRESSIVE EVALUATION

A dimension related to provisionality is *progressive evaluation*. The dimension of progressive evaluation describes how easy it is in a given system to check or execute partial work. As we have seen, a system with a lot of provisionality allows the user to sketch out incomplete ideas. A system with progressive evaluation allows the user to also execute incomplete or imperfect code.

Some programming systems allow programmers to do *live programming*: the programmer can change and then rerun code without stopping the code's execution. An example of such a programming system is Smalltalk.

Smalltalk was the first language tool to support live programming and allowed on-the-fly inspection and code changes during execution of code. Scratch, a programming language for children heavily inspired by Smalltalk, also allows kids to change code without recompiling.

When designing a codebase or library, you can also allow users to run partial code and gain insight into it. An example of a design that allows for progressive evaluation is the use of optional parameters. When a function has optional parameters, a user of the library can first compile and run the code with the default values, and then update the parameters one by one while the system is in a working state at every step of the way. Another example is Idris's hole system, which lets you run partial code, after which the compiler suggests valid solutions that could fit the hole. You can then iterate and refine your types, which then leads to smaller holes, and the compiler becomes a tool to explore the solution rather than a constraint that blocks the exploration.

A system with less progressive evaluation does not allow the user to run code in a less than complete or perfect state, which might inhibit provisionality.

### ROLE EXPRESSIVENESS

The dimension of *role expressiveness* indicates how easy it is to see the role of different code parts in a program. A simple example of role expressiveness is the fact that in almost all programming languages, calls of functions without parameters are still written with two round brackets at the end; for example, `file.open()`. While the language designers could have decided that users are allowed to omit the brackets, the brackets now indicate that `open()` is a function. Brackets at the end of a function are an example of role expressiveness.

Another famous example of role expressiveness is syntax highlighting. Many IDEs color variables differently from keywords, which also helps you to see the roles different code elements play in a program.

Role expressiveness can also be achieved with syntax. For example, calling a function that returns a Boolean value `is_set` rather than `set` helps the reader to understand the role of the variable.

We saw a similar concept in chapter 9, in linguistic antipatterns. When a codebase suffers from linguistic antipatterns, constructs like functions and methods mislead the reader about their role. This means the codebase has lower role expressiveness and can be harder to understand.

### CLOSENESS OF MAPPING

The dimension *closeness of mapping* means how close the programming language or the code is to the domain in which problems are solved. Some programming languages have a good closeness of mapping. From chapter 1 on, we have seen the programming language APL, shown again in the next listing. While you might have thought APL was a very confusing language, it, in fact, has a great closeness of mapping to the domain of vector calculus.

---

**Listing 12.1   Binary representation in APL**

```
2 2 2 2 2 T n
```
A program converting number n into binary representation in APL. The confusion here lies in the fact that you might not know what T means.

For example, all variables are by default vectors, as we can see in listing 12.1 from the fact that T works on the list of 2s. This design is nice if you are used to thinking in vectors and if the problems you are solving can often be solved with the use of vector calculus. COBOL is also often named as a language with a good closeness of mapping to the domain of business and finance. Excel is another example of a programming language with a good closeness of mapping. The layout in rows and columns is precisely how financial calculations were done even before we had computers.

Most modern programming languages, including Java, Python, and JavaScript, do not have a good closeness of mapping; there aren't any problems we can't solve with these languages. Of course, that is not always a bad thing. It can be very helpful to be able to solve any given problem with Python or Java, and to not have to learn a new programming language for each new project or customers.

Codebases can also have a good closeness of mapping to their business domain. Codebases that reuse concepts and words of their target domain are typically easier to understand for customers than codebases that use more generic terms. For example, a method called `executeQuery()` has a lower closeness of mapping than the function `findCustomers()`.

In our field over the last few years, we have seen a growing interest in better incorporating domain into code. For example, the domain-driven design philosophy prescribes that the structure and identifiers in code should match the business domain. This is a move toward better closeness of mapping in codebases.

**EXERCISE 12.2**   Make a list of all variable, function, and class names in your codebase. For each of the names, investigate the closeness of mapping. You can ask yourself these questions for each identifier name:

- Is the variable name expressed in the language of the domain?
- Is it clear what process outside the code this name refers to?
- Is it clear what object outside the code this name refers to?

**HARD MENTAL OPERATIONS**

Some systems require a user to think very hard, to perform *hard mental operations* outside of the system. For example, a language like Haskell requires a user to think about types of all functions and parameters. You cannot ignore type signatures of functions or it will be close to impossible to write working code in Haskell. Similarly, C++ requires the user to use pointers in many situations and reason with them rather than objects.

Hard mental operations are, of course, not all bad. The thinking you require a user to do might pay off, for example, in fewer errors in a strict type system or in better performance or more efficient memory usage in pointers.

However, when you ask the user to perform these hard mental operations in a system you design, you have to be aware of this and consider the operations with great care.

Examples of hard mental operations people might perform within a codebase are often situations that ask a lot of the memory of users. For example, asking users to memorize a large number of parameters to call in the right order is a hard mental operation because it places a heavy demand on STM.

We saw that vague function names have poor closeness of mapping. These names also create hard mental work. Having to memorize non-informative names of functions like execute() or control() require these functions to be stored in the user's LTM and thus can also be hard mental operations.

Finally, some operations are hard because they take a toll on the working memory, for example, if data has to be downloaded from two difference sources in two different formats and converted into a third format. The user will then have to keep track of the different streams and their corresponding types.

## SECONDARY NOTATION

The *secondary notation* dimension indicates the possibility for the programmer to add extra meaning to code, which is not in the formal specification. The most commonly occurring example of secondary notation is the possibility to add comments to source code. Comments are not formally part of the language, at least not in the sense that they change the behavior of the program. However, comments can help readers of code understand it better. Another example of secondary notation is named parameters in Python. As shown in the next listing, arguments can be passed together with a name, and in that case, the order of the parameters may be different at the call site than in the function definition.

---

**Listing 12.2  Keyword (named) parameters in Python**

```
def move_arm(angle, power):
    robotapi.move(angle,power)
# three different ways to call move_arm
move(90, 100)
move(angle = 90, power = 100)
move(power = 100, angle = 90)
```

**Python program demonstrating three different ways to call a function: with the arguments in order, with names in order, or with names in any order.**

---

Adding a named parameter to a function call in Python does not change the way the code is executed, but it does enable the IDE to express the role of each parameter when the function is called.

### ABSTRACTION

The *abstraction* dimension describes whether a user of your system can create their own abstractions that are as powerful as the built-in abstractions. An example of abstractions that most programming languages allow for is the creation of functions, objects, or classes. Programmers can create functions, which are in many ways similar to built-in functions. User-defined functions can have input and output parameters and work in the same way as regular functions. The fact that users can create functions means that users can shape the language with their own building blocks and add their own abstractions. While the power to make your own abstractions is now available in almost any language, many programmers today have never worked in prestructured programming systems like assembly, or some BASIC dialect where such abstraction mechanisms weren't available.

Libraries and frameworks can also offer their users the option to create their own abstractions. For example, allowing a library user to create a subclass to which additional functionality can be added has more power of abstraction than a library that just allows API calls.

### VISIBILITY

*Visibility* indicates how easy it is to see different parts of a system. In a codebase, it can be hard to see what classes the codebase consists of, especially if code is divided over different files.

Libraries or frameworks can also offer their users different levels of visibility. For example, an API that fetches data might return a string, a JSON file, or an object, which each have a different visibility. If a string is returned, it is harder to see the form of the data, and the framework offers the user lower visibility.

## 12.1.2 *Using CDCB to improve your codebase*

We have looked at different dimensions that programs can have. These differences can greatly impact how people interact with a codebase. For example, if a codebase has a high viscosity, future developers working on the codebase might be reluctant to make changes. This can lead to more complicated patches rather than deep changes to the codebase structure. If an open source codebase requires hard mental operations, people might be less likely to become maintainers. Therefore, it is important to gain a sense of how your codebase is performing on the different dimensions.

The list of cognitive dimensions can be used as a sort of a checklist for a codebase. Not all dimensions matter for all codebases, but regularly investigating each one and deciding how your codebase is doing will help you maintain useability. Ideally you analyze the dimensions of a codebase on a regular basis (for example, once a year).

> **EXERCISE 12.3** Fill out the following table to gain an understanding of the dimensions at play. What dimensions matter to your codebase? Which of those can be improved?

| Dimension | Relevant? | Could be improved? |
|---|---|---|
| Error-proneness | | |
| Consistency | | |
| Visibility | | |
| Hidden dependencies | | |
| Provisionality | | |
| Viscosity | | |
| Progressive evaluation | | |
| Role expressiveness | | |
| Closeness of mapping | | |
| Hard mental operation | | |
| Secondary notation | | |
| Abstraction | | |
| Visibility | | |

### 12.1.3 Design maneuvers and their trade-offs

Making changes to a codebase to improve a certain dimension in a codebase is called a *design maneuver*. For example, adding types to a codebase is a design maneuver that improves error proneness, and changing function names to be more in line with the domain of the code is a design maneuver that improves closeness of mapping.

**EXERCISE 12.4** Examine the list you created in exercise 12.3 for the dimensions that could be improved. Do you see design maneuvers you could apply? What would the effect of those maneuvers be on other dimensions?

| Dimension | Design maneuver | Impacts dimensions positively? | Impacts dimensions negatively? |
|---|---|---|---|
| | | | |
| | | | |

Often a design maneuver (that is, a change to one dimension) causes changes to another dimension. How the dimensions interact precisely can depend heavily on your codebase, but there are a few dimensions that are often at odds with each other.

### ERROR PRONENESS VS. VISCOSITY

If you want to prevent the user of your library or framework from making errors, you will often do that by making the user enter additional information. The most well-known example of a dimension that decreases error proneness is allowing a user to add types to entities. If the compiler knows the type of an entity, that information can be used to prevent mistakes, such as accidentally adding a list to a string.

However, when everything in a system is typed, this might present the user with extra work. For example, you might need to cast variables to a different type to be allowed to use them in the way you want. When people dislike type systems, even in light of their benefit in preventing types, that is often because of the extra viscosity a type system adds.

### PROVISIONALITY AND PROGRESSIVE EVALUATION VS. ERROR-PRONENESS

A system with a lot of provisionality and progressive evaluation allows the user to sketch out and execute incomplete or imperfect code. While those dimensions might help someone think about the problem at hand, incomplete programs might not be deleted, and imperfect programs might never be improved, leading to code that is hard to understand and thus hard to debug, impacting error-proneness.

### ROLE EXPRESSIVENESS VS. DIFFUSENESS

We have seen that role expressiveness can be created by adding additional syntactic elements such as names parameters. However, the extra labels cause the code to be longer. The same is true for type annotations, which also express the roles that variables play, but increase a codebase's size.

## 12.2   Dimensions and activities

In the previous chapter, we discussed five different programming activities: searching, comprehension, transcription, incrementation, and exploration. Each activity places different constraints on the cognitive dimensions a codebase needs to optimize for. The relationship between dimensions and activities is shown in table 12.1.

### 12.2.1   Impact of dimensions on different activities

In chapter 11, we described five different activities people do when they program. In fact, these activities also stem from the original version of the CDN framework. Blackwell, Petre, and Green described these activities because the different activities interact with the dimensions. Some activities require a certain dimension to be high, while others work best if a dimension is low, as shown in table 12.1.

### SEARCHING

When searching, some dimensions play an important role. For example, hidden dependencies can harm the activity of searching, because if you do not know what code is called from where, it can be hard to decide what to read next and thus slow down the search. Diffuseness causes code to be longer, which also harms search simply because there is more code to search through.

On the other hand, secondary notation can help searching because comments and variable names can indicate where information can be found.

## COMPREHENSION

Some dimensions are especially important when comprehending code. For example, low visibility in a codebase can harm comprehension because it makes it harder to see, and thus understand, how classes and function relate to each other.

Role expressiveness, on the other hand, can help comprehension. If the type and role of variables and other entities is clear, comprehension can be easier.

## TRANSCRIPTION

When transcribing (that is, implementing a feature based on a predefined plan) some dimensions that are otherwise good can be harmful—for example, consistency. While a consistent codebase can be easier to comprehend, you will have to make the new code fit into the codebase when implementing a new feature, which can lead to extra mental effort. Of course, that effort might be worth it in the long run, but it is still effort that needs to be spent.

## INCREMENTATION

Adding new features to a codebase is mostly supported by closeness of mapping to the domain. If the codebase enables thinking about the code's goal, rather than about programming concepts, it will be easier to add new code. Codebases with high viscosity, on the other hand, makes adding code harder.

## EXPLORATION

Exploring new design ideas while in the codebase (i.e., exploring) is supported most by systems that have good provisionality and progressive evaluation.

Hard mental operations and abstractions can harm exploration because they place a high cognitive load on the programmer, limiting the load that can be spent on exploring the problem and solution space.

**Table 12.1  Overview of dimensions and the activities that they support or harm**

| Dimension | Helps | Harms |
| --- | --- | --- |
| Error-proneness | | Incrementation |
| Consistency | Searching, comprehension | Transcription |
| Diffuseness | Searching | |
| Hidden dependencies | | Searching |
| Provisionality | Exploration | |
| Viscosity | | Transcription, incrementation |
| Progressive evaluation | Exploration | |
| Role expressiveness | Comprehension | |

**Table 12.1  Overview of dimensions and the activities that they support or harm (continued)**

| Dimension | Helps | Harms |
|---|---|---|
| Closeness of mapping | Incrementation | |
| Hard mental operations | | Transcription, incrementation, exploration |
| Secondary notation | Searching | |
| Abstraction | Comprehension | Exploration |
| Visibility | | Comprehension |

### 12.2.2  *Optimizing your codebase for expected activities*

We have seen that different activities place different constraints on a system. Therefore, you must understand the most likely actions people will perform in your codebase. Relatively old and stable libraries are more likely to be searched through than incremented ones, while new apps are more likely to be incremented and transcribed. This means that over the lifetime of a codebase, design maneuvers might be needed to make the codebase more in line with most likely activities.

> **EXERCISE 12.5**  Think of your codebase. What activities are most likely to occur? Have the activities been stable over the past few months? What dimensions play a role is these activities, and how does your codebase perform on these dimensions?

## Summary

- CDN is a framework that helps programmers predict the cognitive effect programming languages will have on their users.
- CDCB is an extension of CDN that helps programmers understand the impact their codebases, libraries, and frameworks will have on their users.
- In many cases, trade-offs between different dimensions must be made. Improving one dimension might decrease another dimension.
- Improving the design of existing codebases according to the notations framework's cognitive dimension can be done with a design maneuver.
- Different activities place different demands on the dimensions a codebase optimizes for.

# How to onboard
# new developers

*13*

**This chapter covers**

- Comparing the ways experts and beginners think
- Improving onboarding new developers into a codebase
- Supporting new developers while learning to use a new programming language or framework

So far we have examined how to read and organize code. As a more senior developer, however, you will likely struggle with your own confusion and the confusion of other more junior people you work with. In many cases, you will want to manage the cognitive load junior people are experiencing to make sure they learn more effectively.

In this chapter, we will examine how to improve your onboarding process, whether that concerns onboarding an experienced developer into an unfamiliar codebase or a novice programmer.

To do so, first examine how experts and beginners think and behave differently. We will then cover a variety of activities a team can perform to onboard new team

205

members. By the end of this chapter, you will be familiar with three techniques and activities to support newcomers more effectively.

## 13.1   *Issues in the onboarding process*

As a more senior developer, you likely have encountered several scenarios in which you had to onboard newcomers. This can be a newcomer to a team or to an open source project. Many programmers are not necessarily trained in teaching or mentoring, making the onboarding process frustrating for both sides. In this chapter, we will dive into what happens in the brains of newcomers during the onboarding process and how you can better manage that process.

Onboarding processes I have witnessed worked more or less as follows:

- A senior developer throws lots of new information at a newcomer. The amount of information is too much to process, causing high cognitive load. For example, the onboarder introduces new people, the codebase's domain, the workflow, and the codebase all at once.
- After the introduction, the senior developer asks the newcomer a question or gives the newcomer a task. The senior developer often sees this as something extremely simple, for example, fixing a small bug or adding a tiny feature.
- The newcomer fails because of the high cognitive load, caused by a combination of a lack of relevant chunks for the domain and/or the programming language and a lack of automatized skills relevant.

What's the problem with this senior developer's interactions with a newcomer? The deepest problem in this scenario is that the senior developer is overloading the capacity of the working memory of the newcomer by asking them to learn too much at the same time. Let's refresh our memory with a few of the key concepts covered in earlier chapters. In chapter 3, we covered cognitive load, which is the brain's effort on a given problem. We saw that when the brain is experiencing too much cognitive load, thinking effectively is inhibited. In chapter 10, we saw that when you experience too much intrinsic and extraneous cognitive load, you have no room for germane load, meaning you will not be able to *remember* new information.

Because the newcomer's working memory is overloaded, they cannot program effectively in the new codebase, nor can they retain new information properly. More than once I have seen this lead to frustration and wrong assumptions on both sides. The team lead might assume the newcomer is not very bright, and the newcomer assumes the project will be very hard. That is not good ground from which to start further collaboration.

One of the reasons more-senior people often struggle with effectively teaching and explaining is the "curse of expertise." Once you have mastered a certain skill sufficiently, you will inevitably forget how hard it was to learn that skill or knowledge. You will, therefore, overestimate how many new things a newcomer can process at the same time.

I am sure somewhere in the last few months you have said that something was "not that hard," "actually quite easy," or "trivial." I would guess that in many of those cases you were talking about knowledge that took you quite some time to acquire. Moments where you say, "Wow, that is easy!" might be moments where you fall into the curse of expertise. The first thing you can do to make the onboarding process easier is to realize that it is probably not all that easy for the person who is learning.

## 13.2 Differences between experts and novices

Often experts think that novices can reason in the same way they do, but maybe slower or with an incomplete picture of the whole codebase. The most important takeaway of this chapter is understanding that experts and novices think and behave in very different ways.

Earlier in the book, we covered reasons why experts can think differently. First, an expert's brain stores a large collection of related memories that their working memory can fetch from LTM. These memories include strategies they have deliberately learned, such as writing a test for the issue first, or episodic memories of things they attempted in the past, such as rebooting the server. Experts don't necessarily have all the answers. They also might need to weigh different options, but generally they already know things about problems and have some idea of how to approach them.

Second, an expert can very effectively chunk code and all sorts of code-adjacent artifacts like error messages, tests, problems, and solutions. An expert can probably glance over a part of the code and recognize that it is, for example, emptying a queue. A beginner might need to read the code line by line. A simple error message like "Array index out of bounds" for an expert represents one concept. To a novice programmer, this might represent three separate elements, leading to more cognitive load. Many situations where people assume a new colleague is "not such a strong programmer" are in fact curse-of-expertise situations where the novice is just overloaded.

### 13.2.1 Beginners' behavior in more depth

To better understand the behavior of beginning programmers, let's consider the useful psychological framework of neo-Piagetism, which explains people's behavior when confronted with new information. Neo-Piagetism builds on Jean Piaget's work, an influential developmental psychologist who focused on the four stages of development for young children. For our purposes, neo-Piagetism describes how programmers behave when they are just getting to know a programming language, codebase, or paradigm.

#### PIAGET'S ORIGINAL MODEL

Before I can teach you how programmers behave in uncomfortable learning scenarios, let's go over the behavioral stages that started in childhood. I first have to explain Piaget's original model for young children, shown in table 13.1. At the first level, which describes the behavior of children aged 0 to 2 years of age, children cannot make plans or oversee situations. They simply experience things (sense) and act (motor) without too much strategy involved. In the second level, when children are between 2 and 7 years of age, children start to form hypotheses, but these hypotheses are often not very strong. For example, a 4-year-old might hypothesize that it is raining because clouds are sad. This is not precisely correct, but you can see they are trying to find explanations for their observations.

At the third stage, ages 7 to 11, children start to form hypotheses that they can reason about, but only in concrete situations. They can, for example, decide on a good move in a board game, but find it hard to generalize their thinking and reasons about whether that move will always be a good one for different boards. That type of formal reasoning happens in the final stage—the concrete operational stage—when children are over 11 years of age.

**Table 13.1   Overview of Piaget's stages of cognitive development**

| Stage | Characteristics | Describes children aged |
|---|---|---|
| Sensorimotor stage | Children lack a plan or strategy; they simply feel and grab onto things. | 0–2 years |
| Preoperational stage | Children start to form hypotheses and plans but don't use them reliably in thinking. | 2–7 years |
| Concrete operational stage | Children can reason about concrete things they can see, but find it hard to draw general conclusions. | 7–11 years |
| Formal operational stage | Children can engage in formal reasoning. | 11 years and older |

### NEO-PIAGETIAN MODEL FOR PROGRAMMING

Piaget's model received some criticism, mainly because he used his own children to create the model. However, his work laid the basis for neo-Piagetism, which has great value in understanding the thinking of beginning programmers. The core idea of neo-Piagetism is that the levels of Piaget are not general but domain-specific. People can operate at the formal operational stage in one domain, like programming in Java, while they still behave at the sensorimotor level for programming in Python. It can even be the case that someone operates at the formal operational stage for a certain codebase but falls back to a lower level in a new codebase. Table 13.2 describes the neo-Piagetian model and its implications for programming, as described by Australian professor Raymond Lister.[1]

**Table 13.2   Overview of neo-Piagetian stages of development and corresponding programming behavior**

| Stage | Characteristics | Programming behavior |
|---|---|---|
| Sensorimotor stage | Children lack a plan or strategy; they simply feel and grab onto things. | The programmer has an incoherent understanding of program execution. At this stage, a programmer cannot correctly trace a program. |
| Preoperational stage | Children start to form hypotheses and plans but don't use them reliably. | The programmer can reliably manually predict the outcome of multiple lines of code, for example by making a tracing table. A preoperational programmer often makes guesses about what a piece of code does. |

---

[1] Raymond Lister, "Toward a Developmental Epistemology of Computer Programming," https://dl.acm.org/doi/10.1145/2978249.2978251.

**Table 13.2** Overview of neo-Piagetian stages of development and corresponding programming behavior

| Stage | Characteristics | Programming behavior |
|---|---|---|
| Concrete operational stage | Children can reason about concrete things they can see but find it hard to draw general conclusions. | The programmer reasons about code deductively by reading the code itself rather than using the preoperational inductive approach. |
| Formal operational stage | Children can engage in formal reasoning. | The programmer can now reason logically, consistently, and systematically. Formal operational reasoning includes reflecting on your own actions, which is essential for debugging. |

At the first level, illustrated by the left-most programmer in figure 13.1, programmers cannot correctly trace a program (that is, they cannot create a tracing table as we described in chapter 4). Behavior at this stage is common for people who have no or little programming experience, but can also occur when programmers switch between very dissimilar languages (e.g., from JavaScript to Haskell). Because program execution is so different in those two languages, an experienced JavaScript programmer may have difficulties tracing a Haskell program. Because they are so focused on the code, which for them is still not easy to comprehend, explaining general principles separate from code is not a useful way of teaching. For example, a sensorimotor programmer who is stepping through database code is not helped if you start explaining how the database is configured elsewhere in the code. First, they need an understanding of the execution model.

The second stage is the preoperational stage, in which a programmer can trace small pieces of code, but this is also the only way they can reason about code: by using their newly learned tracing skills. Preoperational programmers find it hard to explain the meaning of that same code. The preoperational programmer is very focused on the code itself and finds it difficult to look at other artifacts, most notably diagrams. Supporting preoperational programmers in their reading or writing of code by giving them diagrams will not be helpful. Because these programmers reason inductively about code, they often guess the code's behavior based on a few traces.

The second stage, I think, is most frustrating for programmers, but also for the people onboarding or teaching them. Because it is hard for programmers at the preoperational stage to understand the deeper meaning of code, they are often guessing. That can make programmers at this level seem erratic. Sometimes their guesses are spot on, based on prior knowledge that transfers (or luck), but five minutes later they utter entirely unreasonable ideas. This can be the situation in which the person being onboarded gets frustrated and thinks the junior programmer is not smart or not trying their best. However, the preoperational stage is a stage that is needed to advance to the next stage. Training newcomers by expanding their code vocabulary with flashcards can help them advance.

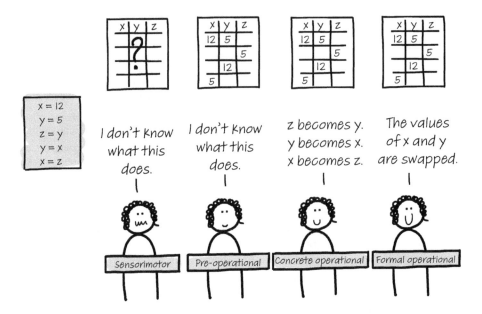

**Figure 13.1  Overview of the four different neo-Piagetian levels for programming**

At the third stage, concrete operational programmers can reason about code without meticulously tracing it. They do this using prior knowledge: by recognizing familiar chunks in code, reading comments and names, and tracing code only when it is needed (for example, when debugging). Lister notes in his study that it is useful for programmers to use diagrams to support their thinking only at the concrete operational stage. Concrete operational programmers start to behave like proper programmers: they can reason about code, and they can make a plan and execute it when writing code. However, sometimes they can still lack the global understanding of a codebase, and they can also struggle with reflection on whether something is a good strategy to follow. This can show itself in an overcommitment to a first strategy (for example, a junior programmer who has tried for a full day to fix a certain bug and keeps failing and trying again rather than stepping back and reflecting on whether the chosen strategy is the right one).

The final stage is formal operation. This is an experienced programmer who can reason about code and about their own behavior comfortably and is thus not so interesting for the onboarding process. These programmers will likely be comfortable learning the details of codebases themselves and can ask for help when needed.

### LEARNING NEW INFORMATION CAN MAKE YOU TEMPORARILY FORGET THINGS

The four stages are presented as discrete stages, but in reality they are not. When learning a new programming concept or a new aspect of a codebase, learners might temporarily fall back to a lower level. If someone can reliably read Python functions without tracing, but is then exposed to variadic functions using `*args`, they might need to trace a few function calls to see what happens before they can comfortably read them without tracing again.

**EXERCISE 13.1** The four different behaviors occur commonly in learning processes within companies. Reflect on the neo-Piagetian levels by coming up with an example you have seen happen in practice. Fill out the following table.

| Stage | Behavior | Example |
| --- | --- | --- |
| Sensorimotor stage | At this stage, a programmer cannot correctly trace a program. | |
| Preoperational stage | The programmer can reliably manually predict the outcome of multiple lines of code, for example, by making a tracing table. A preoperational programmer often makes guesses about what a piece of code does. | |
| Concrete operational stage | The programmer reasons about code deductively by reading the code itself rather than using the preoperational inductive approach. | |
| Formal operational stage | The programmer can now reason logically, consistently, and systematically. Formal operational reasoning includes reflecting on your own actions, which is essential for debugging. | |

## 13.2.2 Difference between seeing concepts concretely and abstractly

We have seen that beginning and expert programmers act and think differently. Research also shows that experts often talk about concepts in different ways, in very generic and abstract terms. For example, when explaining a variadic function in Python to someone new to the concept, experts might say that it is a function that can take in a varying number of arguments. However, they can leave many questions unanswered, for example, how to access all the different arguments, give names to each argument, or whether there is a limit on the number of arguments.

However, novices at a language or codebase benefit from both forms of explanation. Ideally, a beginner's understanding follows a *semantic wave*, a concept defined by Australian scientist Karl Maton, as illustrated by figure 13.2.[2]

Following the semantic wave, first beginners need to understand the generic concept: what it is used for and why you need to know it. For example, a variadic function is useful because it allows you to use as many arguments in a function as are required.

---

[2] Karl Maton, "Making Semantic Waves: A Key to Cumulative Knowledge-Building," *Linguistics and Education*, vol. 26, no. 1, pp. 8–22, 2013, https://www.sciencedirect.com/science/article/pii/S0898589812000678.

After beginners have seen what the concept does in general, they follow the curve down, a process known as *unpacking*. The beginner is then ready to learn details about the concept. For example, they can now learn that a * is used to indicate a variadic function in Python and that Python implements the list of arguments as a list, so in reality there are not multiple arguments; there is one argument that can contain all arguments of the function as elements.

Finally, the beginner needs to come back up to the abstract level, stepping away from details and feeling comfortable knowing how the concept works in general. This phase is called *repacking*. When a concept is properly repacked, the learner can think about it without focusing on concrete details. Repacking also involves integrating the knowledge into the LTM in relation to prior knowledge—for example, "C++ supports variadic functions, but Erlang does not."

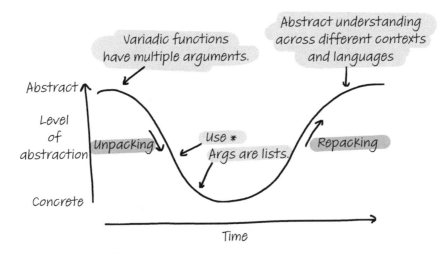

**Figure 13.2   The semantic wave representing the ideal explanation that starts abstractly, allows the learner to unpack knowledge by going through concrete details, and allows the learner to then repack the learned knowledge into their LTM.**

To beginners, there are three distinct antipatterns they use in their depth and a variety of explanations, each illustrated by figure 13.3. The first antipattern is called a high flatline and means you only use abstract terms. A newcomer to Python can learn that Python has variadic functions and why they are useful, but if they never see the syntax, there is a lot to learn later on.

The second antipattern is the reverse, a low flatline. Some experts overload beginners with details without explaining why the concept is relevant and useful. Starting with "You can make a variadic function with a * and then Python sees all arguments as one list" is not going to mean a lot when the beginner does not know when to use a variadic function.

**Figure 13.3**  Three different antipatterns: high flatlining (only abstract explanations), low flatlining (only concrete explanations), and downward escalators (starting from high to low but forgetting to leave room for repacking)

The final antipattern starts at the abstract, and then goes down to concrete, following the semantic wave. But after the concrete details, in this antipattern the expert forgets to allow newcomers to repack meaning. In other words, the expert shows the beginners the why and then the how of the concept but does not give them the time to integrate the new knowledge into their LTM. You can support this repacking by explicitly asking for commonalities people see between the new concept and preliminary information.

> **EXERCISE 13.2**  Choose a concept you know well and find explanations that fit all three locations on the semantic wave, as shown in figure 13.1.

## 13.3 *Activities for a better onboarding process*

In the remainder of the chapter, we will dive into how to improve the onboarding process. The first and most important thing you can do is deliberately manage the cognitive load of the people you are onboarding. It is, obviously, also very useful if the newcomer can also manage their own cognitive load. Introducing concepts such as memory types (e.g., long-term, short-term, and working memory), cognitive load, and chunks can ease a team's communication. It is a lot easier if a newcomer can say, "I experience too much load while reading this code" or "I think I lack chunks for Python" rather than "I am confused." We will now dive into three onboarding activities in more depth.

### 13.3.1 *Limit tasks to one programming activity*

In chapter 11, we described five activities people might do in a codebase: transcription, exploration, comprehension, searching, and incrementation. One of the issues with onboarding is that newcomers are asked to perform at least four different activities: searching for the right place to implement the feature or for relevant information, comprehending new source code, exploring the codebase to gain a better understanding, and incrementing the codebase with a new feature.

As we also saw in chapter 11, the different activities place different cognitive requirements on both the programmer and the system. Switching between the different activities is a lot to ask of a newcomer. Even though they know the programming language and maybe even the domain, performing a lot of different tasks is unnecessarily hard.

During the onboarding process, it is best to specifically choose activities in each of the five categories and have newcomers do them one by one. Let's explore the five activities in more detail and study examples of how each activity can support newcomers.

Table 13.3  Overview of programming activities and how they can be used to support newcomers in a project

| Activity | Examples used to support onboardees |
| --- | --- |
| Exploration | Browsing the codebase to get a general sense of the codebase |
| Searching | Finding a class that implements a certain interface |
| Transcription | Giving the newcomer a clear plan to implement a certain method which has to be implemented |
| Comprehension | Understanding aspects of the code, for example summarizing a specific method in natural language |
| Incrementation | Adding a feature to an existing class, including the creation of the plan for the feature |

The different activities can build on each other and work on related parts of the code. For example, a first task could be searching for a class, followed by transcribing a method within that class into code, and then incrementing the class in a more complex way. You can also alternate tasks in which the focus is on learning new programming concepts with tasks that focus more on getting to know the domain, depending on the existing prior knowledge of the onboardee.

**EXERCISE 13.3**  Think of a concrete activity a newcomer could do in all five categories when new to your codebase.

One can also imagine that a team might create and maintain documents to further help newcomers (e.g., support exploration with good comments and architecture documents explaining modules, subsystems, data structures, and algorithms used in the system).

## 13.3.2  *Support the memory of the onboardee*

As we explained, the first thing that matters in onboarding newcomers is to understand things are not easy. As we covered in chapter 2, newcomers see and remember different things than experts. It might not need saying, but empathy and patience are important!

In addition to having a shared vocabulary of cognitive science concepts, there are three phases in which you can improve the process, which relate to the three forms of confusion that we studied in chapter 1.

#### SUPPORT THE LTM: EXPLAIN RELEVANT INFORMATION

First, you can prepare the onboarding process for newcomers by deeply understanding the relevant information that plays a role when working with the codebase. This can be done with the exiting team, before the newcomer even arrives.

For example, you might want to document all the important domain concepts people are likely to encounter in the code. Another piece of relevant information is all libraries, frameworks, databases, and other external tools used in the code. A sentence like, "We use Laravel for this web app, which we deploy on Heroku with Jenkins" might not take an existing developer any effort, but if you do not know what even one of those tools is, you might miss all meaning in the sentence. And of course, the newcomer might know what a web framework or an automation server is in the abstract, but if they do not know these specific names, it is hard to grasp meaning and remember.

**SEPARATE DOMAIN LEARNING FROM EXPLORING CODE**  Going over all relevant concepts separately from introducing the code will make it a lot easier to learn more about the code. This looks like a small thing but can make a large difference. You could even make a deck of flashcards with relevant domain and programming concepts for the newcomer to practice with.

As a side note, even separate of the onboarding process, having an up-to-date list of all domain and programming concepts relevant to a project is also likely to help existing developers.

**EXERCISE 13.4**  Choose a project you work on often. Create two lists that could help newcomers: one containing important domain concepts and their description, and one with all the important libraries, frameworks, and programming concepts that the codebase uses. Fill out the following table.

| Domain concepts | Programming concepts/libraries |
| --- | --- |
| Concept | Definition |
| Concept/module/library | Use/definition |
|  |  |

### SUPPORT THE STM: PREPARE SMALL, FOCUSED TASKS

Another thing I see happen in onboarding processes, which does not go perfectly, is that the newcomer explains the code. The team lead clicks through the code, showing relevant parts of the code. After the explanation session, the newcomer is asked to start on a relatively simple feature to "get to know" the codebase. The same can happen in open source projects where simple feature requests are labeled beginner-friendly. While this sounds very welcoming, it might present a cognitive problem.

The newcomer will be asked to do multiple programming activities and thus the newcomer's brain is now doing several things: getting to know the code, searching through it, and also implementing a feature. That is likely to overload the newcomer's STM because they cannot (yet) easily navigate the codebase. They spent a lot of time searching for code, and reading code distracts from the task at hand. It is better to split the schemes into multiple phases.

> **UNDERSTANDING IS A BETTER WELCOME TASK THAN BUILDING**   If you want a newcomer to understand a certain piece of the code, ask them to understand a piece rather than giving them an implementation task. For example, ask them to write a summary of an existing class or write down all classes involved in executing a certain feature.

Giving newcomers a focused task will be less heavy on the STM and thus more likely to leave room for germane load to remember important things about the code. In addition to being easier and more effective for the novice, having good summaries of code will be helpful as documentation for other newcomers, more so than more features.

Should you choose to have a newcomer implement a small feature, that is, of course, possible too. But in that code, it is best to remove other aspects that create cognitive load, such as searching through code. You could prepare the relevant code beforehand. You could use the techniques we described in chapter 4, such as refactoring the relevant code into the class at hand to prevent searching.

### SUPPORT THE WORKING MEMORY: DRAW DIAGRAMS

Chapter 4 proposed a number of techniques that can support the working memory, including using diagrams. It can be hard for someone new to a codebase to create these artifacts. In the onboarding process, the onboarder can consider creating tables that aid the working memory.

However, as we described, diagrams are not always helpful for absolute beginners who might be reluctant to step away from the code and view a larger picture. Monitor the helpfulness of diagrams often and abandon them when the technique is not (yet) helpful.

### 13.3.3  *Read code together*

Another technique you can use to onboard newcomers is to read code as a team collaboratively. In chapter 5, we proposed seven techniques from natural language to be applied to code reading:

- *Activating*—Actively thinking of related things to activate prior knowledge
- *Determining importance*—Deciding what parts of text are most relevant
- *Inferring*—Filling in facts that are not explicitly given in the text
- *Monitoring*—Keeping track of your understanding of a text
- *Visualizing*—Drawing diagrams of the read text to deepen understanding
- *Questioning*—Asking questions about the text at hand
- *Summarizing*—Creating a short summary of the text

In chapter 5, we proposed these activities as things to do when you read code as an individual developer. However, these tasks can also be used when you onboard a new developer into a codebase. When the team performs these activities, it lowers the newcomer's cognitive load, and they can then focus on the code with more working memory.

Next we will detail how each of the seven activities can be used with collaboratively reading code.

### ACTIVATING

Before the reading session starts, go over relevant concepts in the code. If you previously did exercise 13.1, you can have this list prepared beforehand. Remind the newcomer of relevant concepts beforehand and relieve confusion about concepts. It is better to discuss details at this point rather than when the newcomer is also trying to understand the code. For example, if you are using a Model-View-Controller model, it is better if that fact is not discovered while browsing different code files.

After the activating phase, the collaborative reading code session can start. Note that the activity being performed is comprehension. That means we want to limit the other four activities.

### DETERMINING IMPORTANCE

If you have low knowledge of something, it can be very hard to distinguish between core knowledge and what is less important. Pointing out the most relevant parts of code supports newcomers. This can be done in a collaborative reading, in which, for example, all team members point out what they think are the most relevant or important lines of the code. Alternatively, you might have a document stemming from previous code-reading sessions in which the important highlights have already been pointed out, which a newcomer can read.

### INFERRING

Similarly, it can be tough to fill in details that are not explicitly stated. For example, a team might have clear understandings of domain concepts, such as that shipments must always contain at least one order, but such decisions might not have been explicitly documented in the code. Similarly, to determine importance you might expressly point out findings in a reading session, or these decisions might have been reported so that they can be easily shared with newcomers.

### MONITORING

As we described, the most important thing you can do in the onboarding process in keep track of the level of understanding the onboardee currently has. Regularly ask them to give a quick recap of the read, define essential domain concepts, or recall a programming concept used in the code.

### VISUALIZING

As described earlier in the book, diagrams serve two purposes. First, they can support the working memory (chapter 4), and second, their creation can help comprehension (chapter 5). Depending on the newcomer's level, the onboarder can either create a diagram and use it to help the onboardee in code reading, or ask the newcomer to draw it to deepen their understanding of the code.

### QUESTIONING

While collaboratively reading code, regularly ask and answer questions about the it. Depending on the newcomer's level, you might ask questions that they answer, or you might encourage them to ask questions you can answer. Relatively experienced newcomers might also benefit from asking questions to find the answers, with your help, but always monitor their cognitive load in such tasks that are less guided. When the onboardee starts to guess or concludes things that do not make sense, their cognitive load might be exceeded.

### SUMMARIZING

As a final step in code reading for onboarding, you can write a summary of the code that was read together. An example of a summary in shown in figure 13.4. Depending on the documentation state in the codebase, this summary could be committed to the codebase as documentation, which is a great and welcoming task for the onboardee to do after the session. In that process, they will get to know the workflow of the codebase (for example, by creating a pull request and requesting a review on it, in a way that is not too scary or too hard on the working memory).

---

Transpiling Hedy is a stepwise process. Firstly the code is parsed using Lark, resulting in an AST. The AST is then scanned for invalid rules. If these appear in the tree, the Hedy program is invalid and an error message will be generated. Secondly, a lookup table with all variable names occuring in the program is extracted from the AST. Finally, the AST is transformed into Python by adding needed syntax such as brackets.

---

Figure 13.4   **An example of a summary of code**

## Summary

- Experts think and act differently from beginners. Experts can reason abstractly about code and have the ability to think about it without referring to the code itself. Beginners tend to focus on details in the code and have a hard time stepping back from details.
- When midlevel programmers learn new information, they sometimes fall back to beginner-level thinking.
- People who are learning a new concept need to learn about it in both abstract terms and in concrete examples.
- People who are learning a new concept also need time to connect a new concept to prior knowledge.
- When onboarding, limit the programming activities newcomers perform to one at a time.
- When onboarding, prepare relevant information to support the onboardee's long-term, short-term, and working memory.

# epilogue

## Some words to close this book

Thanks for making it to the end of this book. Whether you have read the whole text or just a few bits here and there, I am happy you reached this point. Writing this book for been a very rewarding experience. I learned a lot about cognitive science and programming because I dove deeper into the matter than I ever had before. But I also learned a lot about myself. One of the things I take away from this book is that confusion and feeling cognitively overwhelmed is fine, and is part of life and learning. Before I knew all I know about cognition, I used to get upset with myself for not being smart enough to read complicated papers or explore unfamiliar code; now I can be kinder to myself and say, "Well, maybe you have too much cognitive load."

I also started to work on what ultimately became the Hedy programming language. And while I would certainly not recommend anyone create a programming language and write a book at the same time, in my mind these two processes were very connected and went together well thematically. Many of the lessons in this book, like lowering cognitive load, misconceptions, the semantic wave, and spaced repetition, are written about in this book and also implemented in Hedy. If you are teaching kids to program, I would be honored if you'd give Hedy a try on www.hedycode.com. It is free and open source!

To end this book, I want to stress that I have immensely enjoyed exploring, summarizing, and covering the work of great scientists in the field of programming and cognition. While doing my own research is amazing, helping developers gain an understanding of existing research has been tremendously rewarding and might have a bigger impact on programming than my own projects. If you want to read even more, there are a few books I can recommend and a few scientists that you might want to keep tabs on.

If you want to get to know your brain better, I love the book *Thinking Fast and Slow* (Farrar, Straus, and Giroux, 2013) by Daniel Kahneman because it helps you understand your brain in a broader way than this book does. Similarly, the book

221

*How We Learn* (Penguin, 2015) by Benedict Carey dives deeper into topics of spaced repetition and memory. For readers specifically interested in learning math, the book *How the Brain Learns Mathematics* (Corwin, 2014) by David Sousa is packed with research on learning math and abstraction. In the realm of programming, I can recommend the book the *Philosophy of Software Design* (Yaknyam Press, 2018) by John Ousterhout. It is not an easy read, but it is filled with in-depth insights about how we design software. I also very much love the small book *Software Design Decoded* (MIT Press, 2016) by Andre van der Hoek and Marian Petre, which summarizes 66 ways programming experts think, which can be seen as a deck of flashcards you can apply in various situations. I have also covered this book in an episode of SE Radio.

If you are eager to read scientific papers on topics related to this book, I can recommend two papers that impacted my thinking extensively: "Why Minimal Guidance During Instruction Does Not Work" by Kirschner et al.,[1] which challenged everything I knew about teaching, and "Toward a Developmental Epistemology of Computer Programming" by Raymond Lister, which channeled my experience of teaching programming badly and taught me how to do better.[2]

This book covers the work of a range of amazing scientists, but the few hundred pages this book became surely have not been enough to cover all their great work. If you want to dive deeper into program comprehension research, you want to follow these great people: Sarah Fakhoury (@fakhourysm), Alexander Serebrenik (@aserebrenik), Chris Parnin (@chrisparnin), Janet Siegmund (@janetsiegmund), Brittany Johnson (@DrBrittJay), Titus Barik (@barik), David Shepherd(@davidcshepherd), and Amy Ko (@amyjko).

---

[1] Paul A. Kirschner et al., "Why Minimal Guidance During Instruction Does Not Work: An Analysis of the Failure of Constructivist, Discovery, Problem-Based, Experiential, and Inquiry-Based Teaching," *Educational Psychologist*, vol. 41, no. 2, pp. 75–86, 2010, https://www.tandfonline.com/doi/abs/10.1207/s15326985ep4102_1

[2] Raymond Lister, "Toward a Developmental Epistemology of Computer Programming," 2010, https://dl.acm.org/doi/10.1145/2978249.2978251

# *index*

## Symbols

&& operator  29
+ operator  29

## Numerics

*500 Lines or Less* (DiBernardo)  175

## A

abbreviations  137–140
Abelson, Harold  14
abstraction dimension  200
activating  84–85, 217
active thinking  42–44
  schemata  43
  using elaboration  44
activities  180–183
  comprehension  181, 203
  debugging  182–183
  exploration  182, 203
  incrementation  181–182, 203
  optimizing codebase for expected activities  204
  searching  180–181, 202–203
  transcription  181, 203
anonymous functions  53
APL program  7
Apps Hungarian  74–75
*Architecture of Open Source Systems, The*
  (Brown, Wilson)  175
association  113
automatization  167–172
  implicit memories over time  168–169
    associative phase  169
    autonomous phase  169
    cognitive phase  168
  improving implicit memories  171–172
  multitasking and  189
  programming quicker with  170

## B

Bartlett, Frederic  43
beacons  28–30, 87, 129
beginners
  activities for onboarding  213–218
    drawing diagrams  216
    explaining relevant information  215
    limiting tasks  213–214
    preparing small, focused tasks  215–216
    reading code together  216–218
  behavior of  207–211
    neo-Piagetian model for programming
      208–210
    Piaget's original model  207–208
    temporarily forgetting things  210–211
  concepts, seeing concretely vs. abstractly  211–213
  expert programmers vs.  83–84
  reading code  22–23
blog posts  175
books  175
boxplot() function  34, 39
brain-based measurements  157
Brodmann areas  79–80
Brodmann, Korbinian  79
Brooks, Fred  185
Brown, Amy  175
bugs  123
  misconceptions  117–123
    about programming languages  120–122
    debugging with conceptual change  118–119
    diagnosing in new codebase  122–123

bugs *(continued)*
    preventing while learning new programming
        language 122
    suppressing 119–120
  naming and 141–142
  transfer 111–117
    difficulties of 116–117
    existing programming knowledge benefits
        113–114
    forms of 114

## C

calculate() function 52
call patterns 78
camel case 140–141
CDCB (cognitive dimensions of code bases) 200
CDN (cognitive dimensions) 204
  activities and 202–204
    comprehension 203
    exploration 203
    incrementation 203
    optimizing codebase for expected activities 204
    searching 202–203
    transcription 203
  properties of 192–202
    abstraction 200
    closeness of mapping 197–198
    closeness of mapping, exercise 12.2 198
    consistency 194
    design maneuvers 201–202
    diffuseness 194–195
    error proneness 193
    hard mental operations 198–199
    hidden dependencies 195–196
    improving codebase with CDCB 200
    progressive evaluation 196–197
    provisionality 196
    role expressiveness 197
    secondary notation 199
    viscosity 196
    visibility 200
celsius variable 104
checked exceptions 115
chunking 19–21, 25–30
  beacons 28–30
  code clones and 152–153
  design patterns 26
  in code 21
  practicing 30–31
  writing chunkable code 25–26
  writing comments 27–28
chunks 19
class-level code smells 150
closeness of mapping dimension 197–198
code 90
  applying text comprehension strategies 84–90
    activating prior knowledge 84–85

    determining important lines of code 86–87
    inferring meaning of variable names 87–88
    monitoring 85
    questioning 89
    summarizing code 90
    visualizing 88–89
  models for thinking about 92–94
  paradigms 71–75
    benefits of roles 72–73
    Hungarian notation 73–75
  programs 75–78
    stages of comprehension 76–78
    text knowledge vs. plan knowledge 75
  reading code 79–84
    cognitive processes 15–16, 23–31, 79–80
    natural language skills vs. 81–84
    with beginners 216–218
  variables 68–71
    different roles of 68–69
    eleven roles covering 69–71
code clones 153
code reviews 129
code smells 148–153
  catalog of 148–151
    class-level code smells 150
    codebase-level code smells 150–151
    impact of code smells 151
    method-level code smells 150
  harming cognition 151–153
    code clones 153
    god class, long method 152–153
    long parameter list, complex switch
        statements 152
  influence of bad names on cognitive load
    153–159
  linguistic antipatterns 154–155, 158–159
  measuring cognitive load 155–158
    brain-based measurements 157
    EEG (electroencephalogram) 157
    eye-based measurements 156
    fNIRS and programming 157–158
    Paas Scale 155
    skin-based measurements 156
code synonyms 55–56
codebase-level code smells 150–151
codebases
  checking linguistic antipatterns in 154–155
  diagnosing misconceptions in 122–123
  naming
    as part of 129
    consistency with 131
*Coders at Work* (Seibel) 79
coding 12
  cognitive processes affecting 6–12
    interaction of 9
    LTM (long-term memory) 7
    regarding programming tasks 10–12

coding *(cotinued)*
    STM (short-term memory) 7–8
    working memory 8–9
  confusion in 4–6
    lack of information 5
    lack of knowledge 5
    lack of processing power 6
cognitive compiling 60
cognitive load 48
  Germane load 173–174
  influence of bad names on 153–159
  linguistic antipatterns and 158–159
  measuring 155–158
    brain-based measurements 157
    EEG (electroencephalogram) 157
    eye-based measurements 156
    fNIRS and programming 157–158
    Paas Scale for cognitive load 155
    skin-based measurements 156
  techniques to reduce 51–56
    code synonyms as additions to flashcards
      55–56
    refactoring 51–52
    replacing unfamiliar language constructs
      52–55
  types of 49–50
    extraneous cognitive load 49–50
    intrinsic cognitive load 49
cognitive phase, implicit memories 168
cognitive processes 6–12
  code smells harming 151–153
    code clones 153
    god class, long method 152–153
    long parameter list, complex switch
      statements 152
  interaction of 9
  LTM (long-term memory) 7
  reading code 15–16, 23–31, 79–80
    Brodmann areas 79–80
    evidence from fMRI 80
    iconic memory 23–24
  regarding programming tasks 10–12
  STM (short-term memory) 7–8
  with naming 133–136
    evaluating quality of names 136
    LTM 134–135
    STM 133–134
    variable names with information 135–136
  working memory 8–9
cognitive refactoring 52
collaborating with colleague 175
complex code 63
  cognitive load
    techniques to reduce 51–56
    types of 49–50
  reasons for difficulties with 47–50

working memory 56–61
  combining dependency graphs and state
    tables 61
  dependency graphs 56–59
  short-term memory vs. 48
  state tables 59–60
complex switch statements 152
compound beacons 29
comprehension 84–90
  activating prior knowledge 84–85
  activity of 181
  determining important lines of code 86–87
  dimensions and 203
  inferring meaning of variable names 87–88
  monitoring 85
  questioning 89
  summarizing code 90
  visualizing 88–89
concepts, concrete and abstract 211–213
conceptual antipatterns 153
conceptual change 118–119
concrete models 98–99
confusion in coding 4–6
  lack of information 5
  lack of knowledge 5
  lack of processing power 6
consistency
  properties of CDN (cognitive dimensions) 194
  with codebase names 131, 134
containers 70
context 113
control() function 199
counter variable 69, 72
Craik, Kenneth 95
critical attributes 113

**D**

debugging 182–183
declarative memory 164
deliberate practice 30
delocalized code 51
dependency graphs
  combining state tables and 61
  working memory and 56–59
design maneuvers 201–202
  error proneness vs. viscosity 202
  provisionality and progressive evaluation vs.
    error-proneness 202
  role expressiveness vs. diffuseness 202
design patterns 26
determining importance 84, 217
diagrams, drawing 216
DiBernardo, Michael 175
diffuseness dimension 194–195, 202
disruptions 34–35
documentation 129
domain learning 215

drawing diagrams 216
dual-task measure 188
dyadic encode function 7

**E**

Ebbinghaus, Hermann 38
EEG (electroencephalograms) 81, 157
*Effects of Beacons, Comments, and Tasks on Program
    Comprehension Process in Software Maintenance,
    The* (Fan) 27
elaboration 44
emotions 114
encoding 38
error proneness 193
    provisionality and progressive evaluation vs. 202
    viscosity dimension vs. 202
executeQuery() function 198
expert programmers
    beginners vs. 83–84
    reading code 22–23
explicit memory 164
exploration 182, 203
extraneous cognitive load 49–50
eye trackers 83
eye-based measurements 156

**F**

factors variable 69
Fan, Quiyin 27
far transfer 114
fclose() function 111
Feitelson's three-step model 145–146
    overview 145–146
    success of 146
file.close() function 111
file.open() function 197
filter() function 53
fixed values 69, 72
flashcards 35–37
    code synonyms 55–56
    expanding set 36
    thinning set 36–37
    when to use 36
fMRI (functional magnetic resonance imaging) 80
fNIRS (functional near infrared spectroscopy) 157–158
focal poin 76
followers 70
foo() function 153
forgetting 38–39
    forgetting curve 38–39
    hierarchy vs. networks 38
    learning new information and 210–211
formatting names 137–141
    abbreviations 137–140

snake case or camel case 140–141
Fowler, Martin 148

**G**

gatherer 70
Germane load 173–174
GitHub 175
God class 150, 152–153
goo() function 153

**H**

hard mental operations 198–199
hidden dependencies dimension 195–196
hierarchy, networks vs. 38
high-road transfer 114
Hungarian notation 73–75

**I**

iconic memory 23–24
implicit memories 168–169
    associative phase 169
    autonomous phase 169
    cognitive phase 168
    improving 171–172
importance, determining 84, 217
incrementation 181–182, 203
inferring 87–88, 217
inherent complexity 49
inhibition 120
inlining 52
instance theory 170
interruptions 183–190
    at convenient times 187–189
    multitasking 189–190
        automatizing and 189
        research on 190
    preparing for 185–187
        helping prospective memory 186–187
        labeling subgoals 187
        storing mental model 185
    resuming after 184
    warm-up time 183–184
intrinsic cognitive load 49
is_available variable 70
is_error variable 70
is_set variable 70, 197
isMember variable 54–55
isValid variable 154, 159

**J**

JAVA
    attempting to remember 17
    STM (short-term memory) 8

## K

knowledge 5
    activating prior knowledge 84–85
    existing programming knowledge benefits
        113–114
    text vs. plan 75

## L

labeling subgoals 187
lambdas 53
language
    notional machines and 106–108
        conflicting mental models 107–108
        expanding sets of notional machines 106
    replacing unfamiliar constructs 52–55
        lambdas 53
        list comprehensions 54
        ternary operators 54–55
linguistic antipatterns 154–155, 158–159
    causing confusion 159
    checking in codebase 154–155
list comprehensions 54
live programming 197
long method 152–153
low-road transfer 114
LTM (long-term memory) 7
    APL program 7
    explaining relevant information 215
    mental models 100–101
        in working memory and 102
        of source code in 101–102
    names and 134–135
    problem solving, role in 162–166
        resolving cognitive process question 162–164
        types of memories 164–166

## M

main() function 59, 76–78, 152
mastery 113
max_benefit_amount 143
max_interest_amount 144
max_points 146
max_prime_factors variable 69
maximum value 120
memory 37–44
    active thinking 42–44
        schemata 43
        using elaboration 44
    forgetting, reasons for 38–39
        forgetting curve 38–39
        hierarchy vs. networks 38
    forms of remembering information 40–41
        retrieval strength 41
        storage strength 41

    memories 164–166
        overview 165–166
        unlearning 166
    seeing information and 41
    spaced repetition 39–40
    strengthening memories 42
mental models 94, 97–102
    concrete models 98–99
    in LTM 100–102
    in working memory 98, 102
    learning new 97
    notional machines creating conflicting 107–108
    of source code in LTM 101–102
    of source code in working memory 99–100
    overview 96
    storing during interruptions 185
*Meta-Programming* (Simonyi) 74
method-level code smells 150
minimum variable 121
minimum() function 152
misconceptions 117–123
    about programming languages 120–122
    debugging with conceptual change 118–119
    diagnosing in new codebase 122–123
    preventing while learning new programming
        language 122
    suppressing 119–120
models 109
    for thinking about code 92–94
    mental models 94–102
        concrete models 98–99
        in LTM 100–101
        in LTM and working memory 102
        in working memory 98
        learning new 97
        of source code in LTM 101–102
        of source code in working memory 99–100
        overview 96
    notional machines 102–105
        defined 103
        examples of 103–104
        language and 106–108
        levels of 105
        schemata and 108–109
monitoring 85, 218
most recent holders 69–70
most wanted holders 69–70
multiples() function 152
multitasking 189–190
    automatizing and 189
    research on 190
Mythical Man-Month (Brooks) 185

## N

naming 128–146
    choosing better names 142–146
        Feitelson's three-step model 145–146

naming *(continued)*
    name molds 142–144
    cognitive aspects of 133–136
        evaluating quality of names 136
        LTM 134–135
        STM 133–134
        variable names with information 135–136
    formatting 137–141
        abbreviations 137–140
        snake case or camel case 140–141
    inferring meaning of variable 87–88
    influence on bugs 141–142
    influence on cognitive load 153–159
    lasting impact of practices 131–133
    perspectives on 129–131
        consistency within codebase 131
        syntactic rules 130–131
    reasons for 129
        form of documentation 129
        part of codebases 129
        role in code reviews 129
        serving as beacons 129
*Nature of Explanation, The* (Craik) 95
near transfer 114
negative transfer 115
neo-Piagetian model 208–210
networks, hierarchy vs. 38
Node class 29
notional machines 102–105
    defined 103
    examples of 103–104
    language and 106–108
        conflicting mental models 107–108
        expanding sets of notional machines 106
    levels of 105
    schemata and 108–109
        are notional machines semantics? 109
        importance of 108–109

**O**

onboarding new developers 219
    activities for 213–218
        drawing diagrams 216
        explaining relevant information 215
        limiting tasks 213–214
        preparing small, focused tasks 215–216
        reading code together 216–218
    beginners' behavior 207–211
        neo-Piagetian model for programming 208–210
        Piaget's original model 207–208
        temporarily forgetting things 210–211
    difference between seeing concepts concretely and abstractly 211–213
    issues in process of 206–207
open() function 111, 197
operation tables 88–89

operator 29
organizers 71
Ousterhout, John 185

**P**

Paas Scale 155
paradigms 71–75
    benefits of roles 72–73
    Hungarian notation 73–75
parameter list, long 152
Petzold, Charles 75
*Philosophy of Software Design, The* (Outerhout) 185
Piaget's original model 207–208
plan knowledge 75–76, 90
positive transfer 115–116
practices, naming 131–133
problem solving 176
    automatization 167–172
        implicit memories over time 168–169
        improving implicit memories 171–172
        programming quicker with 170
    elements of 161
    learning from code and its explanation 172–175
        Germane load 173–174
        using worked examples in working life 175
    models 109
        for thinking about code 92–94
        mental models 94–102
        notional machines 102–105
    role of LTM with 162–166
        resolving cognitive process question 162–164
        types of memories 164–166
    state space 161–162
processing power 6
programming languages 120–122
*Programming Windows* (Petzold) 75
programs 75–78
    stages of comprehension 76–78
    text knowledge vs. plan knowledge 75
progressive evaluation dimension 196–197, 202
prospective memory 186–187
provisionality dimension 196, 202
public class 8
public static void main 8

**Q**

questioning 89, 218

**R**

reading code 32, 79–84, 216–218
    activating 217
    chunking 19–21, 25–30
        beacons 28–30
        design patterns 26

reading code *(continued)*
    in code 21
        practicing 30–31
        writing chunkable code 25–26
        writing comments 27–28
    cognitive processes 79–80
        Brodmann areas 79–80
        evidence from fMRI 80
    cognitive processes affecting 23–31
    complex code 63
        cognitive load 49–56
        reasons for difficulties with 47–50
        working memory 48, 56–61
    determining importance 217
    expert programmers vs. beginners 22–23
    inferring 217
    monitoring 218
    natural language skills vs. 81–84
        beginners vs. expert programmers 83–84
        eye trackers 83
        strategies for reading 82–83
    questioning 218
    quickly reading 14–18
        cognitive processes when 15–16
        difficulties of 18
        reexamining reproduced code 16–17
    summarizing 218
    visualizing 218
refactoring 51–52
*Refactoring* (Fowler) 148
refactorings 148
repacking 212
reproduced code 16–17
    JAVA 17
    second attempt 17
retrieval strength 41
retrieveElements() function 159
reverse refactoring 52
reverse() function 163
roadblock reminders 184
role expressiveness dimension 197, 202
roles of variables framework 68
root variable 28–29

**S**

schemata 43, 108–109
    as semantics 109
    importance of 108–109
searching 180–181, 202–203
secondary notation dimension 199
Seibel, Peter 79
semantic memory 165
semantic wave 211
semantics 109
sensory memory 23
similarity 113
Simonyi, Charles 74

skin-based measurements 156
slices of code 77
snake case 140–141
source code
    books or blog posts about 175
    mental models in working memory 99–100
    mental models LTM 101–102
spaced repetition 39–40
state space 161–162
state tables
    combining dependency graphs and 61
    working memory and 59–60
steppers 69, 72
STM (short-term memory) 7–8
    JAVA program 8
    names and 133–134
    preparing small, focused tasks 215–216
    working memory vs. 48
storage strength 41
structural antipatterns 153
*Structure and Interpretation of Computer Programs*
    (Abelson, Sussman, Sussman) 14
subgoals, labeling 187
summarizing 90, 218
suppressing misconceptions 119–120
Sussman, Julie 14
Sussman, Gerald Jay 14
switch statements, complex 152
syntax 45, 109
    building memory 37–44
        active thinking 42–44
        forgetting, reasons for 38–39
        forms of remembering information 40–41
        seeing information and 41
        spaced repetition 39–40
        strengthening memories 42
    learning with flashcards 35–37
        expanding set 36
        thinning set 36–37
        when to use 36
    naming rules 130–131
    remembering 34–35
system Hungarian 74–75
System.out.print() function 33

**T**

temp variable 71
temporary variables 71
ternary operators 54–55
text
    comprehension strategies 84–90
        activating prior knowledge 84–85
        determining important lines of code 86–87
        inferring meaning of variable names 87–88
        monitoring 85
        questioning 89
        summarizing code 90

text *(continued)*
    visualizing 88–89
    reading code vs. 81–84
        beginners vs. expert programmers 83–84
        eye trackers 83
        strategies for reading 82–83
text comprehension strategies 83
text structure knowledge 75, 90
toBinaryString() function 4–5, 8, 47–48
tracing 9, 60
transcription 181, 203
transfer 111–117
    difficulties of 116–117
    during learning 111
    existing programming knowledge benefits
        113–114
    forms of 114
        high- and low-road transfer 114
        near and far transfer 114
        positive transfer 115–116
    of learning 112
transform() function 52
tree variable 28–29
Tree variable name 87
turtle 103
type systems 193

**U**

*Über das Gedächtnis (Memory A Contribution to
    Experimental Psychology)*, (Ebbinghaus) 39
unpacking 212
upperbound variable 69

**V**

variables 68–71
    different roles of 68–69
    eleven roles covering 69–71
    inferring meaning of names 87–88
    names containing information 135–136
    single letters used as 138–140

*Vergleichende Lokalisationslehre der Großhirnrinde*
    (Brodmann) 79
viscosity dimension 196, 202
visibility 200
visualizing 88–89, 218

**W**

walkers 70
warm-up time 183–184
Wilson, Greg 175
working life examples 175
    collaborate with colleague 175
    explore GitHub 175
    read books or blog posts about source code 175
working memory 8–9, 56–61
    BASIC program 9
    combining dependency graphs and state tables 61
    dependency graphs 56–59
    drawing diagrams 216
    mental models in 98
        LTM and 102
        of source code 99–100
    overloading capacity of 152
    short-term memory vs. 48
    state tables 59–60
writing code 190
    activities while programming 180–183
        comprehension 181
        debugging 182–183
        exploration 182
        incrementation 181–182
        searching 180–181
        transcription 181
    chunkable code 25–26
    comments 27–28
    interruptions 183–190
        at convenient times 187–189
        multitasking 189–190
        preparing for 185–187
        resuming after 184
        warm-up time 183–184